CW00555725

# Reading Lessons

# Reading Lessons

*The Books We Read at School,
the Conversations They Spark and
Why They Matter*

CAROL ATHERTON

FIG TREE
*an imprint of*
PENGUIN BOOKS

FIG TREE

UK | USA | Canada | Ireland | Australia
India | New Zealand | South Africa

Fig Tree is part of the Penguin Random House group of companies
whose addresses can be found at global.penguinrandomhouse.com

Penguin
Random House
UK

First published 2024
001

Copyright © Carol Atherton, 2024
The moral right of the author has been asserted

Credits and permissions are listed on p. 391 and are considered a continuation of this copyright page

The author and publisher gratefully acknowledge the permission granted to reproduce the copyright
material in this book. Every effort has been made to trace copyright holders and to obtain
their permission. The publisher apologizes for any errors or omissions and, if notified of any
corrections, will make suitable acknowledgment in future reprints or editions of this book

Set in 13.5/16pt Garamond MT Std
Typeset by Jouve (UK), Milton Keynes
Printed and bound in Great Britain by Clays Ltd, Elcograf S.p.A.

The authorized representative in the EEA is Penguin Random House Ireland,
Morrison Chambers, 32 Nassau Street, Dublin D02 YH68

A CIP catalogue record for this book is available from the British Library

ISBN: 978–0–241–62948–2

www.greenpenguin.co.uk

MIX
Paper | Supporting
responsible forestry
FSC
www.fsc.org    FSC® C018179

Penguin Random House is committed to a
sustainable future for our business, our readers
and our planet. This book is made from Forest
Stewardship Council® certified paper.

To my family

# Contents

# CONTENTS

# Introduction

It's the end of the day. An hour ago, all was noise: thudding feet, hurried conversations, whoops of joy at being released into the wild. But now, everything's still, apart from the dust motes that shimmer in the air.

The smell remains, as you might expect. How could it not, with a thousand teenage bodies crammed into one building? It's a smell I'd recognize anywhere, after nearly thirty years of teaching. Top notes of sweat, cut grass and muddy boots fresh from the playing fields, the lingering traces of whatever experiment was being performed in the Chemistry lab during the last lesson of the day. The occasional, jarring whiff of deodorant from someone who was trying to impress. If it's been raining, a pervasive stench of wet dogs. And, of course, the musty scent of books.

Look at them. They totter in piles in the stock cupboard, some of them still shiny and proud, others rubbed at the edges. They'll have been handled by hundreds of students, the names and dates recorded in their front pages reaching back maybe ten years, maybe twenty. They'll have travelled home in fusty school bags, crammed in with exercise books, scrunched-up letters, sedimentary layers of long-forgotten packed lunches.

Some will have been treated carefully, respectfully. Others will have served their time under beds, amongst crumbs and lost socks, waiting to be retrieved at the end of the year and returned to the light.

Take one down from the shelf. Sniff it. Open it and look through its pages. It'll take you back to your own schooldays, to whichever classroom you sat in all those years ago. Someone has probably underlined the same quotations you underlined, about getting a little place and living off the fat of the land, climbing inside someone else's skin and walking around in it, the fall through the air of a true, wise friend called Piggy. Words will jump out at you, and you'll be fifteen again, doodling on your pencil case, stealing glances at the person you fancy over the other side of the room, counting the minutes until you're set free.

It's in rooms like this, surrounded by books like this and breathing in smells like this, that I've spent my entire working life. *Reading Lessons* is partly the story of how I came to be an English teacher, how I fell in love not just with reading books, but with analysing them and talking about them and getting young people to read, analyse and talk about them too. But it's also the story of the books themselves. Some of these books have had a huge influence on my own life, as both a student and a teacher. Some have been called into question by changing times and changing values. Many are more complex than we might have realized when we first encountered them, sitting in those dusty classrooms and waiting for the bell to go.

The relationships we have with these books can be complicated. For one thing, we don't read them out of choice. They are imposed upon us by a range of forces beyond our control, by the decisions that teachers and exam boards make on our behalf. They might not be books we'd have chosen to read independently; they might not even be books we like. We can't just curl up with these books and enjoy them: we have to answer questions on them, make notes and write essays, revise them for exams. They make other demands of us, as well. We encounter them at a crucial stage in our development, when our identities are being formed and the world is starting to seem more complex and various than it did before. They can spark arguments and frustration. They might be loathed from the bottom of our hearts, thrown in exasperation across our teenage bedrooms, but they might equally, at times, hold our hands and help us to feel less alone. On occasion, they might lead us to look at life in a completely different way.

The books we read at school, and the experiences they gave us, act as touchstones for generations and provide a hoard of shared memories. We'll think of swinging on the front porch with Scout Finch, watching Billy Casper fly his kestrel, waiting with our hearts in our mouths as George approaches Lennie with his gun. But they also play a more important role, in prompting us to think about issues of class, gender, sexuality and race, of justice, power and social responsibility. They show us the world through a different set of lenses and ask us questions that were far more challenging than any we would face in an exam. As teenagers, we might have thought that we knew these books inside out, but often it's only as we go through our lives that we recognize the impact they have. They worm their way into our heads and touch us in a way that's more personal than any other school subject. Their lessons will sit quietly within us for years, until something awakens them: a particular set of experiences, a story in the news, maybe a personal crisis. When we reread them as adults, they can resonate with us in ways that we never dreamed of when we first met them.

These books are important for other reasons too. They can often be a battleground. Politicians and other public figures have a habit of airing their opinions about which books should and shouldn't be taught. It's as if these books represent something – a set of morals, a particular standard of beauty – that all young people must absorb. There are outcries when schools replace familiar classics with texts intended to reflect a more diverse and plural society. People can feel bruised when new light is shone on to books that have been loved by generations, revealing them to be more problematic than previously thought. The subject of English is at the heart of this battleground, and in *Reading Lessons* I explore the significance of what English teachers do, in getting young people to read between the lines, examine texts carefully and look critically at the values that under-pin them – activities that are central to the development of a humane society, and more urgently needed now than they have perhaps ever been.

There are many metaphors for books, and for stories. For the poet Emily Dickinson, a book was a frigate, able to 'take us lands away'. Books allow Roald Dahl's Matilda to travel the world while sitting in her little room in an English village. But books can also be comfort blankets. They are lifebelts and refuges, friends and companions. For Nora Ephron, reading was both 'escape, and the opposite of escape'. Hector, the flawed and eccentric schoolteacher in Alan Bennett's play *The History Boys*, describes the moments in reading when it feels as if a hand has reached out and taken yours. Books are mirrors held up to the world, but they are also lights, something we turn to in moments of darkness.

Books can be all of these things, but they are also something more. They're the start of an argument. They are the crucibles in which ideas are fired. The classrooms in which we encounter them should give us space to question and challenge. They should get us to think about the stories that texts *don't* tell as well as the ones they do: who they include and who they leave out. They should draw us into a conversation. As a teacher of English, I don't always know where those conversations are going to end up. But I know how important they are, and how they begin by taking a book from the shelf, opening the pages and starting to read.

# On power, gender and control: 'My Last Duchess' by Robert Browning

It's an old story. There's a man, and a woman. He's not happy. He's noticed things. Suspicions have taken root in his mind and started to grow. He's nurtured them, cultivated them, and they have twisted back into themselves, trapped inside the rigid case of his skull with nowhere else to go. She is oblivious. Her eyes are bright with the joy of being alive: the world, for her, is a place of kindness and pleasure. Irritation is carved into the set of his brow and the flare of his nostril. Everything she says, everything she does, only adds to the anger that festers inside him. Something has to be done.

I am thinking about this man and this woman as I stand in the front porch of our house waiting for Mrs Roberts, our Head of Year, to pick me up. I'm fifteen, and I've been given a mission. A girl in my English class is in hospital and I've been asked to go and help her with her schoolwork so she doesn't fall too far behind. The man and the woman are in the poem we've been studying. I rehearse the facts of their relationship carefully, hoping I won't forget anything important. It's probably the most complicated poem we've encountered so far, and there's a lot that I need to remember. Rhyming couplets. Iambic pentameter. It's October 1988, and I don't know it yet, but I'm about to teach 'My Last Duchess' for the first of many, many times.

I'm not sure why I've been singled out for this job, because this isn't a girl I know particularly well. She's on the hockey and netball teams, competent and capable. She has proper running shoes with spikes while everyone else makes do with crappy trainers from the local market. Such is my hopelessness at any kind of organized physical activity that when I've had anything to do with her in the past, I've usually been on the receiving end of a scornful comment about missing an important catch or not being fast enough. We occupy different circles, and as a result, I barely noticed her absence from school for the first week or so. But then the rumours started. *She's got anorexia*, one person said. Someone else told us that boys had been teasing her about her appearance, saying she was too sporty and muscular, not feminine enough. And so all that hockey-playing energy, all that commitment, has been diverted into creating a body that might be considered more acceptable.

I've already had numerous awkwardnesses to contend with. There was being kept behind after English, for one thing. I'm never kept behind after lessons, and I had no idea what it was all about until our English teacher told me. Then, of course, all my friends wanted to know what was going on, and why I'd been chosen for this particular job. I'd been told to go and ask the new Head of English for some A4 paper to take with me, but the new Head of English is unknown and therefore scary, so instead I've bought a new writing pad. The biggest awkwardness of all, of course, is still to come. What on earth do you say to someone who's suffering from an eating disorder? Until now, anorexia has belonged in the pages of teenage magazines, something that other people suffer from, at other schools. I bury myself in the security of the poem, reciting its first line under my breath: 'That's my last Duchess painted on the wall'. Our English teacher had described the situation for us, making us picture the Duke, the narrator of the poem, drawing aside a curtain to reveal a painting to a visitor. We'd sat in rows and made careful notes. A shaft of autumn sun had filtered through the first-floor window of our classroom, landing on scratched desks and yellowed posters. I run through all the things I've learned. Will I be able to pass on everything I know?

I wasn't aware of it back then, but there was an odd irony in the situation. 'My Last Duchess' is a poem about the relationship between a young woman and a man who thinks he should be able to dictate how she behaves. I was teaching it to a young woman who was suffering unbearably because men – or, more precisely, teenage boys – thought they should be able to dictate how she should behave, to comment on how she should look, to be the arbiters of whether her appearance was acceptable or not. I didn't recognize this at the time, but I was only fifteen and this was 1988, and feminism was still some way from my consciousness. When we'd studied the poem in class, we'd concentrated on the story it told, rather than viewing it in the wider context of patriarchy and the abuse of power. Our essays focused on the character of the Duke. When we got them back, mine had ticks in red ink, a mark of 18 out of 20 and a short comment: *V. good.* I had no idea why it got 18 out of 20 instead of 17 or 19, or what I would have needed to do in order to improve it. It didn't occur to me to ask, either. We didn't have those kinds of conversations back then.

Nowadays, I don't think you can teach 'My Last Duchess' without setting it against the backdrop of gender politics, because the whole poem is about one man's belief that he should be able to police the way his wife behaved. The bare bones of the poem are simple. At the beginning, this man is telling a visitor about this wife, now his former wife. She was younger than him, and beautiful. She was an innocent soul who liked unassuming pleasures: chatting with a stranger, riding her white mule. A man gave her some cherries, and she thanked him. There was no hint of unfaithfulness in this, nothing in fact but simple gratitude, but her husband wasn't happy. You imagine him glowering and ruminating, churning his suspicions over and over in his mind. She smiled at him, but she smiled at everyone else too: that was the problem. Until he formed a plan that brought all the smiles to an end.

The poem is set during the Italian Renaissance, but the emotions are universal. Change the details and the relationship could be happening in Manchester or

Kolkata or Bucharest; it could be nineteenth-century Pennsylvania or 1950s Ireland or skyscrapered Dubai. It could be any place at any time when men (especially older men) have seen women (especially younger women) less as people than as entities that are theirs to control, to make use of in any way they see fit. The white mule doesn't need to be a white mule. It could be anything that takes her attention away from him: a career she's passionate about, an absorbing pastime, a group of close friends. The man with the cherries could be the guy who delivers the groceries. The jealous husband, the wife who's simply going about her business: it's the stuff of countless stories, from fairy tales to Netflix box sets, and the sad reality that lies behind so many domestic violence statistics.

'My Last Duchess', a poem I've now taught to more GCSE groups than I can actually remember, is a dramatic monologue, a form at which Browning excelled. He frequently used it to reveal character flaws and inconsistencies: his narrators are unreliable, often pompous or self-justifying, sometimes vain and occasionally unhinged. The speaker in this poem is the Duke of Ferrara, and not just any old Duke of Ferrara, either. He's Alfonso II d'Este, the fifth Duke of Ferrara, and if you want, you can – like keen students the world over – look him up on the internet and find out all about him. He was born in November 1533, and in 1558, at the age of twenty-four, he married Lucrezia di Cosimo de' Medici, who was just thirteen years old. ('Ewww, Miss!' my students exclaim.) The Duke apparently considered Lucrezia to be his social inferior, which explains his huffiness about the fact that she treats his gift of a nine-hundred-year-old name like 'anybody's gift'. In April 1561, at the age of sixteen, Lucrezia died. The suspicion, I tell my students, was that she was poisoned.

They like this, my students. They like being able to root a poem in historical truth. It stops it from becoming too nebulous, from dissolving into subjectivity. They also like regular rhyming patterns and stanzas with equal numbers of lines, not for any aesthetic reasons but because these are things that they can count and label, a set of easily demonstrable facts that remind them – almost – of safer subjects like Geography and Chemistry and Physics. What they'd *really* love would be if English involved having to know what kind of poison the Duke used, or the six-figure grid reference for where it happened. The slipperiness of English often troubles them, with its ambiguities and scope for interpretation. For a teacher, there's a difficult balancing act to carry out. I want to encourage them to develop their independence as readers, to build their confidence in responding to texts, but at the same time I have to point out that this independence has limits. Sometimes students think there are no right and wrong answers in English, that you can make a poem mean whatever you want it to mean, but this isn't the case. Reading closely, reading carefully, is a matter of tact: working with the words on the page, what we know of their authors and their historical contexts, and the echoes they have in our own day and age. It takes time to develop the kind of understanding you need to be good at English: there are no quick fixes, no easy wins.

I don't give my students the full story of Lucrezia and the Duke. I leave out the fact that the Duke spent most of his time after their marriage at the French court in Paris, leaving Lucrezia – who was apparently far more devoted to him than the other way round – back in Ferrara. I also don't tell them that the likelihood is that she actually died of tuberculosis. All of this will burst the bubble, introducing too many contradictions: for some of them, it will invalidate the whole poem. And anyway, you don't need to know any of these particular historical details to understand what Robert Browning is doing in this poem. We certainly didn't, back in 1988, when accessing all of this information would have involved not a quick search on Google but a trip to the local library and a pile of dusty reference books. All you really need to know is that an arrogant man has married a younger woman, and is unhappy about the way she behaves.

In the poem, the Duke of Ferrara is talking to an envoy with whom he is negotiating the terms of his next marriage. He shows the envoy a portrait of his last duchess, painted by the artist Frà Pandolf. 'Last': she's one in a sequence. He's clearly very proud of this painting, because he manages to squeeze Frà Pandolf's name into the conversation three times in the first sixteen lines, telling the envoy that he mentioned the artist's name deliberately to save him having to ask who painted such a lifelike portrait. But the realism of the Duchess's image, the delicate flush on her face, is also a source of disquiet. As the Duke says, it was not just her husband's presence that called that 'spot of joy' into her cheek. She was 'too soon made glad, / Too easily impressed'. There's a dark hint in his next words, a suggestion of something improper: 'she liked whate'er / She looked on', we're told, 'and her looks went everywhere.'

When I introduce the poem in class, I read it out loud. I don't do this with every poem, but 'My Last Duchess' is one that needs to be heard. You need the emphasis and studied hesitations, the subtle shifts in tone. At this point in the reading I always pause, and look round the class, checking to see who's taking it in.

'So, she was flirting with people?' one of the students invariably wants to know.

'Well, let's see,' I reply. 'Focus on what the poem says. What is it, exactly, that the Duke doesn't like?'

It's there, on the page. She's happy with everything she sees, the Duchess. The favour – the gift, possibly a brooch – that the Duke has given her. The dropping of the daylight in the West. The bough of cherries that someone – an 'officious fool', the recipient of the Duke's scorn – breaks for her. Her white mule. They're all the same. I make the students think about this. This guy's jealous of a mule, for goodness' sake. He's jealous of the *sunset*. Because his wife likes all of these things, he feels that his gift to her – the gift of a 'nine-hundred-years-old name' – has been devalued. It's not about flirting with other men. It's about *everything*.

The next few lines, for me, are the most chilling. The Duke has clearly considered telling the Duchess how he feels; he's even rehearsed the words in his head. He'd tell her about all the things that displease him, the times when she goes a bit too far or doesn't come up to his expectations, the aspects of her behaviour that disgust him. *Disgust*: it's a strong word, and one you'd be stung by, if it was ever used in anger to describe something you'd done. Maybe she'd obey him. Maybe she'd argue back. But she doesn't get the chance to do either, because the conversation never happens. He won't lower himself by admitting that he's been dishonoured. That would be stooping, says the Duke, and he chooses never to stoop. Instead, he takes another, more final, course of action:

> This grew; I gave commands;
> Then all smiles stopped together.

I could pause, at this point, to look at that line in more detail. I could draw your attention to how perfectly paced and balanced it is, those two semicolons giving you time to take in the full import of what he's saying. I could get you to imagine being the envoy, being taken into the Duke's confidence and slowly realizing what kind of person he is. All of these are so tempting, so easy to do, that it's possible to miss what Browning is telling us here. I make my students work it out, and watch as the penny drops. The Duke has had his wife killed because he didn't like the way she was behaving. She smiled at people, and was friendly, and now she's dead. Some readers might conclude that her death is the result of her own behaviour, but that would be to make it her fault, rather than the Duke's. It's the kind of victim-blaming you see everywhere. *Her skirt was too short. She had too much to drink. She shouldn't have been out on her own, so late at night.* She didn't do what she was supposed to do, didn't stay in her box, and so she had to be punished. What did she expect?

'So, *was* she flirting?' I ask. There's a clamour of voices. Yes, she was. Well, not exactly, she was just being friendly, but she should have known better. Somebody suggests that Frà Pandolf was flirting with the Duchess as he painted her portrait, and somebody else replies that if that was the case, the Duke would probably have had *him* killed as well. Another person argues that the Duchess was being unreasonable if she thought the Duke was just going to stand by and watch her behaving like this. Someone reminds us that the poem is set at a time when values were different, that the Duke was simply a product of his culture, and I ask whether this makes his behaviour acceptable. It's a heated discussion, and I'm pleased that so many students are contributing, but at the same time, debates like this can be difficult to manage. There are some moments, as a teacher, when you have to intervene: to address a misconception, or to challenge a viewpoint that might be problematic, maybe even intentionally provocative. (And difficult decisions to make: do you respond by turning this kind of moment into a teaching point for the whole class, or by keeping a student behind for a conversation after the lesson?) There's a bit of chat about whether the bough of cherries is some kind of sexual metaphor, and I remind them that a cigar is, sometimes, just a cigar; that a bough of cherries can simply be an innocent, generous gift. And just when I'm starting to despair at their apparent support for the Duke, a boy at the back says, 'But she hasn't actually done anything wrong. It's him that's the problem. He just wanted to control everything she did.'

It's true. What's particularly unsettling about 'My Last Duchess' is that once you start looking for it, the Duke's desire for control is everywhere. It's there in the curtain that covers the portrait of the last Duchess, a curtain that nobody but the Duke is allowed to put aside: he's controlling her in death just as he wanted to in life. It's there in the way he tells the envoy what to think. It's even present in those questions that aren't really questions: 'Will 't please you sit and look at her?', 'Will 't please you rise?' I tell my students that this kind of question is called a mitigated imperative – the technical name for a disguised or softened command – and they write it down assiduously, because they like learning new technical terms. I give them examples of mitigated imperatives I use in class: *Do you want to get your books out? Can you turn to page 79?* They're phrased like questions, but you're not supposed to refuse: the envoy is only being given the veneer of a choice. And it's there at the end, in the poem's final image: the statue of Neptune, taming a sea-horse, which, as the Duke tells us, 'Claus of Innsbruck cast in bronze for me!' It's significant, too, that 'me' is the last word in the whole poem. The students love this. What better proof of the Duke's arrogance? They highlight it, and make a careful note.

The genius of 'My Last Duchess', though, is that this sense of control isn't just part of the poem's content. It's also present in its form and structure. It consists of a series of rhyming couplets, twenty-eight of them in total, and each line is written in iambic pentameter, a pattern of ten syllables whose stresses reflect the normal rhythm of spoken English. The Duke is modest about his ability to express himself – he claims to have no 'skill in speech' – but it's a false modesty. His account is measured, controlled, calculated. You can imagine him as the master gaslighter, the person whose complete confidence in his own version of events would leave you with little room to breathe. Browning's manipulation of language is the perfect riposte to people – like some of my students, frustrated by what they see as 'reading too much into things' – who think that poems happen by accident, that they flow on to the page fully formed, an unchecked outpouring of poetic genius. There's no way you could write something like this without hours of hard work. It's a masterpiece of regulation, and this is entirely fitting.

At the end of the poem, the Duke and the envoy head downstairs to rejoin the rest of the company. He tells the envoy that his master is so generous that he is sure that any reasonable request for a dowry will be agreed to – although he adds that 'his fair daughter's self' is really what he's interested in. It's not convincing. Of course it's the dowry that he's most concerned with. The students recognize this, by now: they've got him sussed.

'So why does he tell this envoy guy what he's done?' a student asks. 'Won't the envoy just go and tell the Count?'

We think about this. Would the Count call the marriage off, whisk his daughter away and find a more suitable son-in-law? Isn't the Duke taking a risk? Maybe, another student ventures, it's all part of the plan. The Duke's passing on a message about how he expects his future wife to behave. He *wants* the envoy to tell the Count, because then the Count will tell his daughter, and she'll understand what she's supposed to do. Watch your step: don't smile at anyone except him. No looking at the sunset for you. It's extremely calculating, but that's the point.

The real Duke went on to marry Barbara of Austria, daughter not of a Count but of the Holy Roman Emperor, Ferdinand I: she also predeceased him. His third wife, Margherita Gonzaga, who was thirty years younger than him, outlived him by twenty years. Because my students like pictures as well as facts, I show them an image of Lucrezia, the Duke's first Duchess, painted by Agnolo Bronzino in 1560, a couple of years after her marriage. She looks older than her fifteen years, with thin pencilled eyebrows and angular cheekbones, in a high-collared black dress and a jewelled girdle. She's holding something that might well have been a favour given to her by the Duke. It's a small gold object, oval in shape, inset with precious stones. It could be a brooch, or a pillbox, but what it really looks like is a small ornate grenade. If there's time, we also look at images of Alfonso d'Este, painted at different stages of his life. In one, he's in his twenties, hair slicked back, his hand holding down the pages of an open book. His expression is possibly meant to be contemplative, but to me he looks sullen, a moody grad student who has gone to check a fact and found out that he's wrong. In another, in the Metropolitan Museum in New York, he's older, with a domed bald head, grey beard and natty moustache twisted into points. He's wearing armour of the kind that seems decorative rather than actually useful, in black and gold stripes, with a matching doublet underneath. And then he's there as an elderly man, all in black, his long cloak showing off shapely calves that he's clearly quite proud of. He looks almost benign, an Italian Renaissance Dumbledore, until you notice the sword in his left hand. *Don't mess with me. Do as you're told.*

In Margaret Atwood's short story 'My Last Duchess', published in her 2006 collection, *Moral Disorder*, two teenagers argue over Browning's poem. It's a story I'd love to teach alongside the poem itself, but sadly, the curriculum doesn't allow time for it: all these interesting avenues to explore, and we have to stick to the main road, our eyes fixed straight ahead. The boy in Atwood's story thinks the Duke is a 'smug little pervert', a sick jerk: he should be locked up or hanged. The Duchess was just being friendly. The girl disagrees. The Duchess should have worked out that her husband didn't like her smiling at everyone in the way she did. She was a dumb bunny, a simp. *Simp*: a word that took a while to filter into my students' vocabularies, but is very definitely there now, a dismissive little sneer aimed at anyone who is too friendly and attentive towards someone of the opposite sex. Simpering? Sympathetic? Simpleton? On TikTok – a corner of the internet whose target demographic definitely does not include middle-aged English teachers like me – there is a series of videos called 'Simp Nation', skewering the kind of behaviour exhibited by simps. Giving compliments, being a good listener, offering help, even lending someone a spare pencil in class: any of these actions, which might otherwise just be considered part and parcel of being a normal decent human being, is enough to get you labelled a simp, something you definitely don't want to be. No wonder teenage relationships are such a minefield.

When I teach 'My Last Duchess' today, in the all-boys school where I currently work, I begin by making my students find out about coercive control. This is defined as behaviour within a familial or other close relationship that restricts another person's right to live their own life: it seeks to monitor their actions, limit their freedom and isolate them from friends and acquaintances. It's been a criminal offence in England and Wales since 2015, and carries a prison sentence of up to five years. We look at a diagram, the Duluth Power and Control Wheel, that sets out different forms of controlling behaviour. We talk about economic abuse, preventing people from having access to money or a job. We think about the way that isolation acts as a form of abuse, about the way that casting aspersions on someone's friendships or activities outside the home could eventually become so suffocating and unpleasant that they decide it's not worth the hassle and simply stay indoors. Some of them, inevitably, sneer at the Power and Control Wheel's reference to male privilege. There'll be a highly predictable remark about feminists taking things too far. These kinds of comments, though, are exactly why, in a boys' school, I should be teaching 'My Last Duchess' in this way. Somewhere, in my class, there might well be someone whose dad won't let his mum go to evening classes, or whose sister is made to feel ashamed of herself because of the clothes she wears or the friends she wants to see outside of school. If any of this makes them realize that this isn't the way things should be, it's worth doing. If Robert Browning helps to break the cycle in just one family, it will be worth it.

And if all of this makes my students think about the way they themselves treat girls and women, that will be worth it too. Because somewhere in my class there might also be a boy who thinks it's okay to track his girlfriend's social media accounts and find out exactly who she's interacting with and in what way. There might be a boy who doesn't respect boundaries and doesn't take no for an answer. There will inevitably be boys who think it's okay to comment, sometimes very publicly, on what girls look like and how they should behave. There will be boys who catcall, boys who trade laddish banter and claim that it's 'just a joke'. At some point, they will go out into a world where there are men who still think they're entitled to be paid more and shout more loudly, that it's acceptable to grope and intimidate and behave in ways that make women feel less secure about the spaces they occupy and the freedoms they should enjoy. I want them to know that this isn't the way things should be.

In recent years, toxic masculinity – and the violence against women that it so often leads to – has been brought under the microscope. Social media has allowed women to share experiences. Campaigns such as Everyday Sexism, founded in 2012 by Laura Bates, have drawn attention to the constant exhausting drip of comments and assumptions that women face, including the 'small, so-used-to-it-you-almost-just-accept-it sexism' that can become so ingrained. And it is clear that schools are part of the problem. In June 2020, the women's rights activist Soma Sara founded Everyone's Invited, a campaigning organization whose website invites women to post accounts of misogyny, harassment and rape culture. A year after it was launched, Everyone's Invited published a list of all the UK schools and colleges that had been named in its testimonies. Almost 3,000 schools were listed, including 2,556 secondaries and, heartbreakingly, 406 primary schools. Eight of the schools named were infant schools, for children up to the age of seven.

Between 2020 and 2023, during her tenure as UK Shadow Minister for Domestic Violence and Safeguarding, the Labour MP Jess Phillips marked International Women's Day in March by reading out the names of the women and girls who, in the previous twelve months, had died at the hands of men. In doing so, she ensured that their names were placed on permanent record, that their fates were not forgotten. The list that Phillips read out in 2021 contained 118 names, equating to one woman every three days. The final name was that of Sarah Everard, a 33-year-old marketing executive who was walking home from a friend's house in London when she was abducted by a serving police officer. Her murder brought an outpouring of stories from women about the times when they had been made to feel unsafe and the things they'd done in the hope of not becoming another victim. But it also brought questions from men. What could they do to be an ally? How could they make sure they weren't part of the problem?

In December 2021, Andy Burnham, the Mayor of Greater Manchester, launched #IsThisOK, a ninety-second film designed to prompt men to examine the patterns of behaviour that make women feel threatened. The film – part of Greater Manchester's ten-year strategy to reduce gender-based violence – highlights the impact of catcalls and wolf whistles, unwanted attention and invasions of space. *Smile, love! I bet you're prettier when you smile. Look at her. Have you got a boyfriend? Don't ignore me, I just want to talk to you.* All the kinds of comments that make women and girls feel they should tailor their behaviour to men's expectations, that they should be careful about where they go and what they do. Burnham's campaign places the responsibility firmly on men and boys – not just to be aware of their own actions, but to challenge those of others too. It aims to start a conversation: one that is much needed and long overdue.

This conversation needs to take place in schools as well. The publicity generated by Everyone's Invited prompted Ofsted, the UK government's schools inspectorate, to investigate the scale of sexual abuse and harassment in schools and colleges. Their investigation found that sexual harassment was so endemic in some schools that it had become normalized. For some children, incidents were 'so commonplace that they see no point in reporting them'. There were calls for boys to be taught about misogyny and its effects on the everyday lives of girls and women, to question ingrained assumptions and consider the impact of long-established modes of behaviour.

But we have a difficult struggle ahead of us. In the summer of 2022, a new name emerged: that of Andrew Tate, a social media influencer and former kickboxer whose videos on TikTok have, at the time of writing, been viewed over twelve billion times. Tate has gained his notoriety from preaching an extreme form of misogyny. He talks about hitting women, choking them, preventing them from going out. If his partner accused him of cheating, Tate declares, he would assault her, violently. In one video, he outlines his attitude to relationships: 'I inflict, I expect, absolute loyalty from my woman. I ain't having my chicks talking to other dudes, liking other dudes.' Tate, with his luxury cars and private jets, and the Duke of Ferrara, with his art collection, have a lot in common: the conspicuous wealth, the desire for complete control. The Duke of Ferrara, though, isn't peddling a particular lifestyle, or being blamed for what many commentators have described as a form of radicalization. There are countless stories of women in schools being confronted with misogynistic attitudes, of teenage boys refusing to do as female teachers tell them. *Get back in the kitchen*, they say. *You shouldn't be telling a man what to do.*

There are few spaces in the curriculum where we can address the challenge posed by Tate and others like him, where we can tackle issues like gender and power and coercive behaviour. So we grab our chances when we can, and use texts like 'My Last Duchess' to open discussions. We challenge and question. We ask: *Is it okay to treat people like this?* We sometimes run the gauntlet of jeers and dismissive comments. *It's just banter*, we're told. *It doesn't matter.* But it's not, and it does.

I think back to the first time I taught 'My Last Duchess', to the girl at my school. I remember her being pleased to see Mrs Roberts and me when we visited her that Monday evening in October 1988, over thirty years ago now. I remember sitting on the edge of her hospital bed, taking her through the poem line by line, telling her about rhyming patterns and explaining what a dramatic monologue was. She came back to school the following year, still thin, but stronger. A few years later, at university, I read Naomi Wolf's book *The Beauty Myth*, and found a passage that resonated so much that I copied it out. I can still remember it, almost word for word.

> What if she doesn't worry about her body and eats enough for all the growing she has to do? She might rip her stockings and slam-dance on a forged ID to the Pogues, and walk home barefoot, holding her shoes, alone at dawn; she might baby-sit in a battered-women's shelter one night a month; she might skateboard down Lombard Street with its seven hairpin turns, or fall in love with her best friend and do something about it, or lose herself for hours gazing into test tubes with her hair a mess.

What if we lived in a world where girls and women were free to take risks, to go wherever they wanted and do whatever they wanted to do, to live life entirely on their own terms?

At the end of Maggie O'Farrell's 2022 novel, *The Marriage Portrait*, a retelling of the events behind Browning's poem, Lucrezia, the Duchess, manages to escape. A young woman who has existed in literature for nearly two centuries, frozen in time, captured in oils, is given agency. Her life so far has been full of restrictions and constraints. She is aware that she is in danger. She wants to walk, to paint, to explore, to let her mind wander free. And so, dressed in her maidservant's clothes, assisted by the young artist who has helped to paint her, she tiptoes quietly through her husband's fortress, eases back the huge heavy bolts on the kitchen door and steps out into the night. Then she runs.

What Lucrezia doesn't know, breathing in the scent of the trees and feeling the delicious chill of the night air, is that someone else will die instead of her: the maid whose clothes she has borrowed, mistaken for her by the Duke and his henchman, who suffocate her as she sleeps. A noblewoman gains her freedom, a servant dies: another inequality, another form of injustice. I want them both to survive. There are too many dead women in literature, just as there are too many dead women in the world, and too many women living in fear, watching what they do, making their lives smaller than they should be.

I lost touch with the girl from my English class after we left school. I have no idea what she's doing now, but I hope that things worked out for her: that she is happy, and has been able to devote herself to building a life that she has chosen. I hope, above all else, that she's been able to rediscover what it is to run, to be sporty, to delight in the freedom of air and movement and space without scornful voices holding her back. I think back to those classrooms we used to inhabit, those dusty rooms with the faded posters, and wonder how much has really changed: how far we've come, and how far we still need to go.

# On social responsibility: *An Inspector Calls* by J. B. Priestley

Early December, and it's Christmas Jumper Day. I'm teaching Year Ten, and their usual navy uniforms have been replaced by an array of brightly coloured sweaters: snowmen and reindeer, a festive Darth Vader, a sinister-looking Grinch. We're studying *A Christmas Carol*, and we've just reached the point where the Ghost of Christmas Present reveals to Scrooge the figures of Ignorance and Want, personified as wretched destitute children. I point out the irony of the fact that Charles Dickens, in 1843, was giving his readers a warning about neglecting the poor, and yet here we are, almost two centuries later, wearing Christmas jumpers to raise money for the local foodbank.

If I'd made the same point a few years ago, I'd have been met with eyerolls. *She's off again on one of her rants*, students might have thought. But in this particular year, the young people I teach know all too well how challenging life has become for many. I'm aware that some of my own students come from families who must make difficult choices between heating and food. I know that we have sixth-formers who are doing multiple paid jobs outside school, sometimes at the expense of their academic work, to help their parents make ends meet. I'd told my department, at the start of term, to remember that we'd have students who were doing their homework in cold houses with limited internet access. A thin draught rattles the windows in my classroom, and I think of the hard decisions that school leaders face. Make urgent repairs to school buildings, or buy new textbooks? Replace the teaching assistant who is leaving, so that children with additional needs can continue to be supported, or save the money so it can be spent elsewhere? In the news, there are stories of nurses having to use foodbanks. It's a winter of industrial action, of anger against a government that has failed to fund and safeguard vital public services. I think of Dickens, sending out his message about the need for charity and compassion, and wonder what he'd say if he could see the state we were in.

I want to believe that books can change the world. I've been teaching English for nearly three decades now, and I could hardly have done this if I didn't believe in the power of literature to make people engage with the lives and situations of others, immersing them in stories that might make them see things differently. There are voices, though, that disagree. I remember a section of W. H. Auden's poem 'In Memory of W. B. Yeats', his tribute to the great Irish poet. 'Mad Ireland hurt you into poetry', Auden wrote, thinking of Yeats's early years in an Ireland that saw the rise of nationalism and increasing demands for home rule. 'Now Ireland has her madness and her weather still, / For poetry makes nothing happen'. They're lines that play on my mind, taunting me. But Auden also reminds us that poetry survives. The poet can 'let the healing fountain start'. He, or she, can write the words that make people think. It might not seem much, but it's one of the most important things that anyone can do.

Novelists and playwrights make people think too, of course, and every year thousands of teenagers will read a play that has sought, ever since it was written, to act as a rallying cry for social change. This is J. B. Priestley's 1945 play, *An Inspector Calls*, and the message it contains – that we do not live alone, that we live in a society where we bear a collective responsibility towards each other – is one of the most important literary calls to activism that teenagers will encounter. It sparks debate and invites audiences to examine their own actions. And its dominance in schools says a lot, I think, about the desire of English teachers to believe that literature can indeed make something happen, that we can actually make a difference.

Students enjoy *An Inspector Calls*. This is partly, I'm sure, because it's a relatively easy play to study, short and pacy, with a simple structure and a small cast of characters. It also draws on a very particular social context, interrogating the privilege and ignorance of the upper classes in the early twentieth century, and there's something about this historical specificity that students find reassuring. There's a body of facts to be learned, a set of notes to be made and memorized. Any teenager who has studied the play will be able to tell you the significance of its dates, first performed in the year the Second World War ended but set two years before the First World War began. The action takes place at the home of Arthur Birling, a wealthy factory owner, and his wife, Sybil. The Birlings are celebrating the engagement of their daughter, Sheila, to Gerald Croft, the son of titled parents. All is well in the Birlings' world. They are dressed in their best evening clothes. They have just had an excellent meal, and Arthur is expounding his philosophy of life to his future son-in-law over port and cigars. They have no idea, on that spring evening, of the cataclysmic events that will unfold over the next few decades. The horror of the trenches, the Blitz, the death camps: all are still to come. Priestley plays on the gap between the Birlings' ignorance and his audience's knowledge, revealing how short-sighted and complacent they are. There is, Birling declares to his family, no chance of war. There is talk of discontent amongst the workers, but Birling brushes this off. All these silly little war scares and all these capital-versus-labour agitations will be forgotten in a few years' time. The future will be one of progress, of new inventions and peace and prosperity. It's a masterpiece of dramatic irony, and students can see this so easily that the play gives them a feeling of cleverness, a confidence boost. Just to drive home how ignorant Birling is, Priestley has him mention a new liner, the *Titanic*, that is about to set sail: 'forty-six thousand eight hundred tons – New York in five days – and every luxury – and unsinkable, absolutely unsinkable.' We imagine Birling loosening his collar and pouring himself another glass of port, his face red with the glow of good food and self-satisfaction. We might think of Birling's equivalents in our own time, scoffing about the threat of climate change or the seriousness of Covid-19. And then, the doorbell rings, and the servant Edna appears with the news that an inspector has called, to make enquiries about the events leading to the death of a young woman. (Another dead young woman, I observe ruefully, thinking back to 'My Last Duchess': the GCSE set text lists are full of them.)

I teach the play by beginning with this death. I present my students with an outline. A young woman has ended her own life. Two years ago, she was working in a local factory, but was dismissed from her post after leading a strike for higher wages. She managed to find a job as a sales assistant in an expensive clothes shop, but was sacked after being accused of laughing at a customer. Understandably, she became very depressed. She met a rich young man who took pity on her, and they began a relationship. This ended when he became engaged to someone else. She then met a younger man whose behaviour towards her seems to have been somewhat coercive. As a result of this relationship, she became pregnant. She appealed to a local charity for help, there being no other sources of support at the time, but the head of the charity dismissed her appeal. Alone and in despair, she felt she had only one possible way out. She drank a bottle of disinfectant and died in agony at the local infirmary. Which of these events, I ask, would have had the biggest impact on her? Who is responsible for what has happened?

Over the years, I've had a huge range of responses. There are some, perhaps inevitably, that make me despair. It's her own fault. If she'd kept quiet and not gone on strike, there wouldn't have been a problem. Nobody's entitled to higher wages. (I intervene at this point with a little lesson about fair pay, and ask if it's right that ordinary workers should struggle while fat-cat bosses cream off the profits of their labour. Sometimes, depressingly, a student will reply that this is absolutely fine, and I have a private moment of anguish.) Some say that she should have chosen her partners more carefully, and I ask them if they think it's possible to predict how a relationship will turn out when it first begins. There's always someone who will comment that the young woman shouldn't have got herself pregnant, and when I've dealt with the obvious absurdity of this, I drop into the conversation the suspicion that the young man who got her pregnant might actually have raped her. Their sympathies shift, although there's still the occasional person who will opine that she shouldn't have got herself into that situation anyway. Mercifully, though, there will also be students who sympathize. It was a downward spiral, they say. She had no support and no reason to hope that anything would change. Her confidence would have been crushed by so many things going wrong, one of my quieter and more thoughtful students comments, and I thank him, grateful that he felt brave enough to speak up.

It is this situation, this sequence of events, that the Inspector has come to investigate. Slowly, methodically, he questions the Birlings and Gerald, one member of the family at a time, peeling back the layers of their complacency and revealing that all of them, in some way, have helped to make this young woman feel so hopeless that her life was no longer worth living. There are twists and turns and revelations, and a masterly shock at the end. The lives of the Birlings will never be the same again. And neither should those of the audience, we sense, because Priestley's message is that all of us should examine the way we treat others and the consequences our behaviour might have. By the time the curtain falls, we should all be less comfortable than we were at the start of the play.

Priestley sets the scene carefully, even before the action begins. In class, we look at the clues he gives us about the Birlings and their social status. They live in the manufacturing city of Brumley, in the north Midlands, placing them firmly in a region that would have prospered from the mills and factories of the Industrial Revolution. Their house is a 'fairly large suburban house', with 'good solid furniture of the period'. Not antique furniture, though: this is new money, not inherited wealth. Birling is a self-made man and proud of it. He refers to himself, several times, as a 'hard-headed, practical man of business'. Significantly, Priestley tells us that he is 'rather provincial in his speech', and I imagine his wife, who is 'her husband's social superior', twitching with disapproval at any slips in his accent and manners. The members of the family are sketched in brief but telling strokes. Sheila is pretty and 'rather excited'. Her younger brother, Eric, is awkward, feeling perhaps a little on the margins of this family celebration. Gerald Croft, 'very much the well-bred man-about-town', is clearly quite a catch. The son of Sir George and Lady Croft, business rivals of Mr Birling, he represents the future, when the two firms can work together to secure lower costs and higher prices. There is excitement in the air. But, interestingly, while the atmosphere should be 'substantial and comfortable', it is not 'cosy and homelike'. We're not supposed to like these people, or look up to them, the women in evening dresses, the men in white tie and tails. (They're in their own home, one boy points out: why is everything so formal?) We wouldn't want to be in this room.

Into the midst of this walks the Inspector. His surname, which he spells out, is Goole. Priestley uses the stage directions to draw our attention to the impact he should have, telling us that he need not be a big man, but should create 'an impression of massiveness, solidity and purposefulness'. The lighting changes, becoming harsher and brighter. The Inspector takes control. The Birlings are discomfited, wrong-footed on their own territory.

Over the course of the play we see each of the Birlings, plus Gerald, being questioned by the Inspector about their involvement with the young woman whose death is under investigation. The first member of the Birling family to come under the Inspector's critical gaze is Arthur. He doesn't like being questioned at all. My Year Elevens, studying the play for GCSE, enjoy spotting Birling's attempts to intimidate the Inspector. He's a magistrate. He used to be an alderman, and we find out what this is: a member of a local council, elected by other members, with attendant hints of cronyism. He was Lord Mayor two years ago. He plays golf with the Chief Constable, for goodness' sake: how dare the Inspector turn up at his house and start asking questions? We imagine him puffed up with outrage, strutting like a turkey. But the Inspector is implacable, and is not impressed at all by Arthur's social status.

Arthur knew the young woman as Eva Smith, although that wasn't always the name she went by. He remembers her as a 'lively, good-looking girl', but her liveliness led to trouble. She helped to lead a strike for higher wages, demanding twenty-five shillings a week instead of twenty-two and six. A student asks how much that would be in today's terms, and we look it up. One website, thisismoney.co.uk, tells us that Eva and her fellow workers would have been earning the equivalent of just under £160 a week, and that they were asking for another £17.70. I sense a bit of cross-curricular maths coming on. I ask the students to work out how much Eva would have been earning per hour if she got her pay rise, assuming that she worked a forty-hour week. There's a flurry of calculators, and then someone announces that it would have been about £4.42 an hour. We'd have to do a lot more research to find out what Eva would have been able to afford in 1910 for her twenty-two and six a week, but the key takeaway point, for the students, is that she would have been earning well below today's minimum wage. I remind them that it was Eva's hard labour, and that of her fellow workers, that was keeping the Birlings in champagne and port, and I am gratified by their growing outrage.

Eva's protest didn't work. She had far too much to say for herself, Arthur Birling blusters. Far too much. And so she had to go, because why listen to the grievances of an uppity member of the working classes – especially an uppity young female member of the working classes – when you have the privilege of being able to ignore them? Eva has broken that part of the social contract that keeps her in her place: turn up, follow orders, take your wages and be grateful. Whatever you do, don't complain. And for this, she needed to be punished. According to Arthur, 'If you don't come down sharply on some of these people, they'd soon be asking for the earth.' I love the Inspector for his tart response: 'it's better to ask for the earth than to take it'.

Gerald Croft, that dashing young paragon of manliness, fully supports his future father-in-law's actions. The younger Birlings, however, do not. Eric thinks it is 'tough luck'. Sheila describes it as a 'rotten shame', and protests – in one of the play's many highly quotable lines – that 'These girls aren't cheap labour – they're *people.*' The Inspector sketches Eva's hand-to-mouth existence, living in lodgings, hungry and alone. He says, drily, that

> There are a lot of young women living that sort of existence in every city and big town in this country, Miss Birling. If there weren't, the factories and warehouses wouldn't know where to look for cheap labour . . . it would do us all a bit of good if sometimes we tried to put ourselves in the place of these young women counting their pennies in their dingy little back bedrooms.

It's a plea not only to Sheila, but to the audience. And also, of course, to the teenagers studying the play, invited by the Inspector to consider the situations of those less fortunate than themselves. (Some, of course, will feel the situations of their own families reflected in Eva's plight, and I am glad that the Inspector, one of the most powerful characters they'll encounter in the whole of their GCSE English Literature specification, is very firmly on their side.)

The women – and men – who worked in the mills and factories would have been very familiar to Priestley. He was born in 1894, in the Bradford suburb of Manningham, less than half a mile from Lister Mill, the silk factory that was then the largest textile mill in Europe. His mother, who died when Priestley was just two years old, had been a millworker. Priestley's first job, at the age of sixteen, was as a junior clerk in a wool firm. Wool – along with worsted, alpaca, mohair and silk – had, by the time of Priestley's childhood, made Bradford one of the wealthiest cities in Europe, and the West Riding's textile mills employed an estimated quarter of a million people. But this wealth would have rubbed shoulders with extreme poverty, and there were outbreaks of cholera and typhoid. Georg Weerth, a German pamphleteer and friend of Marx and Engels, had opined in 1846 that 'Every other factory town in England is a paradise in comparison to this hole.'

The gap between rich and poor, and the conditions endured by ordinary workers, were frequent themes of Priestley's writing. His 1934 book *English Journey* recounts the travels that he had made throughout England the previous year. It takes in a broad sweep of English society – towns and cities, boarding houses and country inns, Nottingham's Goose Fair and Blackpool Promenade – and describes the conditions in a number of factories. Priestley writes approvingly of the employers who, like the Wills Tobacco Factory in Bristol, provided their workers with subsidized canteens, medical and dental treatment, and bonuses and pensions. He praises businesses such as the chocolate manufacturer Cadbury for spending 'a good part of their money on their factory and its employees, instead of racing stables and yachts and Monte Carlo'. In West Bromwich, less than ten miles from the Cadbury factory in Bournville, he witnesses the poverty of families to whom the rich had not been so paternalistic, describing the slums of an area called Rusty Lane. Here he is, in tones that prefigure those of the Inspector:

> There ought to be no more of those lunches and din-
> ners, at which political and financial and industrial
> gentlemen congratulate one another, until something
> is done about Rusty Lane and West Bromwich ... if
> there is another economic conference, let it meet there,
> in one of the warehouses, and be fed with bread and
> margarine and slabs of brawn. The delegates have seen
> one England, Mayfair in the season. Let them see
> another England next time, West Bromwich out of the
> season.

The anger that animates Priestley's description of the self-congratulatory governing classes would also run through his famous series of *Postscripts*, short radio talks to the nation that were broadcast by the BBC after the nine o'clock news on Sunday evenings during the summer and early autumn of 1940. The *Postscripts* were ostensibly a way of raising the nation's spirits and promoting a sense of collectivity, but Priestley also used them to focus on the kind of country that Britain needed to become after the war. Hitler, he said, was not a 'solitary evil giant', but a malignant dwarf, perched on top of 'a gigantic toad-stool of mess and misery', thrown up because the world had refused to reform itself after the First World War. Britain must fight the Nazis, but it must also fight the conditions that produced them – conditions that could fester at home just as they had on the Continent. But people needed to know what kind of country they were fighting for. Those who had returned from the trenches had been badly let down when the promised 'land fit for heroes' had never materialized. The nation's future, believed Priestley, needed to be radically different from what had gone before. On 28 July 1940, at the height of the Battle of Britain, he attacked the cheap sentimentality of those who waved farewell to the RAF's pilots without thinking about what Britain had to offer them on their return. Reading his words, I can't help wondering what Priestley would have made of those politicians who clapped on their doorsteps for NHS keyworkers during the lockdown of 2020, yet consistently denied them both funding and pay rises.

> It's all right feeling a lump in the throat and saying 'God bless you', but what are we going to do about it? I will tell you what we did for such men and their young wives at the end of the last war. We did nothing ... After the cheering and the flag-waving were over, and all the medals were given out, somehow the young heroes disappeared, and after a year or two there were a lot of shabby, young-oldish men about, who didn't seem to have been lucky in the scramble for easy jobs and quick profits.

According to Priestley, the British public were definitely not all in it together. Speaking in the middle of the Blitz on London, he attacked those with private incomes who could flee London for the safety of the countryside. He quoted *The Communist Manifesto*, causing consternation in government and at the BBC. The Prime Minister, Winston Churchill, remarked scathingly that Priestley's war aims were not *his* war aims, and Priestley's stint on *Postscripts* was brought to an end. But his desire for change was felt by many of his fellow Britons, and in the general election of June 1945, Labour scored a landslide victory.

A short Pathé film of 1944, one of a series titled *Personalities*, shows Priestley at work in his study. He is wearing a three-piece pinstriped suit and smoking one of his many pipes. He types with two fingers, stabbing at his typewriter, pecking at the keys. When he speaks to the camera, traces of Bradford are still evident around the edges of his voice. Sitting in a leather armchair, he outlines his views as to what writers should aim to do:

> I believe that a writer's job right now is to try and understand the whole wide social scene, to understand what people are thinking and feeling, fearing and hoping, and then to express, as vividly and dramatically as possible, that understanding and those feelings. A writer now should speak for the people.

It's a speech that chimes perfectly with *An Inspector Calls*, which he might well have been working on at the time.

I like to think that Sheila Birling would have spent the war years agitating for change. She is deeply distressed when she realizes that she, too, is implicated in the young woman's death. She went to Milwards, sometime in the winter of 1910, to try on a dress. It didn't suit her, but it definitely would have suited the young woman who brought it up from the workroom for her. The young woman smiles, and Sheila, already frustrated by the disappointing dress, interprets this as mockery. She was clearly feeling very sorry for herself. The young woman, who is dismissed as a result of her unlucky smile, was very pretty, Sheila remembers. She 'looked as if she could take care of herself. I couldn't be sorry for her.'

The way Sheila is treated – by her parents, and by Gerald – forms an important counterpoint to the experiences of the young woman at the heart of the play. Sheila is cosseted, protected. Both Mr and Mrs Birling refer to her as a 'child', even though she is in her early twenties, the same age as Eva Smith when she was sacked from the factory. Her father rubbishes her views, and objects to her being 'dragged into this unpleasant business'. Her mother passes on condescending guidance about married life. And Gerald wants her to be excused 'any more of this questioning', on the grounds that she has had 'a long, exciting and tiring day'. It's all too much for her to be expected to cope with. It's nothing like as tiring, though, as a day's work in a factory, hard physical work surrounded by noise and dust, then home to prepare a meal and do her own housework, early to bed before rising at dawn to repeat the process next day. We get the sense that Sheila herself chafes against all these restrictions, and that she recognizes how different her experiences of the world are from those of Eva Smith. As the Inspector proceeds with his investigation, she also recognizes the need for her family to change: 'You mustn't try to build up a kind of wall between us and that girl. If you do, then the Inspector will just break it down. And it'll be all the worse when he does.'

Things become murkier. We learn that Gerald was also involved with the young woman, who he knew as Daisy Renton. This part of the Inspector's interrogation is more complex than his questioning of Mr Birling and Sheila, because Gerald's relationship with the young woman was itself far less clear-cut. It begins with what might appear to be entirely commendable motives. Gerald is in the bar at the Palace Theatre one night – a bar that is, as he puts it, 'a favourite haunt of women of the town'. And amidst what Gerald describes as 'those hard-eyed dough-faced women', he spots someone who seems quite different, with 'soft brown hair and big dark eyes', being harassed by a local dignitary, Alderman Meggarty, with his 'obscene fat carcass'. Gerald swoops in and rescues her, takes her for a drink and something to eat, and, on finding out about her circumstances, sets her up in a friend's flat. Quite the knight in shining armour.

Students are sometimes sympathetic towards Gerald. At least he's kind to Daisy, they argue: he doesn't actually do anything wrong. He gives her a few months of happiness in an otherwise bleak life, such a bright spot that when Gerald ends their relationship Daisy goes away to the seaside to 'be quiet and remember', to make it last just a little while longer. Others push back. If Daisy hadn't been so young and fresh and charming, would Gerald have bothered rescuing her from Alderman Meggarty's sweaty clutches? If you're hard-eyed and dough-faced, do you have to put up with being sexually assaulted? Gerald knew that his relationship with Daisy wasn't going to last. And yet he used her, became the most important person in her life, allowed her to fall in love with him. Sheila is scathing: 'You were the wonderful Fairy Prince. You must have adored it, Gerald.' In class, we cheer when she gives him back his engagement ring.

Then there's Eric. We get the sense, right from the beginning of the play, that he's hiding something. He is shifty and nervous, touchy, resorting a little too often to his father's decanter. He goes out, slamming the door behind him, while the rest of the family reels from the revelations about Gerald. The Inspector turns to Mrs Birling, and asks about her role as a prominent member of the Brumley Women's Charity Organization, to which women in distress can appeal for help. Just two weeks earlier, Mrs Birling had rejected an appeal from a young woman who had found herself pregnant, and had gone to the charity – friendless, alone and feeling desperate – to ask for help. Mrs Birling is dismissive of the Inspector's questioning. The baby's father had offered the young woman some money, but she had refused to accept it, for reasons that Mrs Birling doesn't believe. Girls of that sort, she opines – *that sort*, and we pause to make a note of her dismissiveness – would never refuse money. And so the young woman's appeal is turned down. The father, Mrs Birling asserts, should be made to pay. He's the chief culprit, and should be dealt with very severely. Sheila is agitated. The penny has dropped. She warns her mother to be careful, but Mrs Birling goes on insisting. The father should be compelled to confess in public. He must be made an example of. And into the room comes Eric, pale and distraught, and the shell of respectability that Mrs Birling has built around her family is torn apart.

Eric used Eva Smith too. He was less subtle about it than Gerald. He met her in the Palace Bar and went back with her to her lodgings. She didn't want him to come in, but he was – he admits – 'in that state when a chap easily turns nasty'. When he found out that Eva was pregnant, he stole money for her from his father's office – money that Eva refused to accept once she found out where it came from. He is filled with remorse for his actions. Some students are prepared to forgive him, noting how deeply he is affected by what has happened and how he sides with Sheila in insisting that his family must learn from their experiences. Others see him as yet another example of toxic masculinity, willing to use his physical strength to get what he wants, acting without any thought for the potential consequences.

All the Birlings react differently, with varying degrees of shock and distress and anger, to what they have learned. Students like to speculate as to whether they'll ever be able to repair their relationships with each other, after this: you can certainly imagine the family waking next morning, sore-eyed after a night of broken sleep, contemplating the ruins of the previous evening's celebration. But the Inspector isn't interested in how they feel. He urges them to remember what they did. He twists the knife, pointing out that they can't even tell Eva Smith that they're sorry. And then he delivers a sobering warning that would have reminded audiences of Priestley's wartime *Postscripts*, telling the nation that change was needed, that the status quo could not be allowed to continue:

> But just remember this. One Eva Smith has gone – but there are millions and millions and millions of Eva Smiths and John Smiths still left with us, with their lives, their hopes and fears, their suffering and chance of happiness, all intertwined with our lives, and what we think and say and do. We don't live alone. We are members of one body. We are responsible for each other. And I tell you that the time will soon come when, if men will not learn that lesson, then they will be taught it in fire and blood and anguish.

One of the most powerful performances of this speech I've ever seen, in over twenty years of teaching and watching this play, was given by David Thewlis in the BBC's 2015 production. It's accessible on YouTube, and definitely needs a look. There are the Birlings, reeling. Ken Stott, as Mr Birling, is breathing heavily. If he could, he says, he'd give anything. Thousands and thousands. The Inspector shakes his head. He's offering the money at the wrong time. Serious, flat-vowelled, he leaves the Birlings in no doubt whatsoever as to what he thinks of them. And then he goes, leaving the room in a state of devastation.

The impact of the Inspector on the lives of the Birlings is also captured in one of the most famous stage revivals of Priestley's play, Stephen Daldry's 1992 production for the National Theatre. In this production, the contrasts between 1912 and 1945 are brought into sharp focus. The Birlings' house is perched on stilts, a fragile doll's house whose inhabitants are too big, too clumsy and too loud. Around it is a bleak landscape where children squabble, air-raid sirens sound and ghostly figures shiver. As the family's secrets are exposed, the house collapses. Crockery smashes; sparks fly. Rain lashes the cobbles. The Birlings themselves are left amidst the ruins.

But in the play, there are twists, established through a series of phone calls: the Inspector was not a real inspector, and no young woman has died. The older Birlings are triumphant, off the hook. No death, no public scandal: no need to worry. Sheila and Eric are appalled. Have their parents learned nothing? And then the telephone rings. A young woman has died after swallowing some disinfectant, and a police inspector is on his way to ask some questions.

'Who was that first inspector, then, Miss?' a student wants to know. 'How did he know all of that stuff?'

It's a mystery, I tell them. What was the Inspector's surname?

'Goole.'

I make them say it again. Goole. Ghoul – 'Oh, right! And a ghoul's a ghost, isn't it, Miss? So the Inspector's a ghost, and that's how he knows it all?' A shiver runs round the room. They like a mystery, this particular group.

We talk about what Priestley might have intended by this ending. Was he giving the Birlings the chance to prepare themselves, to approach the visit of the second Inspector with more humility? Was he suggesting that history was doomed to repeat itself unless people were prepared to change?

And this is where I struggle. Because no matter how powerful Priestley's message is, no matter how many teachers take their students to see Daldry's production or show them the BBC version, things haven't changed. Arthur Birling's words about 'community and all that nonsense', and his exhortation that people must look after themselves and their families, were echoed in Margaret Thatcher's 1987 statement about there being no such thing as society, that 'there are individual men and women, and there are families, and no government can do anything except through people, and people must look to themselves first'. Nearly forty years later, OECD figures show that the UK has one of the highest levels of income inequality in Europe. There are many examples that could be used to illustrate the divisions between rich and poor, the haves and the have-nots, but here's just one: in 2020, in the year when Boris Johnson spent an estimated £200,000 on refurbishments for his flat in Downing Street, a two-year-old boy, Awaab Ishak, died in Rochdale from prolonged exposure to black mould in his family's rented accommodation. *We are members of one body.* Given these widening gaps in society, and despite all the best efforts of English teachers, maybe there is a limit to the difference that literature can make. Maybe W. H. Auden was right all along.

Over the last few years, there have been stirrings in the English teaching community about the stranglehold that *An Inspector Calls* has over the GCSE English Literature curriculum. At GCSE, all students in England and Wales must study one play by Shakespeare, one nineteenth-century novel, one play or novel written after 1914 and one collection of poetry. Each exam board (there are four altogether) offers a slightly different list of set texts for each unit, and individual schools choose their texts from these lists. *An Inspector Calls* is on the set text list for the Post-1914 Prose and Drama component of all four GCSE English Literature courses and is the text studied by the vast majority of students nationally. And this is, arguably, a pity. Post-1914 Prose and Drama is the part of the course that offers the richest and most varied range of texts, especially now that exam boards have started to inject some much-needed cultural diversity into lists that have, until now, been relatively static. So many exciting choices, all there waiting to be explored.

And yet, year after year, it's *An Inspector Calls* that teachers return to.

There are a number of reasons for this. An obvious one is funding. A full set of new texts will set you back a considerable amount of money, and given how squeezed school budgets are at the moment, your school leadership team might well wonder why they should invest in new texts if it means that a perfectly decent set of books will be left unused in your stockroom. People baulk, too, at the thought of the planning and workload involved. The exam boards are doing a huge amount of work to support schools who want to introduce new texts, providing resources and webinars, but introducing a new GCSE text is a major undertaking, something that many departments will consider only in a year when nothing else is changing and there is nothing stressful on the horizon – such as an impending Ofsted inspection – to take up energy and headspace. And there's another, less obvious factor: the perception of risk, the fear that changing texts might lead to a drop in grades. Such is the pressure on schools to produce results that it's entirely understandable why teachers stick with the tried-and-tested. I imagine the questions senior leaders might ask: if *An Inspector Calls* helps to get students their target grades, why change? And so arguments about representation and diversity are overridden by league tables. I wish it were otherwise. But we are stuck within a system, cabined and cribbed and confined by the focus on statistical measures of achievement. Some people have suggested that things will only change if *An Inspector Calls* is removed from syllabuses altogether.

Deep down, though, I think there's also something else. It's that desire all English teachers have to make our students sit up and think, to recognize the relevance of what we teach to the world they live in. It's the thought of all those Eva Smiths and John Smiths who are still with us, many of them in our own classrooms, desperate for something to change. There are also, in our class-rooms, the people who might, in the future, be able to do something about it. For all that things haven't changed in the decades since *An Inspector Calls* was written, for all we've learned about the apparent unwillingness of suc-cessive governments to tackle the problem of social inequality, we still want to make a difference. And teach-ing *An Inspector Calls* – introducing yet another cohort of students to the Birlings and Gerald and shadowy Inspector Goole – helps us to feel, somehow, that we can. It's a triumph of hope over experience. But we keep trying, desperately wanting to believe that books can make something happen, after all.

# On complexity: *To Kill a Mockingbird* by Harper Lee

I grew up in a small town called Newton-le-Willows, in Merseyside. It's a place that's most easily described by where it is in relation to other places: halfway between Manchester to the west and Liverpool to the east, Wigan to the north and Warrington to the south, in a part of the country that's criss-crossed by motorways and where everyone seems to be perpetually on the way to somewhere else. This sense of restlessness would form a backdrop to my childhood. There were huge stretches of time when it seemed that nothing would ever happen in Newton-le-Willows, that it was the kind of place where all you could do was to listen enviously to news of the things that were going on elsewhere and wonder whether you'd ever get to witness them yourself. Nevertheless, the town actually has two major claims to fame. It's the birthplace of 1980s pop legend Rick Astley, who shot to stardom in the summer of 1987, declaring that he was never gonna give us up and setting the whole town singing. It was also the location of the world's first fatal railway accident, back in 1830, when the Conservative MP William Huskisson was mown down by Robert Stevenson's locomotive *Rocket* at the opening of the Liverpool and Manchester Railway. We did a project on it in primary school, complete with bloodthirsty crayoned illustrations, and for me it sparked a bit of an obsession with local history, with the kinds of legends and folktales that seem to cluster around every small town.

My favourite stories were the ones that involved ghosts. There was the patch of land at the end of our road, on the outskirts of the town, where it was said that Royalist soldiers had been executed during the English Civil War. If you went there late at night, and if the wind was in the right direction, you could hear their bodies swinging from the trees. Then there was the story of a medieval noblewoman who had been made to do penance as a result of some long-ago love triangle, and now haunted the lake in the park as a mysterious White Lady. But others were pure rumour. Opposite the church, for instance, there was a cottage whose sole inhabitant was an old man who could kill you just by looking at you. If you were passing by, you had to keep your eyes on the ground and walk as quickly as you could without breaking into a run. He often sat in the window, with his back to the street, but nobody had ever seen his face: nobody wanted to look at him for long enough to risk it. Some people said that maybe he didn't have a face at all. The kinds of stories that are absorbed in the playground, embroidered with every retelling, becoming almost-truth just because they have been passed on so many times.

Growing up in a place like this meant that I was primed for *To Kill a Mockingbird*; and as soon as I started to read it, when I was fifteen, I felt instantly that this was a world

I knew. A town full of its own ghosts and rumours, where the pecans that fall from one family's trees can kill you, and where a man can wither people's flowers just by breathing on them: I was sold, immediately. Add in a young narrator with a vivid imagination, a complex cast of characters and some significant messages about morality and injustice, and it was inevitable that Harper Lee's novel would become one of my teenage favourites. Of all the texts we studied at GCSE, *To Kill a Mockingbird* is the one I remember most clearly. Open its pages now, and I can feel the heat rising from the sidewalks of a small Alabama town, can see the mules tethered under the trees and hear children calling to each other across dusty backyards. Quotations thread their way through me like words through seaside rock. I can't imagine what my life would have been like without it.

I'm not alone. Millions of people, around the world, cite *To Kill a Mockingbird* as one of the most important books they've ever read. It won the Pulitzer Prize for Fiction in 1961, and has never been out of print. By the time I first read it, it was being taught in 74 per cent of US public schools. In 2003, it came sixth in the BBC's Big Read poll of the UK's top hundred favourite novels. In a survey carried out by the Museums, Libraries and Archives Council three years later, it was voted top in a list of books that every adult should read before they die. In 2016, parents responding to a poll carried out by Amnesty International voted it second in a list of books that help children to develop empathy. Atticus Finch, the small-town lawyer whose wisdom dominates many people's memories of the novel, has been hailed as the most inspiring character in the whole of literature. Quotations from the novel appear on posters, T-shirts, tote bags and cufflinks. You can even buy a reusable coffee cup proclaiming that you are Atticus Finch, Attorney at Law of Maycomb County, Alabama.

But it's a complicated one, because over the years, *To Kill a Mockingbird* has also received a considerable amount of criticism. Like that other American classic *Of Mice and Men*, it has appeared consistently in the American Library Association's list of the most frequently banned and challenged books. Detractors argue that its view of race relations is naive, that it promotes white saviourism, and that its use of racist language means that it has no place in the modern curriculum. The arguments that surround it are shifting and uneasy, so much so that many of those who love the novel would rather not confront them. It's as if someone has pointed out that your favourite old auntie has been sending poison-pen letters: an enormity that you can't take in, tipping the familiar on its axis.

Our relationships with books can change over time. Sometimes, as we grow older, we see the value of a novel we'd previously dismissed; sometimes, we find out something about a writer that casts an uneasy shadow over their work. And sometimes, a book shows itself to be more complex and problematic than we first realized. This can make us revise our opinions completely. It can also sharpen them. There's that drive to argue and redefine, that eternal *Yes, but* . . . For me, this has been the case with *To Kill a Mockingbird*. I used to think of it purely as a novel that we could learn a lot from, all the lessons about tolerance and injustice that spring to mind whenever the novel is mentioned. More recently, though, I've learned a lot more from the arguments that surround it. I could brush away the complexities and package *To Kill a Mockingbird* up neatly, reduce it to a collection of wise words and principles for living. But that would be a huge injustice.

*To Kill a Mockingbird* was moulded by the seething prejudice of the American South. Its author, Harper Lee, had grown up in the small town of Monroeville, Alabama, where her father, Amasa Coleman Lee, was a lawyer and newspaper editor. During her childhood, Lee would have been aware of a number of infamous miscarriages of justice, where it was clear that the law did not protect Black and white people equally. There was the notorious Scottsboro Boys case of 1931, when nine African American teenagers and young men were found guilty – after a series of rushed and unfair trials – of raping two white women on a freight train in Alabama, despite there being no evidence that any such offence had actually taken place. Two years later, there was the trial in Monroeville of a Black man, Walter Lett, who was sentenced to death for the rape of a white woman. Behind these events was a trial that had taken place seven years before Lee was born, when her father was appointed to defend two Black men who had been accused of murdering a white man. Amasa had no experience in criminal defence, and had less than a fortnight to put his case together. He lost, and the defendants were executed. Horrifically, their bodies were later mutilated. Amasa never fought another criminal case, although he would later take part in a campaign to have Walter Lett's sentence commuted to life imprisonment. But there were more recent events too. In 1955, a young Black boy, Emmett Till, was tortured and lynched by two white men who accused him of flirting with a white woman. An all-white jury found his killers not guilty. That year also saw the arrest of Rosa Parks in Montgomery, and the subsequent bus boycott; the following year, a riot broke out when a Black woman tried to enrol at the University of Alabama. Inequality, ignorance, injustice: a novel tackling these themes in the 1960s could hardly escape controversy.

The story begins when its narrator, Scout Finch, is just five years old, and unfolds slowly, unhurriedly, introducing us to the quirks and complications of Maycomb society. Lee sketches a vivid picture of Scout's world: her home with her father, Atticus, and her older brother, Jem; the games that she and Jem play with their friend Dill; and their mysterious neighbour Boo Radley, the source of both fascination and terror. It's in the second part of the novel that the two defining events of Scout's childhood take place. The first is the trial of Tom Robinson, a Black man accused of raping a young white woman, Mayella Ewell. Mayella is from a troubled background: she and her family live in abject poverty in a shack by the local rubbish dump, and her alcoholic father, Bob, is allowed to hunt and trap out of season – a fact that shocks Scout – so that his children do not go hungry. Atticus has been appointed to defend Tom, and on the face of things, it should be an easy case to defend, as there are clear reasons why Tom could not possibly have committed this particular crime. But this is reckoning without the ignorance and prejudice of an all-white jury, who find Tom guilty. The second event is sparked by the vengefulness of Bob Ewell, who is determined to punish Atticus for making it clear that he was responsible for the attack on his own daughter. He follows Scout and Jem home from school one dark night after a Halloween pageant, and is killed in the ensuing skirmish. Shy Boo Radley is propelled briefly into the limelight, and Scout learns a lot about herself, her father and the complexity of human beings.

There are a number of reasons why *To Kill a Mocking-bird* resonates so strongly with readers, but feisty Scout is one of the most important. Scout is based on Harper Lee herself; Atticus is modelled on her father, and the family's surname, Finch, was Lee's mother's maiden name. Scout's friend Dill, who comes to stay with his Aunt Rachel each summer, is based on the writer Truman Capote, who Lee first met as a child when he was staying with relatives in Monroeville. In some ways, Scout is extremely privileged. She's the daughter of a local lawyer, a member of an established family, not wealthy but certainly comfortable. (This is significant, as there are many families in Depression-era Maycomb who are struggling to scratch a living.) In other ways, she is at a distinct disadvantage. Her mother died when she was just two years old. She's a bright child, which means that she notices things others might miss, but being a bright young girl in a town like Maycomb brings its own problems. She is constantly being told how to behave, what to do and what to think: by her brother, Jem, by her family's maid, Calpurnia, and by the many people in Maycomb – almost all of them female – who seek to pass judgement on her manners and on the way in which Atticus is bringing her up. She shouldn't wear overalls. She shouldn't say a friendly 'hey' in greeting. (According to Charles J. Shields, Harper Lee's biographer, the writer was herself 'a fearsome stomach-puncher, foot-stomper, and hair-puller' as a child, and 'could talk mean like a boy'.) On her first day at school, she also learns that she shouldn't be able to read and write. Scout's early lessons in reading have come from looking at books and papers over Atticus's shoulder, barely noticing the point where the lines of print separated themselves into words and began to make sense. Her teacher, Miss Caroline, has all manner of ideas about how children should learn, and a five-year-old who can already read does not form part of her plan. Scout is told that she needs to start again with a 'fresh mind', and that she should tell her father not to read with her any longer. She goes home bewildered and depressed, insistent that she does not want to go back to school.

I began school as a fluent reader, too, but I was luckier than Scout. I'd had the same experience of looking at print over a parent's shoulder, tucked in next to my mum, following her finger across the page and realizing that the shapes she pointed to actually made sense. I took a book to school on my first day and couldn't be separated from it. One of the classroom assistants insisted that I was just 'looking at the words', but I explained that I could actually read. Our teacher, Mrs Woods, asked me to read out loud, and then brought in the headmistress so that she could listen too. It was all a bit of a puzzle to four-year-old me: couldn't *everyone* read? Rather than being told that I wasn't allowed to read any more, I was sent up to the third-year class to join the Advanced Readers and learn complicated words, but when I read *To Kill a Mockingbird* just over ten years later I understood Scout's predicament, and sympathized. Reading was a physical compulsion to me, just as it was to Scout. 'Until I feared I would lose it, I never loved to read,' Scout famously observes. 'One does not love breathing.'

Scout has a lot to learn in the early chapters of *To Kill a Mockingbird*. Many of these lessons are about Maycomb society, about her fellow townspeople and the nature of her own privilege. At school, she shares a class with children whose lives are infinitely tougher than hers, who have 'chopped cotton and fed hogs from the time they were able to walk'. There's Walter Cunningham, who comes to school without any lunch, and Burris Ewell, younger brother of Mayella and the filthiest human Scout has ever seen, his hair alive with lice. There's also Miss Caroline herself, twenty-one years old and fresh out of college, trying to get to grips with a class more varied and perplexing than her training could possibly have prepared her for. At home, talking to her father, Scout puzzles over the oddness of people. From Atticus, she gains an important lesson in empathy: 'You never really understand a person until you consider things from his point of view . . . until you climb into his skin and walk around in it.'

There is also Boo Radley. Boo is a shadowy figure, the local bogeyman. People have woven so many rumours around his life that it is hard to know where facts end and fiction begins. Maycomb children grow up hearing about Boo. As a teenager, he got in with a bad crowd: after one particular incident, he and his companions were charged with various offences including disorderly conduct and using abusive and profane language. Boo's father promised the judge that his son would cause no further trouble. The other boys were sent to the state industrial school. Boo went home with his father, and has barely been seen since.

The story of Boo consumes Jem and Scout, in much the same way that I was consumed by the legends of my own small town as a child. They pass on their knowledge to Dill, who becomes obsessed with the idea of trying to lure Boo out of his house. There's a heady mixture of excitement and fear, with dares, games and blood-curdling stories of a phantom who dines on raw squirrels. Jem wonders if Boo is kept chained up, but Atticus says that no, there are other ways of turning people into ghosts.

Gradually, Scout learns about grey areas, about compromise, and about the endlessly complicated nature of human behaviour. These are hard lessons for her to learn, but they are important ones. She learns that fairness is a difficult concept and that sometimes it is necessary to bend the truth in order to keep people happy. She learns, too, about her own father. She dismisses Atticus as feeble, because he is nearly fifty and doesn't play football like other fathers, but when there's a mad dog roaming through the streets of Maycomb, it's Atticus who picks up a gun and shoots him. Atticus himself, however, doesn't see this as something admirable. When the revolting old Mrs Dubose is trying to break herself of her morphine addiction, he sends Jem to go and read to her, because he wants his children to see 'what real courage is, instead of getting the idea that courage is a man with a gun in his hand'. Atticus recognizes Mrs Dubose's failings: she is bigoted, mean and bad-tempered, and she expects children to respect her simply because she is old. But he also recognizes that there is something to admire in her determination to die free of her addiction, and wants his children to be aware of the importance of this struggle.

These lessons, laid down carefully during the first part of the novel, provide the groundwork for the event that dominates many readers' memories of *To Kill a Mocking-bird*: the trial of Tom Robinson, the Black man accused of raping Mayella Ewell. The first rumblings of this case, like the threat of distant thunder, are heard months beforehand. Scout is taunted – by other children at school, by horrible Mrs Dubose, and then, at Christmas, by her cousin Francis – because Atticus is defending Tom. There's a tension surrounding the case, a feeling that Maycomb will never be quite the same again. Atticus tells his brother that Scout and Jem 'will have to absorb some ugly things pretty soon'. The case is a difficult one, but it is 'something that goes to the essence of a man's conscience'. Atticus knows that he has to fight, because he will never look at himself in the same way if he doesn't: 'I couldn't go to church and worship God if I didn't try to help that man.'

In defending Tom Robinson, Atticus is taking up an unpopular position. A Black man, accused of an assault on a young white woman: the odds are stacked against Tom from the start. Except, as becomes patently obvious, there is no way that Tom could have committed this crime. The person who attacked Mayella was left-handed, and Tom's left arm – caught in a cotton gin when he was a young boy – is twelve inches shorter than his right. The only thing he is guilty of is showing compassion and sympathy to a young and friendless white woman, the oldest of eight children in a family struggling to make ends meet, who invites him into her house on the pretext that she wants him to break up an old cupboard for firewood. It becomes clear, during the trial, that Mayella has tried to kiss Tom, and that the person guilty of abusing her is her own father, Bob.

Whenever I've taught *To Kill a Mockingbird*, my students have read the description of Tom Robinson's trial with their breath held. There are times when they feel sorry for poor ignorant Mayella, convinced that Atticus is making fun of her. He's simply being polite, addressing her as 'Miss Mayella', but she isn't used to courtesy and perceives it as ridicule. Their sympathy is limited, though, because of course the person we're supposed to feel most sorry for is Tom. The evidence sings out clearly: Tom is innocent. Of *course* he is. How could any jury possibly find him guilty? But the Maycomb jury does. And just about everyone who reads *To Kill a Mockingbird* feels stung by how outrageously unfair their verdict is.

This appalling miscarriage of justice is one of the reasons why *To Kill a Mockingbird* has taken up so much space in so many people's imaginations. It gives many teenage readers their first insight into the fact that the law does not always protect the innocent; that justice is not necessarily neutral. The shock is like a punch to the gut.

Some of my students, of course, will have personal knowledge of the colossal imbalances of power that exist in the world. They'll have experienced discrimination, poverty, even outright bigotry. What they read about in *To Kill a Mockingbird* won't come as news to them. Others, however, will enjoy the luxury of privilege. Studying *To Kill a Mockingbird* forces them to confront the reality of prejudice: twelve men ignoring the evidence and deciding instead to convict a man who could not possibly be guilty. And this is important.

I remember, in my first term as a teacher, attending a welcome event for all of Lincolnshire's newly qualified teachers. One of the speakers reminded us that as teachers in a rural county, we would be distanced from many of the issues faced by schools in urban environments. It was our job, he stated, to make sure that our students weren't protected from the realities of elsewhere. We needed to expose them to other lives, other experiences, to prepare them for the world beyond school. They weren't going to stay in sleepy Lincolnshire for ever.

Lincolnshire isn't quite so sleepy any more, and it has its own social issues to contend with. Students in rural areas also experience deprivation, and isolation, and prejudice: they and their families might also have to contend with the particular kind of social exclusion that comes from living miles from anywhere, with infrequent public transport, and with a lack of access to services and cultural opportunities. But it's still a long way, literally and figuratively, from the Deep South of the first half of the twentieth century, and from the world in which *To Kill a Mockingbird* is set. It's important, then, to make them aware of the injustices of this part of American history. I remember, teaching the novel nearly twenty years ago, playing Billie Holiday's haunting 'Strange Fruit' over a montage of images from the segregation era: separate waiting rooms and drinking fountains, whites-only swimming pools, protests and lynchings. These images were deeply uncomfortable, but this was precisely why students needed to see them. There was silence for a long time afterwards, a sense of people struggling to process the realities of a world much uglier than they'd previously recognized.

Atticus's struggle to have Tom acquitted is often seen as one of the most significant legal battles in the whole of literature. Read it, and you're transported to the hot stuffy courtroom, jostling for space, desperate not to miss the tiniest bit of the action. Watch the 1962 film, with Gregory Peck on Oscar-winning form as Atticus, and you're similarly held, up there on the balcony with Scout and Jem and Dill, leaning on the railings with your chin on your hands. Yet to many of the novel's critics, this is part of the problem, because all of our focus is on Atticus, the good white liberal. For decades, Atticus was held up as a shining example of humanity, proof that not all white people in the South were racist, that some white people fought against prejudice. But, as a number of commentators have pointed out, this is as far as the novel's sympathy goes. It remains resolutely in the world of Maycomb's white inhabitants, and makes very few attempts to explore the lives and viewpoints of their Black counterparts. Osamudia R. James, writing in the *New York Times* on the publication of Lee's second novel, *Go Set a Watchman* (written before *To Kill a Mockingbird* but not published until 2015), remarked on the irony of

Black characters being 'relegated to the margins even in stories about their own oppression'. The novelist Tanya Landman describes the Black characters in *To Kill a Mockingbird* as 'a group of simple, respectful folk – passive and helpless and all touchingly grateful to Atticus Finch'. All this is in spite of Atticus's advice to Scout about getting into a person's skin and walking around in it. Maycomb's Black citizens, says Landman, are two-dimensional: their fears and griefs and resentments go unexplored.

It is certainly striking that in a novel so bound up with the history of race relations in twentieth-century America, we have to look hard for details of the everyday lives of Black characters. Once we do, though, we can see that the divisions in Maycomb run deep. They are apparent in the fact that so many of Maycomb's white families – the Finches included – have Black servants, in the different churches attended by the two communities, in the way that Black people are addressed and spoken about. Maycomb's white citizens frequently describe their Black counterparts in terms of their laziness and sulkiness, their unwillingness to conform. Miss Merriweather, proud member of the local missionary circle, is very open about how little she pays her Black servant. Yet Maycomb could not function without the labour of its Black population, who work in the fields (sometimes, in the case of women, with their babies strapped to their backs), bring up the children of white families and tend the sick.

There are a few occasions when Black characters are

allowed to express their dissatisfaction with conditions in Maycomb. One of the most significant is when Jem and Scout accompany Calpurnia to her church. Inequality is apparent in the way that many of the Black adults greet the white children: 'the men stepped back and took off their hats; the women crossed their arms at the waists, weekday gestures of respectful attention'. Yet one woman, Lula, objects. Calpurnia, she says, has no business bringing white children to a Black church. 'They got their church, we got our'n' – the two communities, according to Lula, should remain separate. It will take far more than Atticus's defence of Tom to bring about harmony to such a divided town.

If, like me, you have fond early memories of *To Kill a Mockingbird*, then reading the novel again, with these objections in mind, is quite a difficult experience. But it's an important thing to do. To read against the grain, to rub things up the wrong way: it's surprising what can emerge. And I can see why it is that *To Kill a Mockingbird* – lauded for decades as one of the most important American novels of the twentieth century, a powerful voice against racial inequality – has also been seen as much more problematic in its view of race relations. It has been dropped from the curriculum in a number of US school districts, and students in others are only allowed to read it with parental permission. In July 2021, the James Gillespie High School in Edinburgh announced that it would no longer be teaching *To Kill a Mockingbird* because its white saviour narrative and use of the N-word meant that it was 'dated and problematical in terms of decolonising the curriculum'.

Nonetheless, for every suggestion that the novel should be 'cancelled', there are equally vehement arguments for its retention. It's important – such arguments say – to see *To Kill a Mockingbird* in the context of the racism of its time, to explore the novel's problematic nature rather than simply getting rid of it. Get students to look at both sides, to decide for themselves. This kind of critical thinking is central to the study of literature: we're not holding up a model, but opening up a discussion.

A powerful contributor to these debates is the playwright and screenwriter Aaron Sorkin, who adapted *To Kill a Mockingbird* for the stage in 2018. Sorkin wanted to point out the story's relevance to the present, rather than seeing it as belonging firmly to the past. He drew heavily on the far-right news website Breitbart for much of Bob Ewell's dialogue, turning this character into a man who snarls with anger at his marginalized position. The kind of resentment that drives Ewell, in Sorkin's play, is what drove millions of Americans to vote for Trump in 2016: Bob Ashby, writing for the DC Theater Arts website, comments that 'If there had been MAGA hats in 1934, Ewell would have worn one.'

Sorkin made a number of other significant changes in adapting the novel. One of his main concerns was to give Tom Robinson and Calpurnia more agency: in his version, Calpurnia becomes Atticus's conscience and critic, pointing out that the Black community has had enough of waiting patiently for change. He also turns Atticus's desire to understand everyone – that facet of his character that has been viewed, for so long, as his biggest virtue – into his main flaw. There comes a point, Sorkin's adaptation argues, where you can't carry on trying to understand Bob Ewell and Mrs Dubose, and their modern equivalents. You simply have to condemn their repugnant behaviour for what it is, and hold them to account for it.

Lee's Atticus is definitely a problematic character, one whose idealism prevents him from taking the urgent, forthright stand that Sorkin's version of Atticus is able to make by the end of the play. Yet he is by no means naive. He admits to his brother, Scout's Uncle Jack, that his defence of Tom is unlikely to succeed. But what Atticus *does* do is to try, and it's this act of trying – trying to achieve something, against all the odds – that carries one of the novel's most significant messages. Courage, as Atticus asserts, is about 'when you know you're licked before you begin, but you begin anyway and you see it through no matter what. You rarely win, but sometimes you do.' It's as if he knows, right from the start, that he has no chance. And this is important. *To Kill a Mockingbird* is a flawed novel, it's true, but it would be even more flawed if the jury had agreed with Atticus. As it is, it succeeds in exposing the ugliness of racism for what it is. It reveals Maycomb as a place where people will cling to their prejudices even when all the evidence is pointing in a different direction. Maycomb isn't sealed off from reality, and the world of the novel is not one where just-ice prevails. It's a world where good people suffer terribly and ignorant people go about their daily business as if nothing had happened. Life doesn't always work out the way it should.

Is it enough, though, to tell readers that the world's a nasty place, and they'd better get used to it? Well, no. And that's not what *To Kill a Mockingbird* does. Instead, it tells us to take a deep breath and to put one foot in front of the other. And to keep going. Because you might feel as if you're getting nowhere, but every inch of progress is worth it. It's a war of attrition, this fight against prejudice, and ignorance, and stupidity. Every flippant comment challenged, every assumption contradicted, is important. All rise, as Scout says directly to the audience, at the end of Sorkin's stage adaptation. It's up to you, now.

It might seem as if I'm swerving the issue here, focus-ing on individual attitudes rather than the need for systemic change. But let's remember that at the heart of *To Kill a Mockingbird* is a little girl who hasn't even reached double figures by the end of the novel, still trying to make sense of the world in which she is growing up. Stu-dents reading *To Kill a Mockingbird* for the first time are in a similar position. They might be a few years older, and the world in which they live might be in some ways unrec-ognizable, but they are still learning about issues of injustice and inequality, how to cope with the fact that not everybody thinks like they do or experiences the world in the way they do, and how to handle their own complicated feelings about life. All of these are big things. Any support you can get with this – anything to help you brace yourself and keep fighting – is important.

There is also, of course, another innocent victim in the novel, one who is sidelined by the focus on Atticus's defence of Tom. This is Boo Radley, who is revealed to be not the squirrel-eating monster of Maycomb legend but a shy man profoundly damaged by the way he has been treated. Boo is the victim of a number of injustices. He has been deprived of his freedom and prevented from living a normal life: the people of Maycomb have made him the object of rumours and the stuff of nightmares. We cannot explore prejudice in *To Kill a Mockingbird* – the way in which people are treated as Other, perceived as a threat – without acknowledging that Boo is on the receiving end of a good deal of othering too. And, just as the lauding of Atticus and the sidelining of Maycomb's Black community tells us a lot about race relations, the othering of Boo tells us a lot about the ways in which mainstream society treats those who are in any way different. For all the scaremongering that surrounds him, Boo poses no threat to anyone. In fact, quite the opposite. He leaves trinkets in the hollow of a tree for Jem and Scout to find. He mends Jem's torn shorts and places a blanket around Scout's shoulders on the night when Maycomb's citizens gather in the cold to watch as Miss Maudie's house burns down. And at the end of the novel, when Scout and Jem are attacked by Bob Ewell, it is Boo who saves their lives.

The emergence of Boo from the shadows, in the novel's final chapters, is halting and reluctant. Scout has to coax him quietly. He is thin and pale, as if he has never seen the sun. In the 1962 film, he is played by a nervous-looking Robert Duvall, his eyes shadowed by dark rings, shrinking himself into a corner. There are too many people in the room, and the lights are too bright. He's happier sitting out on the porch, with Scout. Meanwhile, Atticus frets over who stabbed Bob Ewell, believing that it was Jem, and Heck Tate, who knows that it was Boo, insists that Bob fell on his own knife. Heck is adamant that it would be a sin to drag Boo into the limelight for what he has done. Scout agrees: 'It'd be sort of like shootin' a mockingbird, wouldn't it?' And, as we know because the novel has already told us, it's a sin to kill a mockingbird: all mockingbirds do is to sing their hearts out and make music for us to enjoy.

Looking back, the most important thing about studying *To Kill a Mockingbird*, for me at fifteen, was something that fell into place during my reading of those last few chapters. This was the realization that books weren't just about stories. They could also be a space for allowing you to work out complicated moral problems, for reflecting on why people make the decisions they do and considering whether you'd do the same thing if you were in their shoes. And these problems – with all their knottiness and grey areas – were far more satisfying, for me, than solving equations or mastering chemical formulae.

There weren't any right and wrong answers, and things weren't always left tidy and complete. But that didn't matter. It was what made books so absorbing. Different people could look at them in different ways. You could even look at them in different ways yourself, holding multiple arguments in your mind and weighing them up against each other. It was like a game that could go on for ever without needing to end.

There are stories in *To Kill a Mockingbird* that don't get told. There's the story of what it would be like to be Tom, in that courtroom, knowing that you have been wrongly accused and are facing the electric chair. There's the story of Tom's wife, Helen, and how she copes with what happens to the man she loves, the father of her children. There are stories that are only glanced at. How would Mayella, for instance, tell the story of her life, growing up behind the rubbish dump? How would Calpurnia tell *her* story? What about Boo? These rewritings – taking different characters and exploring the world through their eyes – allow us to examine stories from new angles, thinking about how the world of Maycomb looks if you are not white, not privileged, not accepted. They are brilliant exercises to do in class because they allow students to climb into someone else's skin and walk around in it, opening them up to different perspectives.

In the summer of 2016, I spent a few days visiting local primary schools, meeting the children who would be starting at my school the following September. It was a hot week in Lincolnshire. Fields stretched in every direction: peas, potatoes, broad beans, maize. Polytunnels sheltered soft fruits and herbs, gladioli and lilies. Earlier in the year, there'd been daffodils. Many of these crops need to be harvested by hand. I'd passed daffodil fields on my way to school and seen people at work early in the morning, their bright clothes a splash of colour in the mist, bending low as they worked their way along the rows of flowers. Harvesting daffodils is back-breaking work. It's also a vital part of the local economy. The UK's annual daffodil harvest has a retail value of over £71 million, and over half of these flowers are grown within a thirty-mile radius of the town where I teach. The Fens – an area covering south Lincolnshire, west Norfolk and northern Cambridgeshire – produce a third of the UK's fresh vegetables, a fifth of its potatoes and sugar beet and more than half of its beetroot. Food production in the region contributes an estimated £1.63 billion a year to the UK economy. Thousands of those working in the food industry in the Fens come from Eastern Europe.

And yet. That summer, just before the UK held its referendum on whether to leave the EU, there were billboards in the fields exhorting people to VOTE LEAVE. Those workers would have seen them, telling them they weren't welcome. They'd have sweated and stood up, rubbed their backs, reached for their water bottles and been confronted with signs that must have felt like a slap in the face. Others who have come to the area from EU countries – teachers and care workers, doctors and nurses, factory operatives and builders and members of countless other professions, plus of course their children – would have seen them too. South Holland, the constituency I live in, returned a 73.6 per cent vote in favour of leaving the EU. In neighbouring Boston, it was 75.6 per cent, the highest anywhere in the UK. Lincolnshire was an uneasy place to be, that June, as debates rumbled and resignations took place. I remembered that conference I'd attended, right back at the beginning of my career, when we were told that in areas like ours, our duty to tackle prejudice was all the more important. There was still a long way to go.

So while *To Kill a Mockingbird* is not perfect, Lee's novel is still worth teaching, and worth reading. It teaches us that the important thing is to try, and to try anyway, even when your struggle seems endless and your task overwhelming. And it teaches us to look below the surface of things – to recognize that novels, like people, can be flawed and complex. Next time I teach it, I'll encourage my students to be much more sceptical about Atticus's desire to see the good in everyone, and to think more carefully about Lee's portrayal of her Black characters. I'll present them with a range of responses to the novel, positive and negative, and ask them to weigh these views against each other. Between us, we'll chip away at the neatly packaged wisdom and examine the different stories that *To Kill a Mockingbird* contains, both the ones it's famous for and the ones it doesn't tell. It'll be a difficult process, with no easy answers. Many things will emerge from it, not all of them expected. Its results might not be apparent straight away. But it'll be all the more important because of this, and all the more worthwhile.

# On gaining a voice: *Jane Eyre* by Charlotte Brontë and *Wide Sargasso Sea* by Jean Rhys

A widowed father is concerned about his children. How could he not be? There are six of them, and they lost their mother so young, when the smallest was barely eighteen months old. They've become insular, self-sufficient, relying only on each other. His sister-in-law has moved in to help, but it's difficult: the older ones don't trust her, and he can feel them drifting away from him, locked into a private world of plans and secrets. They're clever children, often poring over books and newspapers or lost in stories of their own making. He wants to get to know them better, to hear what they have to say. Somewhere in the house, there is a mask. He will get them to wear it, to stand in front of him and tell him what they think. It will be easier for them to talk this way, he reckons. They will speak boldly.

Many questions surround this story, clamouring for attention. There's the mask, to begin with. Why does the widowed father have such a thing in his house? And the trickery itself. Does he imagine that the children will feel themselves anonymous? Will they really believe that he won't know which one of them is speaking, given that there is only one mask, and they so varied in size? Will they be honest with him or play a trick of their own, dissembling and deceiving? We don't know. The only account of this incident we have is in a letter written over thirty years later, and by then, so much has happened that the widowed father could be forgiven for not remembering things clearly, for embellishing, for making up a story of his own.

It is 1824, and the widowed father is not to know that in little more than a year's time, his two oldest daughters will be dead, carried away by an illness caught at school. (He will, in fact, outlive all his children, the five girls and the boy, all of them dead by the age of forty.) He has no inkling, at this stage, that his three surviving daughters will write books and poems, that these books and poems will be published, and that they will include two of the most famous and well-loved novels ever written, translated into many languages and taught in schools across the globe. He does not know that the town where he lives, a spill of cottages and cobbled streets high up in the Pennines, will be transformed, its lanes filled with tourists, his home a memorial to his daughters and all that they achieved. What would he think, the Reverend Patrick Brontë, if he could see all of this?

It's tempting to see a direct line running from that huddle of children standing in the parsonage at Haworth, given the freedom to speak by the simple donning of a mask, to the passionate voices that Charlotte, Emily and Anne expressed in their writing. You could trace it through the little books that they wrote with their brother, Patrick Branwell, charting the complicated histories of the imaginary worlds of Verdopolis, Gondal and Angria; through the letters and plays and poems to the novels, captured on screen by innumerable television and film adaptations and living their own vivid existence in the minds of millions of readers. There were difficult times, of course. There was the letter Charlotte received from the poet laureate Robert Southey in response to her request for advice. Southey praised her writing, but warned her against wanting to make it a career. 'Literature cannot be the business of a woman's life, and it ought not to be,' he wrote. 'The more she is engaged in her proper duties, the less leisure will she have for it, even as an accomplishment and a recreation.' There were the disagreements that the sisters had over Charlotte's desire to seek publication: Emily would quite happily have kept her work to herself. There was the failure of Charlotte's first novel, *The Professor*, to find a publisher: there were negative reviews and discouraging responses. But then there was the huge success that was *Jane Eyre*; and if *Jane Eyre* is about anything, it is about the importance of being given a voice.

It is tempting, too, for me to draw a line that runs from *Jane Eyre* to the development of my own voice, since it was reading *Jane Eyre* that first led me to think about doing English at university. It was a plan that hatched the summer after GCSEs, a year after *To Kill a Mockingbird* had fired something in my mind about complexity, and ambiguity, and how much more interesting it was to lose myself in books – with their endless possibilities for argument – than to spend time looking for the answers to problems that had already been solved. My exams had ended in the middle of June and, to begin with, a huge gap had yawned in front of me: twelve weeks that I needed to fill somehow. But then we'd gone back into school for an A-level induction day, to find out about the subjects we'd be studying in September. Our English Literature session had been led by the scary Head of English who'd started at our school the previous autumn, back when I was studying 'My Last Duchess', and it was clear that she expected us to work hard. She'd told us that we should spend the summer reading as much as possible, and had given us some ideas of what to read, starting with the classics and going on to contemporary fiction by writers I'd never heard of, like Ian McEwan and Julian Barnes and Margaret Atwood. It all seemed a long way from the comfortable world of GCSE, where we didn't really need to read anything at all except the texts we were actually studying. I'd spent the next few days immersed in David Lodge's novel *Nice Work*, the story of an unlikely relationship between the MD of a manufacturing company and a university lecturer in nineteenth-century English literature. At one point – while travelling along the M62 and spotting a sign for Haworth, the home of the Brontë family – the lecturer muses on the fact that there must be millions of civilized, intelligent people who have never read *Jane Eyre* or *Wuthering Heights*. What must it be like, she wonders, 'never to have shivered with Jane Eyre at Lowood school, or throbbed in the arms of Heathcliff with Cathy?' I'd never read *Jane Eyre* or *Wuthering Heights*. I'd heard of the Brontës, of course I had, but I'd only recently got the difference between *Jane Eyre* and Jane Austen sorted out in my mind, and what I knew about *Wuthering Heights* came mainly from the Kate Bush song. And so, partly because the scary Head of English had said that we needed to read as much as possible and partly because I wanted to be intelligent and civilized, I decided that what I was going to do that summer was to read *Jane Eyre* and *Wuthering Heights*.

It was actually *Wuthering Heights* that I started with. I wanted to do things properly, so I bought the black-spined Penguin Classics edition and began with the Introduction, which told me a lot about narrative structure, stories within stories, and names that repeated themselves across generations. I got a bit stuck on the Biographical Notice of Ellis and Acton Bell, until I realized that Ellis, Acton and Currer were not three random men but the actual Brontës, writing under pseudonyms to keep their identities hidden. I pushed on, and my head filled with heather and harebells, grim stone cottages and miles and miles of moor. Then, on holiday in Devon, I read *Jane Eyre*, and that was it, as far as I was concerned. When we got home, I went to the local library and unearthed Winifred Gérin's biography of Charlotte Brontë from a shelf in a corner of the Reference section, and walked home in a haze of ideas. I was half-way through *Villette* by the time the new school year started in September. The story of the sad sisters and their complicated brother took over my life. Up until then, when people had asked me what I wanted to do in the future, I'd muttered something non-committal about possibly studying law. Law sounded safe, and respect-able. But from that point, I knew that what I really wanted to do was to study English.

Nobody in my family had been to university. It was all a great unknown. My mum had left school at fifteen, and had spent a few years working in a factory before training to be a nurse. She'd given up her job when my brother was born, when she was twenty-two, and had never gone back, devoting herself to bringing up my brother and my two older sisters – all of them born within four years, three children by the age of twenty-six – and then, nine and a half years later, me. My dad had also left school early, when his dad – a coal miner, from a family of coal miners – developed the lung dis-ease pneumoconiosis, the scourge of miners everywhere, and died. His uncles arranged for him to go down the pit, too, to support his mother and ten-year-old brother: he was the man of the family now. He'd enrolled at the local technical college and completed qualifications in geology and mining technology, and was eventually transferred to the brand-new, state-of-the-art Parkside Colliery, in Newton-le-Willows, where he was appointed Safety Engineer. He helped to formulate the rules that were put in place across the country to make conditions safer for the men who worked underground. Learning and hard work were things that he valued. But he wasn't keen on the idea of university. He had an unshakeable belief in the importance of picking a job, starting at the bottom and working your way up. As far as my dad was concerned, university was distant and rarefied and got in the way of earning a living. I wasn't at all sure how he'd react when he heard of my plans.

It took me a long time to tell anyone at school. Reading wasn't something that people in my year talked about. Even doing English was viewed with suspicion by some of my friends: what was the point of sitting round and discussing books, they reasoned, when you could be learning something useful instead? When the scary Head of English asked us what we were reading, I sat in miserable, tongue-glued-down silence, not knowing where to start. I was sixteen, and had a sixteen-year-old's instinct for the kind of careful self-policing that you need to carry out in order to be accepted by your peers. It was safer to keep quiet.

And so, looking back, it's quite fitting that this pull between discovering a passion and being unable to talk about it was caused by the Brontës, and in particular by Charlotte, whose novels are full of people who struggle with speaking out: sometimes expressing themselves in bursts of emotion that are considered inappropriate, sometimes imposing such rigid forms of self-censorship that they render themselves mute. This is why *Jane Eyre*, with its protagonist who rails so vehemently against her situation, is such a powerful novel, because Jane succeeds in finding a voice. She challenges her cruel Aunt Reed, the hateful Mr Brocklehurst and the voices of convention that see her as a mere governess, incapable of feeling and unworthy of love. Her creator uses her to settle personal scores and to draw attention to the plight of young women who lacked connections and opportunities. Her defiant words – 'I am no bird, and no net ensnares me; I am a free human being with an independent will' – are emblazoned across T-shirts and tote bags, fridge magnets, posters and key rings; a quick look on Google reveals that they're also a popular tattoo.

*Jane Eyre* hooks you in skilfully, right from the start. It's a bleak, rainy November day, with no possibility of taking a walk. Ten-year-old Jane is the poor relation at Gateshead Hall, the home of her aunt, Mrs Reed, and her cousins. Her face very definitely does not fit: Mrs Reed criticizes her lack of a 'sociable and childlike disposition', and tells her to go away and be quiet somewhere. And so Jane slips into the breakfast room and tucks herself away on a window seat, behind a heavy red curtain, with a copy of Thomas Bewick's *History of British Birds*. The first-person narrative voice draws us in with her, hidden from the rest of the household, looking at the illustrations. There are images of desolate coasts, uninhabited lands, the extremes of the earth. Jane's seclusion doesn't last long. She is discovered by her cousin, the vile

John Reed: he chides her for not addressing him as 'Master John', throws the copy of the book at her, and then attacks her for daring to stand up to him. By the end of the first chapter, Jane has been hauled off unceremoniously to the Red Room to await her punishment, and we're absolutely clear on where our sympathies are supposed to lie.

The first ten chapters of *Jane Eyre* are essentially a story of trauma and neglect. Reading the novel now, through the lens of what I know about the long-term effects of abusive upbringings, I'm struck by just how horrific Jane's experiences are. Jane is constantly reminded of her dependent status, threatened with the poorhouse. She reflects that 'I dared commit no fault: I strove to fulfil every duty; and I was termed naughty and tiresome, sullen and sneaking, from morning to noon, and from noon to night.' In the Red Room, she imagines that she sees the ghost of her uncle Mr Reed, cries out in terror and falls unconscious. The incident 'gave my nerves a shock, of which I feel the reverberation to this day'. There is rarely any affection for Jane at Gateshead, and what little there is comes not from her family but from the nursemaid, Bessie. Mrs Reed is like a monstrous Supernanny, confining Jane to the naughty corner and telling her that she will be freed 'only on condition of perfect submission and stillness'. The servants criticize Jane for not being a 'nice, pretty child', tell her that it is her place to be humble, that she should try to be 'useful and pleasant'. Not surprisingly, Jane is grateful

for the most minor of kindnesses. When the local apoth-
ecary, Mr Lloyd, pronounces that her nerves are 'not in
a good state', it's the first time anyone shows any sign of
understanding the appalling situation she is in.

Jane's biggest punishment is to be sent away to
Lowood School, an institution for charity girls where
she will spend the next eight years of her life. Lowood
was closely modelled on the Clergy Daughters' School
at Cowan Bridge in Lancashire, the school whose impact
on the lives of the Brontës had been so catastrophic.
The school, founded in January 1824, had been established to provide a 'plain and useful education' for the
daughters of clergymen of limited income. The Reverend Patrick Brontë took his two oldest daughters, Maria
and Elizabeth, to enrol at the school in July of that year;
Charlotte would follow in August and Emily in November. Maria was then ten years old, Elizabeth nine and
Charlotte eight. Emily, at just six, was the school's youngest pupil. Patrick Branwell, aged seven, was being
educated at home. Anne, the baby of the family at four
years old, remained at home too.

Students love to find parallels between the books they
study and the lives of their authors, and the Lowood
chapters of *Jane Eyre* offer a rich seam for them to mine.
They seize first upon the character of Mr Brocklehurst,
based on the Reverend William Carus Wilson, the foun-
der of the Clergy Daughters' School. Brocklehurst is
both intimidating and hypocritical, written in a way that
seems guaranteed to engineer our outrage. On one of

his visits to the school, he denies the girls a mid-morning snack of bread and cheese to replace the inedible burnt porridge they have been served at breakfast, saying that it is better to feed their immortal souls than their vile bodies; he insists that their hair must be cut short in order to 'mortify the lusts of the flesh', yet allows his own daughters to sport elaborately curled tresses and swathe themselves in furs and velvet. Once Brocklehurst has been dealt with, students move on to the harsh conditions at the school, the rancid meat swimming in grease, the long hours of prayer and study, the birching and public shaming of pupils who fall foul of the rules. And then they focus on the illness that leads to the death of the saintly Helen Burns, Jane's only friend and one of the most nauseating characters in the whole of the literary canon. This illness is, of course, based on the consumption that led to the deaths of Maria and Elizabeth Brontë, who succumbed within just six weeks of each other in the early summer of 1825. Hardly surprising, many reflect, that Charlotte felt such anger towards Wilson, whose superintendence of the school saw the deaths of some fifteen children in the first eight years of its existence. Entirely understandable that her feelings would smoulder, over the years, until they were given voice in the pages of her first published novel.

But there's a lesson here, because as far as schools went in the first half of the nineteenth century, the Clergy Daughters' School was hardly an exception. If you really want to know more about the Brontës, I tell the keenest students, what you need to do is to read Juliet Barker's magnificent biography of the family, published in 1994 and the result of years of painstaking scholarship. Barker challenges many of the myths that surround the Brontë story – the result of Elizabeth Gaskell's 1857 biography, *The Life of Charlotte Brontë* – and replaces them with a markedly different version of events. The idea of Haworth as an isolated rural community, cut off from the rest of the world, gives way to an image of the town as a bustling centre of industry where, in Barker's words, 'politics and religion were hotly disputed and culture thrived'. Any notion that the Clergy Daughters' School was unusual in its harshness is also dispelled. Barker draws on the records of similar schools, such as Woodhouse Grove in Leeds, to demonstrate that strict regimes and cruel punishments were commonplace. So were outbreaks of illness. The Brontës were unfortunate in the extreme, but they were definitely not unique.

Conditions at Lowood change after the epidemic that leads to Helen Burns's death, and Jane eventually becomes a teacher there. But the day-to-day grind of school life becomes claustrophobic: 'School rules, school duties, school habits and notions, and voices, and faces, and phrases, and costumes, and preferences, and antipathies: such was what I knew of existence. And now I felt that it was not enough.' How many teachers desperate for term to end, how many students longing for the fresh air of a different environment, can read

Jane's complaint without recognizing her need for change? It's that stifling, world-too-small feeling of having been in the same place for far too long, of needing to reinvent yourself. Acknowledging the paucity of opportunities available to her as a young woman with no connections and no hope of marriage, Jane decides to advertise for a situation as a governess in a private household. She cannot hope for liberty: the best that life can offer her is 'a new servitude'. And it arrives, in the shape of a letter from a Mrs Fairfax, offering Jane a post at Thornfield Hall. This is, of course, where Jane will meet Mr Rochester, and where one of the most well known of nineteenth-century love stories will begin.

Jane does not meet Rochester straight away. She settles into her post, explores her new home – complete with its battlements, its rookery and, most importantly, its attic – and ponders again on the difficulty of being young, female and insignificant. Her words are undoubtedly a reflection of Brontë's own feelings, but they definitely resonated with me at sixteen, a hundred and fifty years after they were published, just as they will have done for many other readers.

Women [Jane reflects, pacing on the rooftops at Thornfield] are supposed to be very calm generally: but women feel just as men feel; they need exercise for their faculties, and a field for their efforts, as much as their brothers do; they suffer from too rigid a restraint, too absolute a stagnation, precisely as men would suffer; and it is narrow-minded in their more privileged fellow-creatures to say that they ought to confine themselves to making puddings and knitting stockings, to playing on the piano, and embroidering bags. It is thoughtless to condemn them, or laugh at them, if they seek to do more or learn more than custom has pronounced necessary for their sex.

Poor, frustrated Jane; and poor Charlotte too. You can see, in this complaint, the echoes of that letter from Robert Southey, telling her to occupy herself with her proper duties; you can sense a lifetime's accumulation of slights and restrictions, summed up brilliantly in Virginia Woolf's observation that 'she had been made to stagnate in a parsonage mending stockings when she wanted to wander free over the world'. Jane braces herself for months and years of sameness, the unvarying routine of domesticity. But then, a few weeks later, she and Rochester have their fateful first encounter, and life gives her a very different focus for her emotions.

In some ways, the romance between Jane and Rochester is so laden with cliché as to seem laughable now. How could it not be? It is rooted in Charlotte's own thwarted passion, her unrequited love for Constantin Héger, head of the girls' school in Brussels that Charlotte had attended – first as a pupil, then as a teacher – in the early 1840s. It has given rise to countless rewritings (anyone setting out to explore the reams of Jane and Rochester fanfiction on the internet had better prepare themselves for a long and murky journey) and has been immortalized on stage, film, television and radio over seventy times. The Silver Petticoat Review website provides a helpful rundown of fifteen different screen adaptations, ranking them from worst to best, with the bottom spot taken by a 1957 Matinee Theatre production that is apparently more camp than Gothic. Yet initially, Rochester is not a conventional romantic hero. He is dark, but he is neither tall nor handsome. He is gruff, demanding and sometimes cold and withdrawn. Jane even tells him that she does not find him good-looking.

What Rochester does do – and what, arguably, makes Jane and generations of readers fall in love with him – is to pay Jane the kind of attention that has been absent from her life so far. He encourages her to speak honestly, and asks her about herself, her family and her education. He is, in short, the first person to show any kind of interest in Jane in her own right. Who wouldn't be won over? But he is also sometimes paternalistic (not surprisingly, as he's twice her age) and controlling. Look at the way he describes Jane, at a point when they are still relative strangers:

> The Lowood constraint still clings to you somewhat; controlling your features, muffling your voice, and restricting your limbs; and you fear in the presence of a man and a brother – or father, or master, or what you will – to smile too gaily, speak too freely, or move too quickly: but, in time, I think you will learn to be natural

with me, as I find it impossible to be conventional with you; and then your looks and movements will have more vivacity and variety than they dare offer now. I see at intervals the glance of a curious sort of bird through the close-set bars of a cage: a vivid, restless, resolute captive is there; were it but free, it would soar cloud-high.

It's easy for us, now, to see such descriptions as – well – a bit creepy. *I know you better than you know yourself,* Rochester is saying. *I can help to set you free.* My students pull disgusted faces when I point this out. Equally, though, it's easy to see why Jane falls in love with him. Little Jane, neglected and unloved; glowering Mr Rochester, the wealthy, sophisticated man of the world. And significantly, Jane manages to hold something of herself back. She refuses to comply when he instructs her to speak, reflecting that 'If he expects me to talk for the mere sake of talking and showing off, he will find he has addressed himself to the wrong person.' At one point, when she believes that Rochester is about to marry the rich heiress Blanche Ingram, her words burst forth against his apparent dismissal of her feelings: 'Do you think, because I am poor, obscure, plain, and little, I am soulless and heartless? You think wrong! – I have as much soul as you – and full as much heart!' When Rochester promises to attire her in satin and lace for their wedding day, she resists, saying that this would turn her into 'an ape in a harlequin's jacket – a jay in borrowed plumes'. During their courtship, she deliberately contradicts him and stands up to him, showing that she will be anything but meek and obedient. He accuses her of being cruel, and she assures him that she is 'naturally hard – very flinty'. It's Brontë's two-fingered response to convention, to the people who would happily see women like her submitting to men like Rochester simply because of their wealth, their social power and their gender.

So Jane's voice, then, is also Brontë's own voice. And Brontë, entirely predictably, was criticized for speaking out in such a forthright manner. When *Jane Eyre* was first published, in 1847, it became an instant success, buoyed by glowing reviews in many of the noted periodicals of the day. Yet some critics were more negative. Anne Mozley wrote in the *Christian Remembrancer* in April 1848 of the novel's 'masculine hardness, coarseness, and freedom of expression', commenting that it would be difficult to find 'a book more unfeminine, both in its excellences and defects'. Elizabeth Rigby, writing in the *Quarterly Review* later that year, drew attention to the novel's 'pervading tone of ungodly discontent', linking its 'murmuring against the comforts of the rich' to the same militant spirit that had 'overthrown authority' overseas, and 'fostered Chartism and rebellion' at home. Brontë's protagonist, in Rigby's opinion, would have done better to recognize her lowly status and learn to live with it. Tone-policing, it seems, is nothing new: the novel's challenging of social hierarchies was frequently deemed coarse, vulgar and unnatural. Even Virginia Woolf, that champion of women writers, felt that *Jane Eyre* was marred by its author's resentment of the limitations of her world. In reading *Jane Eyre*, Woolf declared, 'one sees that [Brontë] will never get her genius expressed whole and entire. Her books will be deformed and twisted. She will write in a rage where she should write calmly. She will write foolishly where she should write wisely.' You're allowed to speak up, the implicit message is, as long as you do it in an appropriate way. Calm down, and remember who you are.

This awkward oscillation – between needing to speak out and knowing that you're likely to be slapped down and reminded of your place – is something that clearly strikes a chord with many readers. Whenever I've taught *Jane Eyre*, the students it's resonated with most are those who are just starting to find their own voices, to speak up for themselves. Mostly, they've been girls, but boys as well have responded to that sense of marginalization, of being overlooked. They see something in the lonely girl – and, later, the young woman – that is easily missed by those who are already sure of themselves. The confident, the cocky, don't care how they're perceived. Those who are more diffident know how much it matters. That lurking threat of the whispers at break, the looks, the comments on social media, those online spaces that seem to offer scope for self-expression but all too often mean that young people have nowhere that cannot be invaded by taunts and snipes and insults. It's paralysing, this fear of making your thoughts heard. This was certainly me, at sixteen. Even now, as an adult, I'm cautious, conflict-avoidant, sometimes scared to commit. 'Speak what we feel, not what we ought to say,' go the lines at the end of *King Lear*. But for many of us, it's not that easy. We weigh our words: we're careful. We hang back.

There is, also, a huge irony at the heart of *Jane Eyre*, a novel about a woman who gains a voice and gives voice to so many of her creator's frustrations. Because there's a woman in the novel who is silenced, who is never allowed to speak for herself. This is Mr Rochester's first wife, who has been confined to the attic at Thornfield for over a decade. In Brontë's version of events, she is Bertha Mason, the madwoman in the attic, described in terms that degrade and dehumanize her: she is a 'clothed hyena', a 'goblin' and a 'vampire', her features distorted by rage, her eyes bloodshot and 'fiery'. Brontë states that she is a 'Creole', the Jamaican-born daughter of a European settler, and refers to her 'dark' hair and 'black' face. In the entirely English setting of Thornfield Hall, she is indubitably Other, threatening and mysterious, source of the mocking laugh that Jane hears when she is up on the roof at Thornfield. It would be over a hundred years before the novelist Jean Rhys would give the first Mrs Rochester a voice; and when she did, it was not as Bertha Mason, but as Antoinette Cosway, the central character of her 1966 novel *Wide Sargasso Sea*.

To read *Wide Sargasso Sea* after reading *Jane Eyre* is to be plunged into a very different world. This is Jamaica in the 1830s, shortly after the passing of the Emancipation

Act. The heat and the vegetation contrast sharply with the grey November drizzle of *Jane Eyre*'s opening chapter, but the environment itself is just as hostile. Antoinette lives with her widowed mother and disabled younger brother on the family estate, Coulibri. The estate was once rich, but since the abolition of slavery it has fallen into decay. Antoinette's father has drunk himself to death, and the Cosways are now isolated. The former slaves treat them with scorn, referring to them as 'white cockroaches', and their fellow European settlers keep their distance, sensing trouble. Antoinette observes on the novel's opening page that even 'feeling safe in bed' is something that belongs to the past. The family's horse is poisoned, and there are hints of witchcraft, of obeah. There's a constant feeling of restlessness, of paranoia, made all the more acute by the hum of flies and the sweltering heat. Even the orchids in the garden seem hostile: one looks like a snake, another an octopus with long brown tentacles. It's like the aura that comes before a migraine, a vivid bad trip.

Things change. Antoinette's mother marries the rich Mr Mason, but there is gossip from all the 'smooth smiling people' who can't understand why Mason has chosen this unstable young widow with her two undesirable children and her wreck of an estate. The new Mrs Mason is desperate to leave Coulibri, but her husband refuses. Then, one night, a group of former slaves set fire to the house. Coulibri is destroyed, and Antoinette's brother is killed, but the most horrific image of this part of the novel is of the family's parrot, Coco, trying to fly from the burning building with his feathers alight, his clipped wings unable to carry him.

The clipping of wings seems a highly appropriate image, not just for *Wide Sargasso Sea* but for *Jane Eyre* as well. Both Jane and Antoinette long for freedom, but both are restricted. Birds pervade both novels, from the illustrations that Jane pores over in her window-seat refuge to the shrill cries of the tropical birds in the forests of the Caribbean. The name Coulibri means 'hummingbird'. Both Antoinette and Rochester hear the ominous sound of cockerels crowing, that biblical sign of betrayal, and at one point a heap of chicken feathers in the corner of a room reminds Antoinette of the mysterious rituals of obeah. Jane insists that she is no bird, and that no net can ensnare her, but after she leaves Rochester, she compares her sad heart to 'a bird with both wings broken'. Birds are multivalent symbols. They soar and swoop and glide, but they are fragile, easily damaged. Birdsong can be delicate and beautiful; it can also be intense, piercing, eerie. Between them, Brontë and Rhys use birds in just about every way imaginable, a richly detailed counterpoint to the range of emotions that Jane and Antoinette experience and the situations in which they find themselves.

Like Charlotte Brontë, Jean Rhys drew on aspects of her own early life in writing her novel. She was born on the island of Dominica in 1890: her great-grandfather, the owner of slaves and sugar plantations, had been governor of the island in the 1830s. The family's estate – like Coulibri – had fallen into disrepair after the abolition of slavery, and had been raided in a riot. Rhys was isolated in Dominica, growing up as a white Creole in a predominantly Black community. At sixteen, she was sent to school in England, where she was mocked and treated as an outsider. She married three times, and led an itinerant life, travelling around Europe and writing novels about women who – like Brontë's protagonists – have little money and very few prospects available to them. Eventually, she settled in a small Devon village in a bungalow that had been condemned as unfit for human habitation. When *Wide Sargasso Sea* was published, in 1966, it was Rhys's first novel since 1939.

In *Jane Eyre*, we are reminded many times of the contrasts between Jane and Bertha. Rochester is at pains to point out how different they are: Jane is grave and quiet, Bertha demonic and ferocious, with bloodshot eyes. But reading *Wide Sargasso Sea*, I'm struck by the similarities between Antoinette and Jane. Both begin their stories as essentially unwanted, sent away because their presence is inconvenient. After the fire at Coulibri, Antoinette's grief-stricken mother is sent to an institution, and Antoinette is sent first to live with her Aunt Cora and then to a convent. Children taunt Antoinette and tell her that her mother has gone mad, that she tried to kill Mr Mason and now has eyes like a zombie. Rhys, like Brontë, creates a powerful sense of an isolated young woman living very much inside her own mind. Yet Antoinette, unlike

Jane, has a rich stepfather who can offer a dowry to anyone who will take her off his hands. And consequently, Antoinette is married off to an Englishman, the younger son of one of Mason's friends. In *Wide Sargasso Sea*, this man is never named, but he is Rhys's version of the man known to readers of *Jane Eyre* as Edward Fairfax Rochester. Eventually, he will take Antoinette to England, give her a new name and conceal her in the attic at Thornfield Hall.

When *Wide Sargasso Sea* is taught nowadays, it's often used alongside *Jane Eyre*, at A level, as part of a comparative study or as a way of introducing the concept of post-colonialist readings. Students – especially those who have read and loved *Jane Eyre* – can struggle with it. *Jane Eyre* is a novel to return to, a book to curl up with and lose yourself in. *Wide Sargasso Sea* is a much less comfortable read. There are no lighter moments in *Wide Sargasso Sea*, no points where you feel you can relax. This is appropriate, because the world in which the novel is set is not a place of safety: certainly not for Antoinette, derided, rejected and sold off to someone she has never met, and not for Rochester either, assailed both by fever and by the rumours that surround his new bride. There's also the difficulty of the novel's narrative style. The story is told partly by Antoinette, partly by Rochester. There are flashbacks, shifts in tense, and gaps that the reader must try to make sense of. At times, Antoinette recounts her dreams and imaginings with such vividness that we're not sure what is real and what isn't. It's as if we're being continually kept on guard.

Guiding students through these difficulties takes a lot of sensitivity. Sometimes, students think that it's their own fault. They're not up to the job: the novel has defeated them. Others blame the writer for not making things easier. Why does it all need to be so complicated? Both of these reactions can, if teachers are not careful, end in students rejecting literature altogether. If we're aware of where the stumbling blocks in a text might be, we can help students to tackle them, to see a narrative method that initially seems tricky and off-putting as a way of conveying a particular set of experiences. Difficulty, then, becomes enriching, rather than perplexing. *Trust me*, we're saying. *It'll get easier, and you'll see why they've done it like this.* Meanings are not always immediately available. Opacity is not necessarily a problem. But this takes time, and relies not only on our relationships with our students, but on our relationships with the texts we're teaching. We're helping things to run smoothly, brokering a deal.

In *Wide Sargasso Sea*, the move to England is precipitated by the arrival of a letter. Rochester learns of his wife's family history, of her father's alcoholism and her mother's madness. His disorientation turns to coldness and cruelty. He refuses to call Antoinette by her own name. Instead, he calls her Bertha, an act of control that echoes the renaming of slaves by their owners. There are hints of what Antoinette will be turned into, in her matted hair and swollen face, and a chilling reference to what Rochester has planned, to 'the day when she is only a memory to be avoided, locked away, and like all memories a legend'. The novel's ending sees Antoinette lighting a candle and making her way along the corridor at Thornfield.

Some readers will resist *Wide Sargasso Sea*, and not only because of its challenging narrative style. They'll argue that Brontë's creation should be allowed to stand alone. If she wanted Rochester's first wife to be a monster, who's to deny her? Yet Rhys's novel shows us that, sometimes, the stories we're familiar with – the stories we love – rely themselves on stories that are more damaging. In *Jane Eyre*, Bertha is the dangerous Other; in *Wide Sargasso Sea*, Antoinette is very definitely a victim. In Brontë's novel, she is barely allowed to speak, uttering only 'wolfish cries', fierce yells and – of course – that long, low, eccentric laugh. It is Rochester who tells her story, painting her in the harshest light possible. Rhys gives us a sense of the complexity that lies behind the first Mrs Rochester, allowing Antoinette to speak for herself. In doing so, she teaches us an important lesson: to be alert to hidden histories, and to the ways in which people seek to define both themselves and others.

You can, if you wish, join the millions of people who flock each year to Haworth in West Yorkshire, to visit the Parsonage, pay homage to the Brontë family memorial stone in the parish church of St Michael and All Angels, and explore the shops and cafés that line the steep, cobbled Main Street. You can have lunch at the Villette Coffee House and drink at either the Black Bull, Branwell's former haunt, or the Kings Arms, where – if you're lucky – they'll have the locally brewed Brontë Beers on tap, each of them named after one of the family (Charlotte, apparently, has a fruity start and a hoppy finish). But these paths are well trodden. For something different, you'd need to head across the moors to the A65, and then follow this road north-west through the breezy limestone country of the Yorkshire Dales to Cowan Bridge, just over the border into Lancashire. There, by the side of the road, is the building that once housed the Clergy Daughters' School, marked now by a plaque set into the wall. In a startling reversal of fortune, it's now a beautifully restored holiday cottage, with a wood-burning stove, crisp bedlinen and a luxurious roll-top bath. From there, you can head via the M6 to Manchester and thread your way through the side streets off Oxford Road to a pub called the Salutation. Formerly a boarding house, it is where Charlotte and her father took lodgings in 1846, so that the Reverend Brontë could undergo an operation to remove the cataract from his left eye, an operation conducted entirely without anaesthetic. While he was recovering – lying on his back in a darkened room, with leeches on his temples – Charlotte began to write *Jane Eyre*. The Salutation is proud of its Brontë connection, but all the same, it's odd to think that you can now sit and have a drink, take part in a pub quiz, in the spaces where Jane's lonely childhood was first committed to the page.

I imagine Charlotte watching, her brow furrowed, not entirely sure whether she approved.

The most haunting of *Jane Eyre* locations, though, is situated just over an hour's drive away, in Derbyshire, just outside Hathersage. This is where you'll find North Lees Hall, supposedly the model for Thornfield. In 1845, Charlotte stayed at the vicarage in Hathersage with her friend Ellen Nussey. There, so the stories go, she would have heard the legend of a madwoman who was imprisoned in the attic at North Lees Hall, and who died in a fire. North Lees Hall, like Thornfield, is three storeys high, topped by battlements, the seat of a gentleman rather than a nobleman. It is secluded and surrounded by trees. It was built in the late sixteenth century by a man whose name was Robert Eyre. Various members of the Eyre family were buried in the local churchyard, and just a few miles away, on the road to Bakewell, there's a pub called the Eyre Arms.

Like the Brontë Schoolhouse in Cowan Bridge, North Lees Hall is now – at least in part – a desirable holiday residence. You can stay in a private room with a four-poster bed; you can walk on nearby Stanage Edge. You can even enjoy the rooftop terrace, now with outdoor furniture. I'd defy anyone, though, to stay up there for long without imagining that they can see the shadow of a small, self-contained governess in a plain grey dress, without thinking of her passionate soul and her desire to give women like her a voice, and without listening for the echoes of a long, low laugh that concealed unimaginable pain.

# On not fitting in: *Oranges Are Not the Only Fruit* by Jeanette Winterson

There's a question I'm asked several times a year. *What's the best book you've ever read, Miss?* It's a difficult one. What does 'best' mean, in literary terms? After a lifetime of reading books, not only studying and teaching and talking about them but also retreating into them and using them as a comfort blanket, labels like 'best' and 'worst' seem far too simplistic. There are books that I adore, but that I know are flawed in all manner of ways; books whose brilliance I can appreciate but will never love. *It's complicated*, I say. *What about you?*

If you were to ask me, though, which books have been most important to me, which have made the biggest difference to my life, that would be much easier. There's a children's book called *Charley* by Joan G. Robinson, about a girl who runs away from home after a misunderstanding with her family, that I loved when I was about ten and still reread from time to time. There's David Lodge's *Nice Work*, which prompted me to discover the Brontës, and of course there's *Jane Eyre*, although my favourite Brontë novel is actually *Villette*: if you want solitariness and self-reliance, then it's crabby Lucy Snowe you need, not saintly Jane. And then there's *Oranges Are Not the Only Fruit*; and to explain why *Oranges*

*Are Not the Only Fruit* has been such an important part of my life, we need to go back to 1990, to the year after I first decided to study English at university, but when I was still stuck in Newton-le-Willows and waiting for the future to begin.

By January 1990, I was four months into my A levels, and the discussions we had in class were opening up spaces in my head that had never existed before. Sometimes I needed to go out and walk just to try to outpace the restlessness of what was going on in my mind. I used to make my way the couple of hundred yards from my house to the bridge over the railway, the line from Warrington to Wigan, and stand. From there you could see fields and housing estates, the lights of the distant motorway, the cooling towers of the power station ten miles away at Widnes. I'd kid myself, sometimes, that on a clear day you could see as far as Wales, but that was just wishful thinking, the desire for something other. We were doing Philip Larkin's *The Whitsun Weddings*, and poetry – which, for so long, had seemed like some kind of mysterious code – was finally making sense. Some of the most vivid lines in Larkin's poetry were about the idea of elsewhere, a place to escape to, where you could be out of reach. I didn't know where I wanted to be, but I did know that it wasn't where I actually was.

As I've grown older, I've come to realize that small towns – plus the experience of growing up in them, being shaped by them and eventually getting away from them – have an important and perhaps under-recognized

place in contemporary culture. Small towns can represent comfort and security, but they can also be stifling
and stultifying. In June 1984, the British synthpop band
Bronski Beat released its debut single 'Smalltown Boy',
and gave a voice to teenagers everywhere who wanted to
break away. The video features singer Jimmy Somerville
sitting on a train, the lines crossing over the points, the
tracks veering away into the distance. Scenery flashes by:
trees, offices, what looks like a school. There's a soaring
falsetto and a howl of pain. The song tells a story of
ostracism and violence; of being beaten up down an
alleyway just for loving the wrong people. As the song
ends, Somerville reaches the big city. He steps out on to
the platform, scared but brave, not knowing yet quite
what the future holds.

I don't know where Jeanette Winterson was in the
summer of 1984 when 'Smalltown Boy' was released,
but chances are she was putting the finishing touches to
*Oranges Are Not the Only Fruit*, her novel about a girl who
grew up in a terraced house on a long stretchy street
with a hill at the top and a town – a small town,
obviously – at the bottom. The novel was published in
March 1985, and won that year's Whitbread Award for
the Best First Novel. I first became aware of it in 1990,
when it was adapted for television by the BBC and
broadcast in that January when I was immersing myself
in Larkin's poetry and wondering what my own future
might bring. It wasn't until later that year that I actually
read the novel itself. I can remember where I bought it:

WHSmith, in the Arndale Centre in Manchester. I hoarded it on the train and didn't start reading it because I knew that the sooner I started it the sooner I'd finish, and I didn't want it to be over. Once I did start, it utterly consumed me, and is still one of the best coming-of-age novels I know.

There's another reason why *Oranges* was so important to many of us who were teenagers back in the 1980s and early 1990s. In May 1988, when I was fifteen, Margaret Thatcher's Conservative government introduced an infamous and highly controversial piece of legislation known as Section 28. Section 28 was an amendment to the 1986 Local Government Act, and made it illegal for local authorities and state-maintained schools to 'intentionally promote homosexuality, or publish material with the intention of promoting homosexuality'. Council-run libraries, theatres and community centres could not fund books, plays, films or other materials depicting same-sex relationships, and schools could not present gay relationships as acceptable. Teenagers who were gay, or who were questioning their sexuality, had nowhere to turn. And then, for a whole hour on three consecutive Wednesday evenings, the BBC – that bastion of culture and respectability – broadcast an adaptation of a novel by a young gay woman, about growing up, discovering who you love and breaking away from all you've ever known. It was as if someone, somewhere, was whispering: *It's okay. You're not on your own.*

\*

The essential story of *Oranges Are Not the Only Fruit* is simple. Its narrator, Jeanette, has been adopted at birth by a Pentecostal Evangelist couple living in a Lancashire mill town. Her father is meek and unassuming, but her mother – a northern dragon in a fearsome headscarf – has enlisted Jeanette to join her in 'a tag team against the rest of the world', and is training her to live a life in God. She teaches Jeanette to read from the Book of Deuteronomy, and keeps her away from school, believing it to be a 'breeding ground' of sin, until the authorities intervene. Jeanette is clearly different from the other children, and struggles to fit in. And then, as a teenager, Jeanette meets another girl, Melanie, and falls in love. When their relationship is discovered, they are cast out from the church, with Jeanette being subjected to a disturbing exorcism by a group of elders that includes her own mother.

*Oranges* is narrated in a confiding first-person voice that lures you in with its arch observations and wry humour. There are lovely details: a homemade Noah's Ark with a detachable chimp made from a Brillo pad, a fire-and-brimstone pastor whose anxious wife urges him to 'steady on, Roy'. Yet it is much more than the tale of an unusual upbringing. Its chapter titles are the names of the first eight books of the Old Testament, and stories – both biblical and otherwise – permeate the narrative of Jeanette's childhood. Chapters break off into digressions that draw on fairy tale, Arthurian legend and invented myths such as that of the emperor

Tetrahedron, who lives in a palace made of elastic bands. As you read, it becomes clear that *Oranges* is not only about growing up, but also about being able to write your own story – about working out, from the stories you're told when you're young, what your own story is going to be, and taking control of it.

When you're a teenager, taking control of your story is important. In school, you might think it's about careers: jobs and colleges, apprenticeships and universities. But there are other things too. As teachers, we touch on these in all manner of ways, often arising from chance conversations. We give young people the opportunity, and sometimes the strength and intellectual means, to resist the narratives that are forced upon them. We use chosen names and preferred pronouns; we affirm identities and create a safe space for students to discover the people they're becoming. This might be the only safe space they have, especially in small towns like the one I grew up in and the ones I've taught in, full of people who've known you all your life but don't know the person you're turning into. It's hard to shake things up and show people you're not who you were back when you were five, or eleven, or fourteen. When you're struggling under the weight of all those expectations, you need a place to breathe.

The small town where *Oranges* is set is not actually named, but it is Accrington, twenty miles north of Manchester, where Winterson lived until she left for Oxford. It is vividly drawn, 'a town stolen from the valleys, a huddled place of chimneys and little shops and back-to-back houses with no gardens'. Winterson conjures an image of flagstones and cobbled streets, washing hung out to dry in defiance of the weather. It's a town populated mainly by women – there are very few men in Winterson's novel – and these women have the larger-than-life quality that adults often acquire if you're a particularly observant child, listening to conversations and taking things in. There are the women who run the sweetshop and give Jeanette a free banana bar with her weekly comic; the waitress at Trickett's café whose glasses are stuck together with a Band-Aid because someone put a delivery of beefburgers down on them. There are the places that mark the limits of Jeanette's world, such as Ellison's tenement, where the annual fair is held, and the Factory Bottoms, where Jeanette isn't allowed to go on her own. And there are the snobberies, the minute judgements made in a society where everyone knows not only their own place, but also everyone else's. Shopping at Maxi Ball's Catalogue Seconds, where the clothes smell of industrial glue, is a sign of fecklessness and desperation; but quiche is 'a bit daring' and well-spoken Mrs Clifton, who shops at Marks & Spencer, is the object of both respect and resentment. You don't want to lower yourself, but you don't want to pretend to be something you're not, either.

When I first read *Oranges*, in my own small northern town less than forty miles away, I knew instantly the kind of place Winterson was describing: the market stalls and rainy streets, the factory shop selling bargain clothes, the posh girls who went to Brownies and had music lessons. My nearest reference point was Wigan, the town where my grandparents lived and where my parents had spent the early part of their lives. Neither of my parents drove, and so when we went to Wigan we had to go on the bus, an orange double-decker that jolted its way along narrow roads through yet more small towns: Golborne, Abram, Ince-in-Makerfield. It was a landscape that worked hard, full of red-brick houses and stern-looking pubs, shops and car showrooms and light-industrial buildings. There were occasional fields, tangled hawthorn hedges, a solitary chestnut horse that I always craned my neck to see. The bus, full of smoke and gossip, used to stop at Golborne for an inexplicable ten minutes outside a chemist's shop, and would then stir into life like a grumpy walrus. Eventually we'd arrive in Wigan, outside the old market hall with its smell of vegetables and raw meat. There's a scene in *Oranges* where Jeanette and her mother take the bus into town so that her mother can buy mince at the market, and reading it now I'm transported to the Wigan of my childhood, wrinkling my nose as we passed the fish stalls in the market, trailing along after my mum and wondering if we'd see the horse again on our way home.

There's something really powerful, in adolescence, about reading books that describe places you recognize. It gives you a sense that your surroundings have a deeper resonance, a significance that's been acknowledged by someone else. They have layers; they belong not just to the here and now but to the wider culture. This is especially the case if the places you know aren't ones that are conventionally found in books. For many of my students today, it's reading Susan Hill's novel *The Woman in Black*, with its descriptions of the flat misty landscapes of the east of England. I remember one student showing me photographs of eerie-looking fens that he'd taken from the bus on his journey to school. He'd struggled with the novel up till then, but being able to connect its setting with his own surroundings, that bleak November morning, had flicked a switch in his mind: his route to school made the perfect backdrop for Hill's malevolent ghost. When I was a teenager, studying Philip Larkin, I was reading poems that described ordinary scenes in ordinary towns, dismantled cars and advertising hoardings, chain stores and coach parties and recreation grounds. Even though Larkin was writing about Hull – a city I'd never been to, and would not visit until many years later – his images resonated with me miles away at the other end of the M62, reflecting that particular kind of restlessness that seems to be wherever you are when you're seventeen, stuck in a place that somebody else chose for you and waiting for the rest of life to come along. Reading *Oranges* gave me the same feeling: here was a world I could understand. These were books that I could get inside, that I could inhabit in a way that didn't always feel possible. Between them, the unlikely partnership of Larkin and Winterson represented the security of the familiar.

This sense of security was important, because it was

also about belonging. It's true that literature should open you up to the world beyond your own experience, but it should also help you to feel that what you *do* experience is recognized and valued, held safe. If you don't see yourself in books, if you don't see the world you know reflected in them, you don't feel as if they have anything to do with you. They're part of a conversation that excludes you when it should be trying to welcome you in. Nowadays, we are much more careful about making sure that the texts we read in school represent a diverse world and a variety of lives and experiences. Exam boards have broadened their range of set texts and provided resources to support schools trying to break away from the traditional canon. Pressures of time and funding mean that departments are not always able to make the most of these opportunities, but at least they're a start. We have to try.

The dominant force in Jeanette's life is religion. It shapes the story she has been told about her origins, in which her mother, out walking one night, 'dreamed a dream and sustained it in daylight': a dream of a foundling whom she would adopt, raise, dedicate to the Lord and train as a missionary. It also permeates every aspect of her existence. Jeanette's weekly routine is one of prayer meetings and church services, tambourine lessons and Bible quizzes. Holidays are spent in gospel tents and at church camps. When Jeanette loses her hearing and needs to have her adenoids removed, her mother is convinced that she has simply been filled with the Spirit. She is surrounded by tales of sinners and the converted, and the concept of Hell is a constant presence. At school, she embroiders a sampler with the words 'The Summer is Ended and We Are Not Yet Saved', a quotation from the Book of Jeremiah. The other children snigger at her stories of testifying on the beach at Llandudno, and she is later accused of terrorizing them with stories of eternal damnation. As readers, we recognize that this is a deeply dysfunctional upbringing, but to Jeanette herself, this is simply what life is like. School is full of confusion, whereas church is a source of happiness and belonging. She is proud of her religion, and if her mother does not show her anything that could be described as love, she does not appear to feel this as a lack.

So it's an odd world that Jeanette lives in, her social circle made up largely of members of the Pentecostal Church, her closest friend the elderly Elsie Norris. And into this world, one day when Jeanette is a teenager, comes Melanie. It's hardly an auspicious meeting. It's a rainy day, and Jeanette is being dragged round the local market by her mother. She is mutinous. She wanted to stay at home. She has torn her raincoat and her mother is making her wear an outsized pink mackintosh that she has bought from a box of cheap seconds. And then she spots Melanie. Melanie is working on the fish stall, boning kippers and decorating every fourth fish with a sprig of parsley. Her eyes are 'a lovely grey', like a cat's.

Jeanette goes back week after week to look at her, and talk to her, and eventually invites her to church. It's the first time Jeanette has had a friend of her own age, and her life is about to change beyond recognition.

Winterson prepares the ground carefully for Jeanette's relationship with Melanie. We see other characters start to perceive her as someone whose sexuality is beginning to emerge. Her aunt tells her that she has plenty of time to get a boyfriend. Jeanette replies that she doesn't think she wants one, but this notion is dismissed. The neighbours, Nellie and Doreen, gossip about Doreen's studious daughter, Jane, who spends all her spare time at her friend Susan's house doing her homework: 'If she doesn't get a boyfriend folks will talk.' It's a time and a society where young women – even clever young women – are expected to get married and produce children, rather than going to university or pursuing a career. But sex itself is something to be feared. Men are beasts, with scratchy stubble and incomprehensible desires. Jeanette's mother tells her a cautionary tale of the time she thought she was in love with a young Frenchman called Pierre, having felt a 'fizzing and a buzzing and a certain giddiness'. She slept with Pierre – 'Lord forgive me, but I did it' – and later found out that the fizzing and the buzzing were actually the symptoms of a stomach ulcer. 'Don't let anyone touch you Down There,' she warns Jeanette. There's a feeling of tension, of something unstoppable set in motion.

Jeanette and Melanie hug at the end of their Bible study, and it feels 'like drowning'. Winterson is beautifully opaque about what actually happens when Jeanette and Melanie first sleep together, turning instead to the language of the Book of Genesis and its story of origins: 'And it was evening and it was morning; another day.'

The BBC's adaptation of *Oranges Are Not the Only Fruit* drew praise from many quarters. It won three BAFTA awards in 1990, including those for best drama series or serial and best soundtrack. In 2010, the *Guardian* put the serial as number 8 in its list of the top 50 TV dramas of all time: the journalist Grace Dent praised its 'ferocious cast of womenfolk, huge of faith, hat and handbag'. But not surprisingly, when the drama was first screened, there were angry reactions to its portrayal of religion. Representatives from the Elim Pentecostal Church, the church that Winterson attended as a child, were asked to speak to the cast and producers during filming about attitudes to homosexuality. When the programme was aired, they complained that they had been misrepresented. The Reverend Eldin Corsie claimed that the portrayal of the church was 'absolute nonsense': 'We don't and never have excommunicated people for being lesbian or homosexual. The whole thing was a distortion and a gross caricature. My congregation were made to look like a gang of Bible-thumping morons.' The most significant reaction, however, was undoubtedly that of

Constance Winterson, Jeanette's mother, who died while watching the serial's second episode.

The main omission from the BBC adaptation of *Oranges Are Not the Only Fruit* is that of the digressions that punctuate the story of Jeanette's childhood. There are many of these, featuring characters and places from archetype and mythology: a beautiful princess who is told by an old hunchbacked woman that she is in danger of being burned by the brightness of her own flame; a prince who wants to meet the perfect woman; Sir Perceval setting out from Camelot to find the Holy Grail. These fragments confused me when I first read *Oranges*, and I have to prepare students for them carefully so they recognize the role they play rather than being tempted to skim over them. They're actually really important, because they're used by Winterson to develop and amplify a number of significant themes. Characters resist the roles that have been defined for them. They long for things that do not exist. They are sent on journeys, shut out, forced to find new places to live. The critic John Mullan has described these 'flashes of fairytale and newly minted legend' as signs of the young Jeanette's hungry imagination, and reading the novel again now, I'm struck by the sense of a character wanting to carve out her own story from all the stories that have gone before. There's an energy that emerges from these multiple narratives, and with it a sense of the young Jeanette's own identity, unfolding its wings.

My students often initially see this complexity of style

as a hindrance, something that gets in the way of Jeanette's own story. But once they have spent time with it, many of them come to appreciate that the spaces in the novel – the gaps between the digressions and the main narrative, between the biblical chapter titles and the scenes of Jeanette's early life – invite us to think, to make connections. It's the kind of technique I'd have loved to have explored when I was at school, although, of course, I wouldn't have been able to, because Section 28 wouldn't have allowed it. I talk to my students, now, about the impact of Section 28, and they are appalled when they learn that schools and local authorities were put in a position where they risked prosecution for offering support to vulnerable groups and people in need of help. No prosecutions were ever brought under Section 28, but sometimes, a law doesn't have to be used actively in order to have an impact. It was enough just for Section 28 to exist. Teachers who did try to support students were forced to do this covertly, making it clear that they were risking their jobs in doing so. There was, of course, no internet back then, no networks that could easily be tapped into, no possibility of reaching out and finding friends online. It was a time of loneliness and fear.

The idea of *Oranges Are Not the Only Fruit* being on the curriculum at my own secondary school – a Catholic comprehensive – would have been unthinkable even without Section 28. I remember my GCSE English teacher telling us that Antonio and Bassanio, in our set play *The Merchant of Venice*, were sometimes played 'a bit queer', and another teacher saying – apropos of nothing – that he could understand why two men might want to hold hands in public, but that it wasn't something he thought he should have to see. I remember this, and so does Dermot, one of my oldest friends, who always knew he was gay but didn't come out until he was twenty-one, three years after we left our school and our small town and moved to our respective big cities. Years later, we talk about what it was like to grow up in that environment. He'd had to be constantly on the alert, he said. Insults in the corridors and changing rooms, jokes and comments that might have been aimed at him but might not, keeping him nervous, jumpy. The overwhelming message he received from society, both overtly and more insidiously, was that his sexuality was wrong. So he took on the burden of keeping it quiet, of maintaining a rigid sense of control over everything he did so that nobody would ever find out. He'd had to police his own behaviour to avoid drawing attention to himself. He didn't drink alcohol, in case it caused him to drop his guard; didn't go to parties, to evade the inevitable teenage snogging and its aftermath. Even a glance in the wrong direction could be dangerous. All of this took a toll. 'When I think about who I am now, I'm still nervous about conflict,' he tells me. 'It's over thirty years ago and this is still who I am.'

We talk about escape, about the small town where we grew up and that we both, for our own reasons, wanted to leave behind. 'All you had to do was to sit and wait, and think about another time in the future when things would feel safer.' The future has become safer, but of course he didn't know, back then, that it ever would. School was brutal. There was nowhere that felt unequivocally secure.

Dermot didn't read *Oranges* until he was at university, but he did watch the BBC adaptation, sitting at home with his mum and his older sister. He remembers the fact that neither of them batted an eyelid at its depiction of same-sex relationships. It mattered, he said, to see something that touched on the same sense of longing and loneliness. It let him know that he wasn't on his own.

By the time I started teaching, in 1996, Section 28 no longer held the same fear that it once had. It wasn't repealed in England and Wales until 2003, but I don't remember it ever being mentioned as a reason not to offer support or tackle homophobia. That doesn't mean, however, that the attitudes it represented had gone away. Early in my teaching career, I put in a request to buy copies of both *Oranges Are Not the Only Fruit* and Pat Barker's *The Ghost Road*, as part of an attempt to extend sixth-form reading. *The Ghost Road*, which explores themes of trauma and brutality, won the Booker Prize in 1995: its central character, an officer in the First World War, has a number of relationships with both men and women while he is on leave. My request was turned down. 'They're not really the kind of books we should be encouraging students to read,' I was told.

I was compliant when I was at school, but as a teacher,

I am much more rebellious. I kept both *Oranges Are Not the Only Fruit* and *The Ghost Road* on the list of recommended reading that I gave to students at the beginning of their A-level English Literature course, and in 2001, one of my students opted to write about *Oranges* for an essay that allowed candidates a free choice of texts. '*Oranges* was a revelation,' she told me, when I messaged her to ask about the book's impact. 'Someone talking about relationships and feelings that I didn't even know existed, but instantly understood and related to was exhilarating and terrifying. My first reading made me feel furious and intensely sad. But my overriding memory and the impact it has to this day is a sense of overwhelming hope that she got out of her small section of the world and moved forward and became part of the change. I'd loved reading as a child, but I struggled to find myself or my experiences in books as I went through adolescence. I would say that Jeanette Winterson brought me back to literature.'

Today, *Oranges Are Not the Only Fruit* can be studied in England and Wales at both GCSE and A level. There's a York Notes study guide, and hundreds of online resources. It was included in the American Library Association's Bibliography for Gay Teens in 2000. Thousands of schools now have LBGTQ+ support groups for students, and many have dedicated sections in their school libraries, celebrating diversity and equality. My friend Dermot would never have dreamed of coming out when we were at school. Nowadays, I have students who would never dream of having to hide who they are, who are brilliantly and courageously themselves. But I know there will be others who are more cautious, who need the help of positive role models – and of seeing their lives and feelings reflected in books – in order to reassure themselves that they, too, have a place.

In 2011, Jeanette Winterson published her memoir, *Why Be Happy When You Could Be Normal?* It tells the story of the reality behind *Oranges Are Not the Only Fruit*, and I recommend it to everyone who sees *Oranges* as some kind of nostalgic northern comedy. There are moments in *Why Be Happy When You Could Be Normal?* that make me want to curl up and howl, knowing that the truth was far grimmer, far more loveless, than the fiction. One of these comes just six pages in, when Winterson reveals that the character of Elsie Norris, the elderly lady who is the fictional Jeanette's best friend, is invented: 'There was no Elsie. There was no one like Elsie. Things were much lonelier than that.' Another is when the real Mrs Winterson burns the books that the teenage Jeanette has collected. These are the books that she has bought with her earnings from her part-time job; books that are precious, lovingly covered in sticky-backed plastic. The next morning, Jeanette picks up some of the scraps that have blown along the alley. Fragments, shored against her ruins.

Just like her real-life counterpart, Jeanette, in *Oranges*, manages to leave her small town for an ancient city whose inhabitants spend their time puzzling over the nature of the world and the meaning of life. Once she gets there, the only thing she is certain of is that she can never go back. She is asked, several times, 'When did you last see your mother?' She doesn't know how to answer. She came to the city to escape such questions. At the end of term, despite her misgivings, she takes the train home for Christmas, heading north through the darkness and the worsening weather, to find her mother tinkering with her new electronic organ. Winterson's description of Jeanette's journey home captures the randomness of strangers in a railway carriage:

> There are three of us now; the bundle chanting her complaint round a fat cheese sandwich, one fat hand clasping a thermos like a long lost friend; the muttering man singing a ditty about love and the lack of it; and me, with a copy of *Middlemarch* under my pullover. It is not the one thing nor the other that leads to madness, but the space in between them.

I remember those journeys home from university, caught between worlds. I ended up in the same ancient city as Winterson, where I felt odd and out of place, and went back home in the holidays to my own small town, where I also felt odd and out of place, but for different reasons. I resumed my long moody walks, my head full of books, still wanting to be somewhere else but being even less certain about where that was. In the Christmas holidays after my first term, I got a job in a department store in Warrington, and spent three weeks hanging earrings on racks and being bored. I escaped during breaks to the bookshop that I'd haunted during my years in the sixth form, down a back street by the side of the Co-op, and spent my wages on the books I needed for my next term, Forster and Woolf and Plath. One of my colleagues spotted them when I got back to work. 'What d'you want to read that rubbish for?' she demanded. Not the one thing nor the other, but the spaces in between.

Describing the freedom that reading gave to her as a teenager, Winterson says that literature 'isn't a hiding place. It is a finding place'. Books were my finding place too, and Dermot's, just as they have been for countless people going through difficult times. They held our hands and gave us the courage we needed to move away from those attitudes and those small towns. But the journeys have been hard ones, and it is vital that they are not forgotten.

# On loyalty, empathy and social mobility: *Great Expectations* by Charles Dickens

This is how it begins. Picture a graveyard on the edge of a bleak and lonely marsh, headstones all snaggle-toothed and overgrown with nettles. A small boy is examining one of the graves. Its inscription is weathered, but he can still make out the names: his father, his mother and his five brothers, none of whom he ever got to know. He blinks. His nose runs in the raw cold. He's aware of just how alone he is, the weak winter sun just starting to drop below the horizon, the wind whipping tears from his eyes. And then, there's a voice.

*'HOLD YOUR NOISE!'*

My students jump. They like this. They like the fact I'm reading aloud to them, that I've built it up in advance, telling them that today we're going to have a story. I get them to wriggle in their seats so they're comfortable and do an exaggerated shush, my finger to my lips, before I begin. They're Year Eight, twelve and thirteen years old. There's a knowingness about the way they play along with the preparations for story-time, all of us complicit in the pantomime of making sure we're sitting quietly and paying attention, but they're still young enough to enjoy the innocent pleasure of listening to a story on a Friday afternoon. Amongst all the frustrations of being a teacher, the admin and the targets and the brain-sapping elemental exhaustion, there are still lots of things to love, and this is one of them.

You have to do the different voices. High, quavery and nervous for Pip, rasping and harsh for Magwitch. You exaggerate them so that your students can picture the contrast between the small boy, already a bundle of shivers, and the desperate convict. You bounce through Dickens's description of Magwitch – 'A man who had been soaked in water, and smothered in mud, and lamed by stones, and cut by flints, and stung by nettles, and torn by briars; who limped, and shivered, and glared, and growled; and whose teeth chattered in his head as he seized me by the chin' – and pause for an obvious breath to draw attention to just how long his sentences are, crammed with so much detail that we're almost as over-whelmed as Pip. You linger with relish over Magwitch's demands for a file and wittles – with a brief aside to explain what wittles are – and his descriptions of what he will do to poor Pip if he does not comply. *You fail, or you go from my words in any partickler, no matter how small it is, and your heart and your liver shall be tore out, roasted, and ate!* The students are intrigued by now, wanting to know what happens. But you make them wait till next time, knowing that there is value in a cliffhanger, in leaving your listeners on a note of suspense.

We'd started the lesson by discussing what the phrase

'great expectations' might mean. High hopes, one student volunteered, and others agreed. The ambitions that you have for yourself and that other people might have for you. Another student reminded us that I'd started the year by telling the students what I expected of them and what they could expect from me in return. They needed to underline their headings, respect other people's opinions, not be afraid to make mistakes. We talked about whether great expectations – your own expectations of yourself, or other people's expectations of you – can ever be a burden. We imagined these expectations as both a gift, a sign that someone wants good things for you and is confident that you can achieve them, and as a weight, potentially suffocating. It would be really difficult, one boy commented, if the ambitions you had for yourself weren't the same as the ones that other people had for you, and there were nods around the room, students imagining the pull of loyalties and the sense of guilt.

It's all still in the future, for these students. They're bright-eyed and curious. They want to be computer-game designers and film directors, lawyers and YouTubers, vets and engineers. One wants to be a novelist, and I hope with all my heart that he succeeds. It's the start of a journey. They don't know, yet, what the road ahead will be like, how many twists and turns they'll have to navigate.

*Great Expectations* will take them on a journey too. It's a rollicking good read, full of energy and pace. It contains a fabulous cast of larger-than-life grotesques, many of them distinguished by one or two well-chosen quirks: ferocious Mrs Joe, who never tires of reminding Pip that she has brought him up 'by hand'; fish-faced Uncle Pumblechook with his dull staring eyes; and vengeful Miss Havisham, her heart frozen by the lover who abandoned her, withering away in her dusty wedding dress. There are brilliant set-piece descriptions and audacious plot twists. In the midst of all of this, there's Pip, about seven or eight years old when the novel starts and a man in his thirties, quite a bit sadder and considerably wiser, by its end. The lessons Pip learns, the situations he encounters and the choices he has to make are all part of this journey. As an example of the *Bildungsroman* – the novel of experience, of moral and psychological growth – *Great Expectations* is second to none.

Dickens featured heavily on the reading list that I was sent before I went to university. It dropped through the letterbox in a thick envelope stamped with the college crest, in the early spring of the upper sixth, a couple of months after I'd been offered a place to read English at Oxford. My parents were proud of me – of course they were – but my dad still had his misgivings as to whether an English degree would lead to an actual career. There were occasional hints that I'd be better off looking for a job, something unspecified but safe in a legal office or for the local council, and the idea horrified me. How could I give up now? The reading list gave me a way of proving that what I was doing did involve work: not the kind of work that my dad recognized, but work all the same. If I could devote myself to it in a way that was serious and methodical, with lever-arch files and dividers and tasks to tick off when completed, then – at least in my head – it would show him how dedicated I was. And there was a lot of work to do, because it was a long list. We'd be doing English Literature from 1830 to 1900 in our first term, and as well as novels and poems, we had to read history and non-fiction: *Culture and Anarchy*, *The Communist Manifesto*, Thomas Carlyle and John Stuart Mill. We had to write an essay, too, focusing on either women or the working classes in Victorian literature. Most Saturdays, I caught the train into Manchester so that I could sit in the Central Library and read, and afterwards I'd linger around the bookshops, Dillons and Waterstones and the big Sherratt & Hughes on St Ann's Square. Every book I finished, every page of notes I made, felt like a step closer to whatever the future held.

For Pip, at the beginning of *Great Expectations*, the future seems to be clear. He lives with his sister, the fearsome Mrs Joe Gargery, and her husband, mild-mannered Joe, the village blacksmith. Pip will become Joe's apprentice, working in the forge, shoeing horses and making tools. He doesn't aspire to anything else. Why would he? His is an ordinary life, surrounded by ordinary people, without a hint of anything beyond. He lives in a world where people know their place and expect to remain in it. He is lucky, he knows, to be there at all, given the fate of those five dead brothers.

But then, one day, Uncle Pumblechook arrives with news. The mysterious Miss Havisham, a wealthy recluse, has sent for Pip. Mrs Joe, thinking that Pip is about to make his fortune, is ecstatic. She pounces on him, scrubs him to within an inch of his life, trusses him up in his best suit and sends him off with Uncle Pumblechook, bound for Satis House, where Miss Havisham has lived amidst the relics of her wedding – still wearing her bridal dress and veil, now grimy and tattered – ever since she was jilted by her husband-to-be. And there, Pip falls in love.

The object of Pip's affections is Estella, Miss Havisham's adopted daughter. Estella looks down on Pip with a haughtiness that is apparent right from the start. She addresses him as 'boy', and treats him with disdain. Everything about Pip is wrong: his rough hands and coarse labourer's boots, his shyness and uncertainty. When he and Estella play cards, he calls the knaves Jacks, and receives yet another sneer. For the first time ever, he feels that he is not good enough. A gap opens up between what his life has been and what he wants it to become: the life of a gentleman, a life where he can become worthy of Estella.

With students this young, a novel like *Great Expectations* is too long to be studied in its entirety. You have to be selective, focusing on specific incidents and characters and cutting back on others. Purists would no doubt be horrified, but texts need to be made manageable. And so, with Year Eight, we concentrate on key incidents in Pip's journey. His first visit to Satis House, with all its attendant feelings of strangeness and exclusion, is one of these. It's important because it's a significant moment in the plot, but it's also an opportunity for an exercise in empathy. I get my students to imagine what it would be like to be Pip, there in that dusty house, his throat swollen with tears. What would it feel like, to be invited somewhere so strange and discomfiting, and to be treated with such contempt? We discuss how to develop these ideas into full sentences, using metaphors and similes, focusing on the link between emotions and physical sensations. What would Pip feel in his eyes, in his fists, in the pit of his stomach? Would his legs feel shaky, the ground unsteady? Then we do an exercise called thought-tracking, where we imagine what would be going through Pip's mind as he makes his way home, stung by Estella's cruelty. Students write two or three sentences, in the first person, to capture Pip's thoughts. When they've finished, they stand up and wait – some a bit nervous, others eager and excited – until everyone's on their feet.

'Are we ready?' I ask. 'Okay. One at a time, and listening carefully to everyone else's ideas. Go!'

And starting in the back corner, taking it in turns and working their way up to the front of the room, the boys read their work, putting Pip's feelings into words. *The earth has changed beneath my feet*, one boy says. Other voices follow. *I trudge down the path, fists clenched, eyebrows lowered.*

*Thoughts are buzzing round my head like a swarm of wasps.* And, brilliantly, from one of the quietest boys in the room: *Something in my head has turned against me. It hides in the shadows and when I don't expect it, it jumps out and walks right beside me. I know it's here. It's watching, taking time to tell me my life is worthless. My stomach is closing in on itself.* There are times, in lessons like this, when a student comes out with an idea that is so perceptive, so well phrased, that I'm genuinely in awe: those shiver-down-the-spine moments that make everything worthwhile. It's hard to believe that most of these students are only twelve years old.

In today's educational environment, it can often feel difficult to make time for this kind of activity. The past few years have seen an emphasis on knowledge that can be learned and memorized, revisited at intervals to ensure retention. Sometimes, there's a shadowy Ofsted inspector peering over my shoulder, demanding to know why I'm not drilling Year Eight with facts about Dickens's life and giving them multiple-choice quizzes to check that they can retrieve key pieces of information. But this kind of knowledge doesn't necessarily ensure depth of understanding. Nor does it help to foster what Peter Bazalgette, in his 2017 book, *The Empathy Instinct*, refers to as 'cognitive empathy', the connection with others that draws on a range of intrapersonal and interpersonal skills. Bazalgette highlights the capacity of fiction to encourage reflection on the lives and situations of others, enlarging their experiences and challenging their perspectives. He quotes George Eliot's desire for those who read her works to be 'better able to imagine and to feel the pains and joys of those who differ from themselves in everything but the broad fact of being struggling, erring, human creatures'. And while a lot of what we do in class is dictated by the needs of assessment, laying the foundations for what students will need to do in their crucial exams at the age of sixteen, a good part of it is also dedicated to building this ability to imagine and to understand, through reading closely and carefully, thinking about how characters are created and how they are shaped by the worlds in which they live. Teaching English is a complicated business. It draws not just on students' intellectual capacity but also on their emotional maturity, their willingness to make leaps of imagination and consider why characters think and behave in the ways they do. For Bazalgette, the development of empathy is crucial to the building of a civil society. It's one of the reasons why English is so important, and why I will cling on to getting students to imagine what it would be like to be Pip, or Joe, or any of the characters we encounter, for as long as I continue to teach.

In the story, years pass. Then, one evening, there is an unexpected arrival. A stranger appears in the Three Jolly Bargemen, the local inn, where Pip is drinking with Joe and his companions. The stranger is authoritative and forbidding, with deep-set eyes and dark whiskers, smelling strongly of soap. His name is Mr Jaggers. He is a lawyer, and he has news to impart. Pip has a mysterious benefactor. He is to leave the forge and go to London, to be brought up as a gentleman. In time, he will come into a handsome property. He is now a young man of great expectations, his life utterly transformed. The only condition he must obey is that he must never enquire as to whom his benefactor might be.

All is excitement. Pip is to have twenty guineas to spend on new clothes. He is to have a tutor, one Matthew Pocket. He is lost in a dream of the future. He is certain that all of this has come about because of Miss Havisham. What other explanation could there be? Miss Havisham clearly has a plan, with Pip and Estella at the centre of it. Once he has become a gentleman, Pip will be a suitable husband for Estella. He will achieve his heart's desire.

There is, nevertheless, a touch of uneasiness. For Joe – good, patient Joe, Pip's brother-in-law, mentor, father figure and best friend – is quiet. He is going to lose his apprentice, but he wants no compensation, and will not stand in Pip's way. He is happy for Pip. And yet he struggles. He scoops at his eyes with his hands, dashing away tears. At home, he sits by the fire and gazes into the glowing coals, watching the shapes of the flames, unable to put his feelings into words. He does not know how to treat this new and different Pip, and Pip does not know how to treat him, either. Pip is focused on his future and wants to leave his old life behind. The stars in the sky, Pip observes, are 'but poor and humble stars' for glittering down on his unassuming home. He does not want to go to the Three Jolly Bargemen in his new clothes, to say goodbye, because his former companions will make a fuss, and he will feel embarrassed. He is detaching himself, but does not know how to do so humbly, graciously, without hurting people's feelings.

The last few weeks before I eventually left for university – my own heart's desire – were a similar process of detaching myself, of distancing. I was awkward, all scruffy jeans and short spiky hair, and no doubt I was just as graceless as Pip, with just as many corners to bump against. Home felt too small. I'd been in one place for too long and needed to be somewhere else. In Philip Larkin's poem 'Wires', young steers butt up against electric fences, scenting purer water not here, but anywhere. There comes a time when you have to leave in order to find out who you are.

A couple of days before the start of term, I went to the supermarket with my mum. Making our way down the aisles, picking out bits and pieces that I'd need, we bumped into an elderly lady who'd taught my brother and sisters at primary school. She looked me up and down, stern and still teacherly two decades into retirement. 'Make sure you don't forget your roots,' she instructed. 'You'll go a long way. But don't forget your roots.' It was a warning, an injunction. I felt as if she'd found me out.

In London, Pip has a lot to learn. The amiable Herbert Pocket, his tutor's son, takes him under his wing and makes sure he knows how to behave. Don't put your knife in your mouth, Herbert informs him. When you're drinking, don't turn your glass upside down to drain out the last few drops. Don't stuff your napkin into your tumbler at the end of a meal. Pip acquires the outside appearance of a gentleman. Yet Matthew Pocket opines that this is just a veneer. For Matthew, 'no varnish can hide the grain of the wood . . . the more varnish you put on, the more the grain will express itself'. There are reminders of Pip's former status, too, from others. In the 2011 BBC adaptation of *Great Expectations*, which I watch with my students in class, the odious Bentley Drummle goads Pip about his lowly origins. He is insignificant, a pipsqueak, as mere and trifling as his name. *Pippety-pippety-pip*, Drummle sneers, and you can imagine Pip seething. He teeters astride an abyss and is desperate not to fall. He remembers the small boy he once was, in his coarse boots, finding out for the first time that he is not good enough.

I had coarse boots when I arrived at Oxford, although most students did back in the autumn of 1991. Doc Martens: the great leveller, some green or purple or cherry-red, although mine were just plain black. My boots didn't set me apart, but I'm sure other things did. Other people knew what to do. When I went to the porter's lodge to collect the key to my room, I had to queue behind a girl with a lacrosse stick. I'd never seen a lacrosse stick outside the pages of Enid Blyton. There was a drinks party on our first evening where people talked about gap years and opera and where they'd been over the summer. I hadn't been anywhere over the summer. I couldn't discuss port or Wagner, or share experiences of voluntary work in India. I didn't know *anything*, I realized. I didn't even want to speak in case my northernness and my lack of sophistication were too obvious. I forced myself to breathe slowly, to calm myself down.

I thought everyone would be as keen on their work as I was. I was in for a shock. I was assigned a tutorial partner who tried to rearrange our weekly tutorials around his golf sessions, and got short shrift from our tutor one week when he turned up completely unprepared. He came to find me later, to apologize, but he didn't seem particularly shamefaced. What radiated from him was a much greater sense of belonging than I had, a sense that Oxford was where he was supposed to be. He wasn't the only one. Other people, too, were casual and cavalier. They treated Oxford not as an immense privilege but as a stepping stone, a place to make use of on the way to wherever it was they were headed. So what if they didn't hand in an essay that week? Reading – the whole reason why I was there – didn't really seem to interest them. Who wanted to bury themselves in a library anyway, when there was so much else to do? They were playing a game, expertly. I didn't know the rules.

I did know something. I knew a lot about books. I got encouraging comments on my essays, and it became clear that I was actually quite good. I found friends who were from similar backgrounds to me, and we bonded over how weird it was to find ourselves here, inhabiting quads we'd previously only seen on *Inspector Morse*, wearing gowns for formal hall and hopscotching at midnight down lanes that hadn't changed for centuries. You find ways of belonging, when you need to.

But I was still battling, deep down, with what Lynsey Hanley, in her book *Estates: An Intimate History*, describes as 'the wall in the head', a phrase borrowed from the German expression – *die Mauer im Kopf* – that was used to capture the state of mind of residents of the former GDR who struggled to cope with reunification. For Hanley, who grew up on a council estate in Solihull, this internal wall is a part of working-class existence. It acts as a roadblock, a barrier between one world and another. It stops you thinking that anything on the other side is for you, or for people like you. The people on the other side might not want you there. Even if you manage to make it across, you won't feel at home. (I remember one of the teachers at my school saying that even if I did get into Oxford, I'd probably only fail in the long run.) The people there won't be interested in anything you think. A lot has been done, since I was at university, to widen participation and smooth the path for applicants from 'non-traditional backgrounds', but the obstacles in our way are not just the systemic ones. They're also psychological. That feeling of uncertainty, that you constantly have to watch your behaviour, to keep your table manners and your vowel sounds in check. That sense that there must have been a mistake, that you shouldn't really be there.

My way of dealing with all of this was by working, as hard as I could. If I could prove my worth by being as good as possible, then nobody could say I hadn't earned my place. Imposter syndrome is a difficult burden to carry. By the end of my second year I'd burned myself out and had to take a year off. If being at home had been hard before, it was even tougher now, after two years at university. I still had that wall in my head, grey and forbidding, except now I was back on the other side. I convinced myself that nobody – neither my schoolfriends, nor my family – would really understand what it was like, holding these two different places in my head and trying to cope with everything they demanded of me, Newton-le-Willows on one side of the wall and Oxford on the other. I'm not even sure, at twenty, that I'd have been able to put all of these complicated feelings into words. It seemed easier not to try.

Pip is just as inarticulate as I was, just as self-absorbed and clumsy in his handling of other people's feelings. When Joe visits him in London – completely out of place with his country accent and country manners – Pip does not know how to put him at his ease. Joe is made even more awkward by Pip's discomfort, and tells him that 'you and me is not two figures to be together in London'. They inhabit different worlds. Joe is all wrong in the city, amidst its grand buildings and elegant carriages, its fashionable people. Pip won't find so many faults in him, Joe tells him, if he visits him at the forge, where he belongs. Pip feels guilty. But when he does go back to the village, to visit Miss Havisham, he avoids Joe, and makes excuses as to why he should not go to see him.

The lessons Pip must learn – about accepting all the various elements of himself, and about treating those who love him with a true generosity of spirit – are hard ones. He must sit with the discomfort of guilt and must listen when he is told, gently, of his neglect of Joe. There are many occasions in the novel when he has to reflect on his behaviour and its impact on others. I look at my students and wonder how many bumps in the road there will be for them; how many dark nights of soul-searching, gritty-eyed from lack of sleep. It's all a long way in the future.

The thing that keeps Pip going is the thought of Estella. He has convinced himself that his secret bene-factor is Miss Havisham, that her plan all along has been to turn him into a gentleman so that he can be a worthy husband for her adopted daughter. He casts himself as a young knight from an ancient romance, charged with restoring sunshine to Satis House and setting the clocks going again for the first time since they were stopped at twenty to nine, the moment Miss Havisham learned of her abandonment. He must sweep away the filth and the beetles, the cobwebs, the mouldering wedding cake. Once he has performed all these deeds, he will marry the princess. But when Pip sees Estella again after years of separation, he is cast back into his role as the common labouring boy, his princess disdainful and unreachable.

He learns, too, that Miss Havisham has a different project in mind: that she has brought Estella up to be a breaker of hearts, to be icy and cruel, as a form of revenge for her own fiancé's faithlessness. There are many times when Pip feels that his life might have been better if he had never been to Satis House, if he had remained in the forge, by the fire, with Joe.

Another unexpected visitor. This time, it's Magwitch, the escaped convict who accosted Pip in the graveyard at the beginning of the novel, that incident that left my students desperate to know what happened next. Magwitch was recaptured and transported to Australia. He has been working on a sheep farm in New South Wales and is now a rich man. He has returned to London because he wants to see Pip, and to reveal that he is Pip's mysterious benefactor. He wanted to reward Pip for his bravery in trying to help him, in fetching him a file and stealing food for him from Mrs Joe's pantry. Now, years later, he is keen to see what Pip has made of his gift. He has come to the old country, he says, 'to see my gentleman spend his money like a gentleman. That'll be my pleasure.'

It might well be Magwitch's pleasure, but it certainly isn't Pip's. Pip is horrified. He has suffered a double blow: first, in learning that he is not destined to marry Estella after all, and second, in discovering that his benefactor is a criminal, a transported convict who has returned from Australia illegally and is now in hiding from the authorities. Pip is full of loathing: not just for

Magwitch, but for himself. That old sense of precariousness, of feeling that his status as a gentleman is built on shaky foundations, is multiplied a hundredfold.

For Year Eight, it's a nice moral puzzle. If you'd been given something, and had cherished it for many years, would your feelings about it change if you knew it had been bought with the proceeds of crime? We talk about what you might do, how you could turn the situation into something positive and use it to benefit others. Pip, meanwhile, has reached a crisis. He has been spending his money lavishly, on food and drink and the pursuit of pleasure, and is in debt. The last straw comes when Estella marries the loutish Bentley Drummle, leaving Pip bereft. The life of a gentleman – once full of promise – now seems very hollow.

Gradually, Pip comes to recognize how much his behaviour has hurt those who love him. He is unable, even, to show too much bitterness towards Miss Havisham, who realizes, anguished, how much pain she has caused him. His feelings towards Magwitch soften and he dedicates himself to formulating a plan that will, if successful, secure the convict's safety. There are moments of peril, a tense journey along the Thames, a struggle. The plan fails. Magwitch is recaptured and sentenced to death. Pip, grief-stricken, vows to support him for as long as he can. He no longer sees Magwitch as a criminal, but simply as 'a man who had meant to be my benefactor, and who had felt affectionately, gratefully, and generously, towards me with great constancy through a series of years'. Most significantly, he sees in him 'a much better man than I had been to Joe'.

After Magwitch's death, Pip falls dangerously ill. It is Joe – endlessly faithful and patient – who nurses him back to health and pays his debts, forgiving him for everything that has happened. Pip goes to work in Cairo, and does not return for eleven years. When he does come back, it is to find Satis House demolished, and Estella – now a widow – walking in its moonlit grounds. She asks for Pip's forgiveness and, at the end of the novel, Pip can see 'no shadow of another parting from her'.

This ending is famously ambiguous. Dickens's original version of the final chapter saw Pip and Estella meeting briefly in London, with Pip learning that Estella had married again. In a letter to his close friend and critic John Forster, Dickens commented that he wanted to make the novel's conclusion an unconventional one. Later, he decided that this initial ending had been too sad. His rewritten version needs careful reading. Skim over it and you could be forgiven for thinking that life has a happy ending in store for Pip and Estella, after all their years of pain. But just a few lines beforehand, Estella insists that even though they are friends, they must continue friends apart. What to think? Again, in Year Eight, there is intrigue. Do they never part again because they get married, or do they never part again because they never see each other again? One boy volunteers that while we might want Pip and Estella to marry, life doesn't necessarily work that way. 'It's the difference between real life and stories, isn't it? You can kind of bring everything to a close in a story, like they all live happily ever after. But real life's not always like that.'

Pip's story is often seen as carrying important messages about moral growth and the enlargement of sympathy: the recognition of people's innate worth and the knowledge that social status is not everything. What he also learns to do, ultimately, is to live with himself. And this – the hard lesson of self-acceptance – can take many decades to learn.

My year away from Oxford was the making of me in some ways, but it was also one of the toughest years of my life. I got a voluntary work placement on a community project in Liverpool, and then a paid job as a classroom assistant in a local primary school. And then my dad died, very suddenly, just before Christmas, and I had another set of feelings to cope with. There's an operation, called firing, that is sometimes performed on horses whose tendons have been damaged. A red-hot iron is used to burn lines around the injured leg, and as the burn heals, the tendon is supposedly strengthened. I went back to Oxford similarly cauterized, tougher and less apologetic. I worked hard, again, but was cleverer about it this time. I sat Finals at the end of the year and got a First, and then instead of staying on to do postgraduate work – the ambition that I'd nurtured from the age of sixteen – I headed back up north to train to be a teacher. Postgraduate work could wait. I needed to do something real.

What helped most, in the end, was going somewhere else entirely: neither Oxford nor Newton-le-Willows but Lincolnshire, a different place, where I was able to put the two worlds that had defined me for so long into perspective. The flat neutrality of the Fens gave me a new start, a place not overwritten by expectation. And over the years, I managed to untangle the things in my head that had become so snarled and knotted. I learned to breathe easily, to be at some kind of peace.

I wonder, then, about Pip's years in Cairo, those eleven years that Dickens skims over in the novel's two final chapters. I wonder about the thoughts that would have chased around his head, the memories that would have haunted him in those lonely hours in the middle of the night. I wonder about the point when those thoughts and those memories would have started to ease, to loosen their grip, and when he would have begun to see the past recede and the future open up.

Sometimes, I think that my dad and I were like the poet Tony Harrison and his dad in the poem 'Book Ends': what was between us was not the thirty or so years, but books, books, books, and my desire to study them. Perhaps the best literary equivalent of our relationship, though, is Seamus Heaney's poem 'Digging'. Heaney reflects, with his pen snug in his hand, on how skilfully his father and grandfather had cultivated the land, stooping and straightening, digging tirelessly. Heaney, however, has taken a different path. His talent lies not in digging, but in writing: a different activity, but just as skilful and laudable. When I first read the poem something shifted in my head and I saw the similarities between my dad and me, laid out more clearly than ever before. My dad was a digger too, a keen gardener, and a great believer in an honest job done well. The clean rasping sound of spade in soil, the smell of earth. I was just as stubborn and hardworking as him, just as dedicated and single-minded, but with a different focus. I had a head full of books, and I was doing my own digging.

I can just about visit my former college, when I go back to Oxford, without feeling that I shouldn't be there. The voices in my head – telling me that I didn't fit in, that someone must have made a mistake – haven't entirely gone away. They're definitely quieter, but I know how nagging and insistent they can be, how they hide – as my lovely Year Eight student said – in the shadows and jump out occasionally just to remind you they're still there. I think about my class, sitting there with their eyes bright and everything still waiting to happen, and hope that whatever they do and wherever they end up, they feel that they belong.

# On learning: *A Kestrel for a Knave* by Barry Hines

My son is playing guitar. He plays with the kind of pure, intense concentration in which all space and time fall away: he's in the zone, in the state that psychologists refer to as 'flow', completely absorbed in what he's doing. He adjusts his tuning, moves his capo up a fret, working with an ease that comes partly from instinct and partly from many hours of practice. He's been playing for most of his life. He had his first proper lesson when he was six, but even before then he was drawn to anything with strings. One of my favourite photographs shows him at two years old, clutching a ukulele, his hands splayed across it like little fat starfishes. His face is split by a smile that's the closest to pure joy I've ever seen. 'Look at him!' my best friend exclaimed when she saw the photo. 'It's as if he's seen the future.'

Music is the element in which he moves. Listening to him improvising or riffing on a melody has made me aware of a kind of knowledge that I definitely do not possess. He can pick up an instrument he's never played before – a mandolin or a Cretan lyra – and produce something beautiful, without seeming to think about it. He can spot, within a couple of seconds, what kind of tuning a guitar is being played in: when he was seven, he astonished a busker in York by identifying – correctly – the chords he was using. To me, his completely unmusical mum, his playing is astonishing. I have no idea how talented he actually is, but really, that doesn't matter. What's important is the enjoyment he gets from playing, the headspace and the escape into something beautiful.

Playing guitar has also given him the chance to achieve. This has been important, because school and my son were never really the best of friends. It wasn't a case of open conflict – they generally tolerated each other – but it was clear that this relationship was purely one of necessity. He served his time, got his GCSEs and headed off into the world of work. There was never any question of him staying any longer than he needed to.

I was completely the opposite. Learning – the kind of orthodox, teacher-driven learning that involved a desk and a pen and a pile of books – came easily to me. I was the kind of child who grasped things quickly and ticked all the boxes without really having to try. This was fortunate, because there weren't many opportunities at my school to do much beyond the actual curriculum. I was at secondary school at a time when teachers were striking for better pay and conditions. Activities at lunchtime and after school were non-existent for a while, and there were several years when the outlets provided by this wider curriculum – music, drama, art and photography clubs, student journalism and debating, and a host of different sports – simply weren't available. In some ways, to me, this didn't matter.

I had other ways of achieving, of getting that buzz of success. I was lucky.

My son has been lucky too. He has all the guitars and amps and effects pedals he needs; he's had guitar lessons most weeks ever since he started playing and has people around him who take an interest in what he does. Yes, he's talented, but it's hard to sustain a talent without support. Especially if you're a teenager, and especially if everyone in your life treats you as if you're a waste of space.

This is the situation in which Billy Casper, in Barry Hines's 1968 novel, *A Kestrel for a Knave*, finds himself. Billy is sixteen, growing up in a South Yorkshire pit village on the outskirts of Barnsley, about to leave school. Billy struggles to read and write. He doesn't want to go down the pit, like his older brother, Jud, but he doesn't know what else he can do. His one passion is falconry. He has captured a young kestrel, Kes, and trained her to fly to the lure, teaching himself painstakingly from a book he has stolen from a local shop. Kes blazes like a miracle in Billy's narrow life. His relationship with her is the best thing that has ever happened to him. And then, one day, she disappears.

*A Kestrel for a Knave* is the kind of novel that exists in many people's consciousnesses even if they haven't actually read it. They'll have an image in their minds of greyness and poverty, spoil heaps and narrow horizons. They'll also be able to recall the novel's iconic front cover, taken from Ken Loach's 1969 film, *Kes*: a grainy black-and-white picture of a boy sticking up two fingers, a defiant V-sign to the world. As with Atticus Finch, and as with *Jane Eyre*, there's a whole range of merchandise available: you can buy this image on T-shirts, mugs, key rings, printed on to canvas and framed for your wall. You can even have it emblazoned across a spare wheel cover for your 4x4.

It was this image – later copied by the singer Jarvis Cocker, who cites Hines's novel as a major influence, in a photograph for *NME* in 1995 – that dominated my first encounter with *A Kestrel for a Knave*. I was about seven years old, making one of my frequent raids on my sister's bookshelf for something to read. I knew immediately that it was a Bad Book, because sticking up two fingers was one of the rudest things you could ever do. I'd tried it, once and only once, and been told in no uncertain terms that I should never, ever do it again. The boy had scruffy hair and a thin, pinched face. I put the Bad Book back where it belonged, rubbing shoulders with Jilly Cooper and somebody called D. H. Lawrence, and found something else to read instead.

We didn't do *A Kestrel for a Knave* at school. This surprises me, looking back, because my English lessons in the early years of secondary school were dominated by an outdated kind of social realism, by endless novels about dysfunctional families who all lived jumbled together in tiny terraced houses: *The Family from One End Street, Gumble's Yard, There is a Happy Land, Magnolia Buildings*. There were tales of gritty pragmatism and industrial

towns, feckless adults and tribes of kids banding together
to defeat authority. These books were somehow supposed to reflect our own lives, in what could have been a
precursor of today's attempts to make sure students see
people like themselves reflected in the books they study
in school. Except it didn't work, because the reality
depicted in these novels was nothing like our own. I
resented them because they seemed to send a message
about who we were, or at least who our teachers thought
we were, a misplaced attempt to represent what somebody else imagined our lives and preoccupations to be.
Books about different worlds, different ways of being,
weren't for us: we were only supposed to be interested in
stories about poverty and underachievement, about exist-
ences characterized by the need to pull together and
make do in a slightly exhausted kind of way. I'm probably being very unfair to these novels and the people who
chose them for us, but this was how it felt, to twelve-
year-old me. (Later, of course, when I discovered Larkin
and Winterson, I'd read about a world that I actually *did*
recognize, and it was a revelation.) I could always have
got *A Kestrel for a Knave* out of the library, if I'd wanted to,
but it had become tainted by association, lumped together
in my mind with the tired clichés of all those other books.
It was something I'd read one day, but not now.

My next encounter with *A Kestrel for a Knave* took place
when I was training to be a teacher. By then, the received
wisdom was that the novel was most suitable for the less
academic groups, the students who weren't considered

to be up to the challenge of *Animal Farm* or *Lord of the Flies*. The very mention of the novel gave me the same kind of sinking feeling that I'd had at school when confronted with yet another story about northern poverty. So when I had to observe a Year Ten lesson on *A Kestrel for a Knave* on the first week of my second teacher training placement, it was never going to end well. The teacher was reading the novel out loud. She'd got up to the bit where Billy is taunting his drunken brother, Jud, marching round his bed chanting 'Bas-tard Bas-tard Drun-ken PIG', and if teenagers don't enjoy anything else in an English lesson, they should at least enjoy listening to their teacher engaging in a bit of gratuitous swearing. (*Miss! Miss! Miss said 'bastard'! Miss SWORE!*) But they didn't react at all. The teacher was reading in an endless monotone, and the students were stupefied with boredom, some chewing gum, one boy picking his nose. The teacher carried on, each 'bas-tard' having even less effect than the previous one. I vowed then and there that whatever else I had to teach, I would never teach *A Kestrel for a Knave*.

It took me a long time, then, to finally get round to reading Barry Hines's most famous novel. And I'm glad beyond all measure that I did; and if I had the chance to teach it to my own GCSE students – sadly, it's no longer on the curriculum – then I would. Because it's a cracking story that's about so much more than poverty and hopelessness. It's also a novel about beauty, and nature. It's vivid and angry and raw. It reminds us that people have inner lives beyond the restrictions of their immediate circumstances, and that these inner lives need nurturing. And it prompts us to think about the narrowness of formal education, and the importance of the learning that young people do outside of school – learning that teachers might never get to know about.

Barry Hines was in his late twenties and a PE teacher at Longcar Central School in Barnsley when he wrote *A Kestrel for a Knave*. (One of his colleagues was Brian Glover, who would go on to play the bullying PE teacher, Mr Sugden, in *Kes*.) Hines was writing about people and places he knew intimately. He set the novel in a small mining town based on Hoyland Common, just south of Barnsley, where he grew up. The character of Billy was inspired by his brother, Richard, a keen falconer. As a teacher in a secondary modern school, he wanted to give a voice to the working-class kids, the non-academic kids, the young people who had been written off as failures at the age of eleven. In an interview published in the *Guardian* in July 1970, Hines stated that 'I thought I would like to show that these kids can do something which is in fact very skilful – not the old talk about them being cobblers and joiners, but something that means they have to get books out of the library. And it's a technical skill; they've actually got to read about it before they can do something like training a hawk.'

Falconry is not only technical: it also carries the magical breath of the ancient, the jewel-brightness of an illuminated manuscript. The novel's epigraph, from the fifteenth-century *Boke of St Albans*, lifts Billy out of his mining community and places him in the company of rulers and nobles:

> An Eagle for an Emperor, a Gyrfalcon for a King; a Peregrine for a Prince, a Saker for a Knight, a Merlin for a Lady; a Goshawk for a Yeoman, a Sparrowhawk for a Priest, a Musket for a Holy water Clerk, a Kestrel for a Knave.

When Billy tells his fellow pupils about creances and jesses, lures and bating, he is using terms that have remained unchanged for centuries. Falconry is his access to a different world, a world that contains only him and his kestrel, focusing on each other, concentrating.

Billy certainly needs a different world. Hines tells us the story of a day in his life, with flashbacks revealing how he caught and trained Kes. It's a narrow life, full of everyday cruelties and meannesses that Billy is so used to that he hardly seems to notice them any longer. He wakes up in grimy bedsheets, in the bed he shares with Jud, his older brother, who works down the local pit. He goes off to do his paper round before school, argues with his mum and with Jud, gets the cane for falling asleep in assembly, is picked on by Mr Sugden for having no PE kit, and has a meeting with a condescending careers advisor. There's nothing in the cupboards at home for breakfast, so Billy steals two bars of chocolate from the newsagent's and a bottle of orange juice from

a milk float. (He does this casually – Hines uses the word
'lifted', which carries no moral overtones – and we sense
that this is simply the way things are, for Billy.) Tellingly,
when Billy has to write a 'tall story' in his English class
as part of an exercise on the difference between fact and
fiction, it's a story about being loved and cared for, about
living in a house with central heating and carpet on the
stairs, where his mum brings him breakfast in bed and
the teachers at school are kind to him.

There are very few people on Billy's side. In his After-
word to the 1999 Penguin Modern Classics edition of the
novel, Barry Hines describes him as a 'lonely misfit who
doesn't belong to the gang', and he certainly doesn't have
any close friends. In an early flashback, we see him getting up at dawn for a planned birds'-nesting trip with his
classmates Tibby and MacDowall, but neither is awake,
and Billy has to go on his own. Later in the novel, it's
MacDowall who taunts Billy about his absent father and
then fights him. Jud is a classic bully, showing his dominance in punches and threats; Billy's mother is feckless.
There's no better illustration of how little Billy's family
understand him than when he is poring over his stolen
book on falconry, having been denied the chance to sit
and read the copy in the local library because he is not a
member. Jud snatches the book and throws it across the
room, scornful; when Billy tries to straighten its bent
pages, Jud comments, 'Anybody'd think it wa' a treasure
tha'd got.' And of course, that's Hines's point: to Billy, it
*is* a treasure, a way of unlocking the door to another

world. Billy's mum, meanwhile, doesn't even know what a kestrel is. Jud can't understand why Billy would want to steal such a thing anyway: 'I could understand if it wa' money, but chuff me, not a book.'

Then there are Billy's teachers. The first one we meet is Mr Crossley, a man on the edge with a monumental lack of humour. This is shown in a lovely little vignette when Mr Crossley is taking the register. He calls out 'Fisher', and Billy replies 'German Bight'. It's the kind of joke that makes you warm to Billy even more than you would have done anyway, marking him out as cleverer than he realizes, and cleverer than anyone else realizes too; certainly cleverer than Mr Crossley, who doesn't understand and has to have it spelled out for him: 'It just came out, Fisher – German Bight. It's the shipping forecast, Sir; German Bight comes after Fisher; Fisher, German Bight, Cromarty. I know 'em all, I listen to it every night, I like to hear the names.' (Who can read this without imagining Billy tuning in, night after night, in his horrid curtainless bedroom, comforted by the familiar rhythm of the words?) Crossley clearly has anger-management issues: look how carefully he tries to amend his register with his red biro, 'lapping and lapping the tiny square until he had gouged a mis-coloured egg, the focal point of the whole grid'.

Next, there's the headmaster, Mr Gryce, a man who is inordinately fond of the sound of his own voice and who delivers the kinds of lectures that no teenager ever paid any attention to in the entire history of education.

Gryce despises his pupils and doesn't hesitate to let them know it, telling them that they think they know everything, that they don't know how lucky they are, they've got it all on a plate. His pupils manifestly haven't got it on a plate at all, of course, at least not if Billy's life is anything to go by. But Gryce doesn't have a clue. His bluster helps to heighten the sense of how unsympathetic Billy's day-to-day life is, how Billy is judged for being a particular age, from a particular social class, from a particular educational background. As far as Gryce is concerned, Billy and those like him are a symbol of what is wrong with the world, with nothing to commend them. Billy couldn't change Gryce's perception of him even if he'd wanted to.

And then there's Mr Sugden, the PE teacher, with his spotless football strip, his socks held up with tape. Sugden is the proxy for every hated PE teacher who has ever existed: all those petty tyrants who let the best students pick teams while the weaklings and fat kids shiver miserably on the sidelines; all those sticklers for the rules who force people to wear discarded kit from Lost Property; all those FA Cup-winner *manqués* who thrive on taunting the kids who can't move quickly enough. Sugden is just as ridiculous as Gryce, but he's dangerous too: the kind of sadist who, in real life, would make the school careers of countless children an utter misery. If Sugden was your PE teacher, your whole week would pivot around that hated lesson. You'd barely sleep the night before; you'd wake, rubbing your eyes, and drag yourself off to school hoping against hope that something would happen to mean the lesson was cancelled, like a fire drill maybe, or a smallish meteorite landing on the school. Sugden's lesson isn't really a lesson at all, because it's all about him. He's there in his spotless kit, his boots 'polished as black and shiny as the bombs used by assassins in comic strips', his laces tied meticulously. He captains one of the teams and gets first pick of the best players. His team is Manchester United; he is Bobby Charlton. He's also the commentator, and the ref. He threatens and domineers and takes it all far too seriously. So determined is he to win that he makes the boys play on after the bell, missing their lunches, until the winning goal is scored. Except that it's his opponents who win, the ball allowed in by Billy. And he certainly gets his revenge, forcing Billy into the shower, barring the exit and spraying him first with hot water, then cold. It's the kind of behaviour for which he would nowadays, quite rightly, be sacked.

Only one of Billy's teachers shows him any sympathy at all. This is Mr Farthing, the English teacher, played by Colin Welland in the 1969 film, bluff and burly in his grey tweed jacket. It is in Mr Farthing's lesson that Billy, prompted by the other boys, talks about finding and training his hawk. It's a lesson where I suspect that Mr Farthing – who initially dismisses Billy as 'someone you can't suit, who has to be awkward, who refuses to be interested in anything' – learns more than anyone else. Billy is monosyllabic at first, but once the words come, there's no stopping them: his language takes on a fluency and a lyricism that many a teacher, giving students the chance to talk about something they are passionate about, will recognize. Reading this part of the novel, I'm reminded of the individual talks that my students have given, over the years, on a dizzying range of hobbies and interests: archery and drumming, marine biology and roller hockey, manga and street dance and planes. Years ago, a student brought in her pet rat, and it sat in its cage, all bright black eyes and curious questing whiskers, while its owner talked knowledgeably about pet care and the rest of us looked on, mesmerized by our silent little visitor. One boy spoke about having a deaf parent, and taught us some British Sign Language; another showed us how to ride a unicycle. Giving a presentation like this used to form part of students' overall GCSE grade, and it's a huge pity that it no longer does, because as well as being a valuable life skill it is also an important way of valuing students' experiences outside school: the hours they spend practising instruments and doing voluntary work, the care they put into building a collection, the sporting triumphs and quiet enthusiasms that we might never get to know about otherwise. Glimpses of the world beyond school; a reminder that the six hours a day they spend with us are only a tiny part of their complex, multifaceted lives.

Talking about Kes, having the chance to put his passion into words, is one of the most important experiences Billy has ever had in school. He describes, in detail, how he went about training her – waiting until she was 'hard penned', putting on her jesses, manning her patiently until she was ready to start jumping on to his glove in return for a scrap of meat – and has everyone spellbound, special for what is probably the first time in his life, the centre of attention with his 'eyes animated, cheeks flushed under a wash of smeared tears and dirt'. It's significant that this is one of the few times in the novel when Billy verbalizes his emotions rather than expressing them through his fists, admitting to 'feelin' champion' after teaching Kes something successfully, and commenting that 'I wa' that pleased I didn't know what to do wi' missen'. Indeed, Billy's longest stretches of conversation are with Mr Farthing, not only in his English lesson, but also after his fight with MacDowall, and then later, when Mr Farthing comes to watch him fly Kes at lunchtime. You imagine his shy blushes as he admits to his pride, the quick glances of a boy not used to making eye contact. It's with Mr Farthing that Billy speaks of the strangeness of Kes, and of her silent otherness, managing to articulate why he is so in awe of her:

> It makes me mad when I take her out and I'll hear somebody say, 'Look there's Billy Casper there wi' his pet hawk.' I could shout at 'em; it's not a pet, Sir, hawks are not pets. Or when folks stop me and say, 'Is it tame?' Is it heck tame, it's trained that's all. It's fierce, an' it's wild, an' it's not bothered about anybody, not even about me right. And that's why it's great.

Reading the novel now, I'm struck by the beauty of Hines's descriptions of the natural world. I suspect I'd have skipped them if I'd been reading this book as a fifteen-year-old, but to middle-aged me they're extraordinary. The landscape of *A Kestrel for a Knave* isn't some kind of pastoral idyll. It's a patchwork of waste ground and edgelands, playing fields and grass verges, coloured in watercolour shades of brown and olive rather than lush verdant green, illuminated by the thin sunlight of early spring. But it is alive. As Hines shows us, in flashback, how Billy found his kestrel, he describes buttercups and sorrel, dog daisies and clover, plantains and brambles. All around, there are birds: the 'long undulating notes' of a chaffinch, the coo of a woodpigeon, the *tic-tic-tic* of a robin, the 'loud churrs' of a pair of wrens. I'm reminded of the stretches of wasteland I used to pass on my way to school, ablaze in summer with goldenrod and rosebay willowherb, and think of how good Hines is at evoking the kind of little world that you know minutely, as a child. Especially a child like Billy, whose boundaries – both physical and psychological – would have been very narrow indeed. Through Billy's eyes, Hines draws our attention to tiny details, such as a dewdrop on a blade of grass that explodes, 'throwing out silver needles and crystal splinters', when it catches the sun. He describes the green of a stem of grass, fading to white; the pebbly ridges of a cart track; the persistence of a thrush tugging a worm out of the ground. He performs that important task of making you look at the ordinary world around you through a different set of eyes.

In their obituary of Barry Hines, Mark Hodkinson and Tony Garnett describe Billy as 'half-boy, half-pigeon, disowned by his family and school, left to shuffle through life in a 10-bob anorak and half-mast trousers'. This makes him seem like an object of pity, but he's so much more than this. For one thing, he's a perpetual doer. Read the novel now and you'll be struck by how much motion there is in it, how Billy is always moving. Here he is, hopscotching from one flagstone to the next as he delivers his papers; now he's climbing a wall, testing his footholds carefully to make sure they'll take his weight. Here he's washing himself in the school toilets after fighting the bully MacDowall and getting covered in coke dust, dipping his face in the water, lathering his hands and blowing soap bubbles. Now he's giant-striding across the goalmouth, playing with the netting, pretending to be a monkey at the zoo. Then he's hanging from the crossbar by one hand, scratching his armpit with the other, making chimp noises. We could be told a lot about what's going through Billy's mind, his fears and resentments and hatreds, but Hines keeps us, skilfully, on the surface.

We know, subconsciously, that Billy's relationship with Kes won't last. When it ends, it's horrible. Jud wants Billy to place a bet on two horses for him: Billy spends the money on fish and chips instead. Both horses win, and Jud takes revenge by killing the bird. Reading Billy's search for his kestrel – his rising panic, his desperate combing of woods and fields and undergrowth – is difficult, because we sense what's coming. His surroundings are blurred into unfamiliarity by fear and rain and tears: branches rattle like snakes and brambles become tentacles, grasping at his ankles and slowing him down. When Billy returns home, we are stunned first by Jud's offhandedness and then by Mrs Casper's ineffectuality: she won't even *hug* him. In the novel's closing section, Billy wanders the streets before finding shelter in a derelict cinema, where he sits down, imagining that he is with his dad, eating ice cream and watching a film in which he appears as the hero, flying Kes, the bird alive and breathtaking once again. In the film, he buries Kes up on the hillside. David Bradley, who played Billy in the film, says that he can't watch the last twenty minutes, over forty years later: it still upsets him too much.

It's not clear what Billy's future will be, after the book's brutal, gut-wrenching ending. The actor Greg Davies, in a BBC Four documentary about the film *Kes*, said that he wanted to think that Billy's spirit wasn't crushed after all, that he didn't follow the route that seemed to be laid out for him and go off to work down the pit like so many of his classmates. If he had, one suspects there wouldn't have been a happy ending. Billy, at sixteen in 1968, could well have become Billy at thirty-two in 1984, on a picket line in the miners' strike, worrying about how to make ends meet on his meagre strike pay. He wouldn't have been working at one of his local collieries, though. Rockingham, the closest pit to Hoyland Common, closed in

November 1979; nearby Elsecar Main followed in October 1983. He might have joined the flying pickets who were bussed off to other parts of the South Yorkshire and Nottinghamshire coalfields to lend support; he might even have ended up at the Battle of Orgreave, just twenty minutes away down the M1, in June 1984, although that seems more like Jud's style than Billy's. But there wouldn't have been much of a future for him after that. The South Yorkshire mining communities suffered terribly in the decades after the pit closures, and nearby Grimethorpe, home of the famous colliery band, would, by 1994, become the poorest settlement in the country, with unemployment reaching over 50 per cent for much of the 1990s. It's a part of the country that feels itself forgotten, and betrayed. Tellingly, in the general election of December 2019, three South Yorkshire constituencies elected Conservative MPs, two of them for the first time ever. Stephanie Peacock, the Labour MP for Barnsley East – the constituency that includes Hoyland Common – saw her majority cut by over 10,000.

Today, Billy Casper would attend not a secondary modern, but the bright and airy Kirk Balk Academy, whose website proclaims it to be 'Outcomes Focused, Child Centred'. It is part of a multi-academy trust whose vision is to 'enhance the life chances of the children and young people in our care': it assures the public that 'all young people, irrespective of background or ability, will be successful in our Trust'. Almost a third of its pupils are eligible for Pupil Premium funding, which the school uses to provide one-to-one support and guidance and to reduce the barriers to learning that exist as a result of social disadvantage. It offers a wide range of enrichment opportunities intended to broaden students' horizons and give them the chance to participate in activities beyond their parents' means. There are 'Proud Thursdays', when senior leaders praise students' achievements. In 2022, 54 per cent of its students achieved a Grade 5 or above in both English and Maths, 4 per cent higher than the national average. Its most recent Ofsted report proclaimed it to be 'Good'.

Kirk Balk has a challenging job: very few of its students have parents from professional backgrounds, and many face significant deprivation. But I sense that Billy would have fared well there, with more people to keep an eye out for him and more safeguarding policies and practices to pick up on his unhappy home life. He'd have not just one cursory interview with an Employment Officer, but opportunities to do work experience, explore apprenticeships and attend careers fairs with local employers. He certainly wouldn't reach school-leaving age and still 'have a job to read and write'. I hope that the equivalent of a Mr Farthing would find out about his kestrel and make sure that his amazing achievement was celebrated on a Proud Thursday, using it as a chance to boost his self-esteem and help him to stand a bit taller, feeling a shy glow of satisfaction at knowing someone else had recognized what he'd done.

In a beautiful tribute to Barry Hines, the poet Ian McMillan – himself born and raised in Barnsley – stated that 'here in the former South Yorkshire coalfield *A Kestrel for a Knave* is our *Moby-Dick*, our *Things Fall Apart*, our *Great Gatsby*, our *Grapes of Wrath*'. The slim novel with the scruffy boy on its cover has certainly left its mark. In Hoyland Common, the junior football club is called The Falcons, there's a micropub on King Street called the Knave and Kestrel, and a new development called Kestrel Way where you'll find a carvery, a Motordepot car supermarket and an enormous drive-thru branch of Costa Coffee. In Barnsley itself, there's a Kestrel Road, Kestrel Avenue and Kestrel Rise, plus a Kestrel Van Conversions and an aerial photographer called Kestrel Imaging. McMillan comments that:

> . . . if you speak to anybody in Barnsley they'll tell you they were in the film, even if they weren't born when the film was made. It has become an epic that included everybody who has ever lived in the borough and everybody who ever will: 'You'll see me at the back of the assembly scene,' they'll say; or 'When the milkman's coming down the street at the start I'm just twitching the curtains in the back room.'

*A Kestrel for a Knave* has had an impact in other ways too. It reminds us that schools need to offer more – that society needs to offer more – to young people who don't fit the mould, who aren't destined for university and don't find school an easy place to be. Some of these young people will have adults in their lives who can nurture their interests, spot a latent talent and encourage it to flourish. But many won't. They'll be told – sometimes overtly, but often in more subtle ways – that they don't matter. Hands will be wrung about the fact that they haven't managed to achieve arbitrary targets. Governments will see them as a problem to be solved. The paid work that they're heading for, work that will give them a sense of pride and a feeling of making a contribution, will be described as low-skilled, dead-end.

I collect my son from his weekly guitar lesson, and we go for a walk, afterwards, at the local nature reserve. It's the middle of May: the hedgerows are a tangle of hawthorn and wild roses, and on the riverbank, curious sheep look up from their grazing. My son tells me something complicated about scales that I don't understand. Above, there's a hover of wings: a kestrel, intent on something hidden in the grass. I imagine a skinny boy, bright-eyed and patient, his shirt cuffs frayed, his anorak not fitting. I think of all the things he knew, all the things he'd taught himself, that most of his teachers never realized he'd learned. Because schools are not the only places where learning happens, and often, it's the knowledge we gain outside them that's more important.

# On seeing things differently: *Noughts & Crosses* by Malorie Blackman

I've worked with a lot of people during my career. There's been a huge, Chaucerian variety: the idealistic, the cynical, the young and ambitious and the grizzled old stagers. Some have been so gifted that their skill is genuinely moving. Others, as is the way of things, have been a bit odd. One had a habit of stealing people's lunches from the staffroom fridge, and got into a furious confrontation over a punnet of kiwi fruit. Another, when his students were doing a practice exam, had the genius idea of hiding himself in the classroom cupboard and pretending to be a ghost.

In addition to these real, flesh-and-blood colleagues, I like to think that there's another, shadowier group. I imagine them having their own special corner in the staffroom, where they sit at break, huddled round a plate of biscuits. There's avuncular Seamus with his shock of white hair and his rich, reassuring Irish accent; glowering Ted, frowning at the world from under dark eyebrows. Charlotte, small and short-sighted, embarrassed about her terrible teeth. Bespectacled Philip, who people steer clear of nowadays, with his unpleasant political beliefs and his collection of dodgy magazines. Charles, with his stories of poverty on the filthy streets of London. The seriously old ones, like Geoffrey with his pilgrims, and the younger ones, like Yorkshire Simon. And the three Williams: the one who imagines that he can see angels; the one who dreams about being back in his beloved Lake District; and the one with the domed bald head and the stiff white collar, who sits and observes and takes everything in, a look of polite amusement on his face.

These are the people without whom I couldn't do my job: the writers of the novels, plays and poems that I teach. Some of them have been my companions since my own schooldays. Others I've met more recently, but they've lodged themselves, nevertheless, in my brain and my heart, their words shaping the way I see the world. I imagine them catching my eye when the bell goes, chatting as we set off down the corridor. *What's it today? Year Ten?* Over the years, we've taught the young people of south Lincolnshire about many things. We've wandered through the chartered streets of eighteenth-century London, listening to cries of pain and fear. We've picked blackberries and fished for pike, stolen a boat and murdered a king. We've raged against many kinds of injustice and sat on a dusty train one hot Whitsun, watching the country unfold outside. Once, during a lesson about a mid-term break and a little boy knocked down by a car, we looked up to see one of the toughest lads in the school weeping silently in the back row.

Those shadow colleagues – both the ones I've named above and the many others who've been part of my classrooms over the last three decades – have a number of things in common. Most of them, for starters, are men. Most of them are dead. And the vast majority are white.

Those three Williams are significant here, because they're not the only Williams you might find in that particular corner of the staffroom. There's William Golding, of course. William Butler Yeats. William Congreve, William Wycherley. A fact frequently cited about the gender gap in UK businesses is that there are more men called John on the boards of FTSE-100 companies than there are women. An equivalent fact for English teaching is that many students will go through their entire GCSE English Literature course studying more writers called William than they will writers of colour.

Part of the problem is that, until recently, the GCSE set text lists have included very few texts by non-white writers. In the current GCSE English Literature specifications, the only compulsory texts by non-white writers feature in the Poetry unit, which focuses on a collection of poems from the Romantic period to the present day on a theme such as conflict, relationships or youth and age. The number of Black writers included in this collection will vary depending on which exam board and option you are studying. In some options there might be as many as three. In others, there is only one. There is one route through GCSE, with one exam board, that involves the works of no writers of colour at all.

Things haven't always been this way. In the 1960s and 70s, teachers were able to select texts that reflected the cultures of the students they taught. Organizations such as the London Association for the Teaching of English, the English and Media Centre and the National Association for the Teaching of English worked hard to establish initiatives that promoted anti-racist education. The first version of the National Curriculum, introduced in 1989, emphasized the importance of social and cultural diversity, and the need to tackle the under-representation of writers from particular groups. Novels such as Mildred D. Taylor's *Roll of Thunder, Hear My Cry* and Rosa Guy's *The Friends* made frequent appearances in classrooms. When I started teaching, the GCSE Poetry Anthology included poems by Grace Nichols, Wole Soyinka and Merle Collins. Coursework made up 30 per cent of students' overall grade, and as long as we ticked particular boxes – covering a play by Shakespeare, a text written before 1900 and a contemporary text – we had the freedom to choose whatever we wanted to teach. The next incarnation of the GCSE made it compulsory to study a range of 'poems from other cultures', by writers that included Edward Kamau Brathwaite, Sujata Bhatt, Moniza Alvi, Imtiaz Dharker and Derek Walcott. This was not without its problems. What, people wondered, counted as 'other'? What if one of these 'other cultures' was actually your own? Why not simply make diversity the norm, rather than drawing attention to otherness? Still, it did at least mean that students encountered the works of a number of writers of colour.

One of the Black writers who students meet most

frequently at GCSE is John Agard, whose poems 'Flag', 'Half-Caste' and 'Checking Out Me History' appear on a number of English Literature syllabuses. Agard was born in 1949, in what was then British Guiana, and moved to Britain in 1977. 'Checking Out Me History', which draws on Agard's own experiences of school, is a meditation on the absence of people of Black origin from mainstream school history. It focuses on what the faceless authorities have decided the narrator should be taught, and on the fact that this Eurocentric education has blinded him to his own heritage. The narrator has learned more about characters from myth and nursery rhyme – Robin Hood, Old King Cole, Dick Whittington and his cat – than he has about important figures such as Mary Seacole and Toussaint L'Ouverture. When Agard describes these untold stories, his diction takes on a lyrical tone, using metaphors of light and water, beacons and suns. Nanny of the Maroons, who led a group of formerly enslaved people in a war against the British authorities in Jamaica, is a 'hopeful stream' that leads to 'freedom river'. Mary Seacole is 'a healing star', 'a yellow sunrise'. The narrator ends the poem by saying that in checking out his own history, he is carving out his identity.

'Checking Out Me History' is a fantastic poem, full of spark and energy. But whenever I teach it, there's always a moment when someone will raise an objection. It's happened so many times that I can almost predict it. A hand will go up, and somebody will say, 'But, Miss, I don't agree with what he's saying. Why should every-body have to learn about all these people just because he thinks it's important?'

I can never quite believe that this is still happening. Even now, after Black Lives Matter, after so many years of Black History Month and so much public discourse about the need to examine Britain's imperial past, a stu-dent is going to argue that he shouldn't have to learn about counter-narratives and alternative histories, about the shameful legacy of colonialism or the contributions to world history made by people from the global major-ity. I raise my eyebrows.

'So. Are you saying that what he's writing about doesn't matter?'

Bluff and bluster. 'Well, no. It matters to him, obvi-ously. But why should it matter to me? Why do I need to know all this stuff?'

I pause. I'm rehearsing answers in my mind. There's the fact, for a start, that the curriculum is not built around what happens to matter to individual students, especially ones with strong opinions about what they don't need to know. There's also the fact that colonialism and its lasting impact is something that students *should* know about. I compile a mental list of topics that need to be brought to their attention: the British institutions that continue to profit from the legacy of slavery; the British landowners and industrialists whose wealth was built on the subjuga-tion of others; the fact that decisions about what we learn are made by people in power, and that the curriculum therefore represents not a set of eternal truths, but partial choices, subject to bias. As I think about all of this I am aware of the different responsibilities that weigh on me at this moment. I am responsible to Agard and the urgency of what he has to say: that a history told only by one side is a history that is profoundly unjust. I am responsible to the fifteen-year-old boy who has asked this question, whose views I disagree with strongly, but whom I need to challenge tactfully. Overwhelmingly, I am also responsible to the rest of the class, and in particular to those students whose families have come to Lincolnshire from other countries and continents: from South and East Asia, from Africa, from the Caribbean and Eastern Europe. In the way I approach 'Checking Out Me History', I am not just teaching a poem. I am making clear what my own values are.

And so, we talk. Not just about history, but about roots and identity, and the importance of the stories that tell us who we are. We discuss why Agard's narrator needs to know about his own history, and link this to our own lives and backgrounds. I talk about my great-great-great-grandfather Austin Flynn, who came from the parish of Islandeady in County Mayo and made the journey across the Irish Sea to Lancashire sometime in the 1850s, in the wake of the famine that had ravaged Ireland the previous decade. I tell them how important it has been for me to learn about my Irish heritage, and about the history of Irish migration into Lancashire in the nineteenth century, something I was never taught about at school. I ask them to think about their own family histories. Some of them volunteer stories. One boy's aunt is tracing the family tree. Another tells us about visiting his great-great-grandad's grave in a British cemetery in Normandy. But many stay quiet, listening. It's a complicated topic, a big issue, and often with subjects like this my job as a teacher is to sow the seeds of ideas in the hope that students will come back to them later, to think and examine and reconsider.

In Malorie Blackman's 2001 novel, *Noughts & Crosses*, there's a conversation that mirrors, very closely, the conversations that have gone on in my classroom, and no doubt in many others up and down the country, about 'Checking Out Me History', about Black History Month, and about the important attempts that are being made to decolonize the curriculum. It's between teenage Callum and his History teacher, Mr Jason. Mr Jason has been teaching a version of the subject that emphasizes the contributions made by the dominant ethnic group, the Crosses, and makes very little mention of the subjugated group, the noughts. The Crosses, he asserts, have been 'the explorers, the ones to move entire backward civilisations onwards'. They pioneered the use of gunpowder and weapon-making, writing and the arts. But Callum, a nought, is unhappy. It's not fair, he complains. Noughts only feature in the history books when they're on the losing side. What about the nought explorer who was joint first to reach the North Pole? What about the other noughts, throughout history, who have been important? Another teacher, trying to calm the situation, advises Callum that sometimes it's better to leave things unsaid. But this is wrong, Callum retorts. 'Things that go unsaid soon get forgotten. That's why us noughts aren't in any of the history books and we never will be unless we write them ourselves.'

Callum has already started to check out his history. He reads widely and arms himself with information. He lives in a country called Albion, a reimagined version of Britain that was colonized centuries ago by Cross invaders from the continent of Aprica. The Apricans conquered huge swathes of the world, enslaving millions and imposing their culture. In Albion, slavery has been formally over for half a century, but noughts are still subject to state-sanctioned discrimination. Most schools are segregated, and while Callum has been granted admission to an elite Cross school, many Crosses – and some noughts – are not happy about this move towards integration. The number of noughts in positions of authority is tiny. The message is clear: one race sees itself as superior to the other, and is using every system and institution available to it to enforce this superiority. Except there's a twist. In Blackman's novel, the Crosses, the dominant race, are Black. The noughts are white. And it is 'nought' with a lower-case 'n': they are even denied the dignity of an initial capital. As Callum comments, 'Even the word was negative. Nothing. Nil. Zero. Nonentities. It wasn't a name we'd chosen for ourselves. It was a name we'd been given.'

Nought isn't the worst name, either. There's another: blanker. It's an insult, the worst one imaginable. Blank by name and blank by nature, as one of the Cross students at Callum's school explains. 'Blank, white faces with not a hint of colour in them. Blank minds which can't hold a single original thought. Blank, blank, blank . . . That's why they serve us and not the other way round.' (Crosses, meanwhile, are daggers. Daggers can hurt.) When Callum's friend Sephy, a Cross, accuses some of her Cross friends of acting like blankers, Callum is appalled. It's as if the word is ingrained in the vocabularies of even the most sympathetic Crosses, there to be plucked out and used as an insult whenever it's needed.

In her memoir, *Just Sayin': My Life in Words*, Blackman outlines the experiences that led to her writing *Noughts & Crosses*. She describes wondering why the books she read at school did not feature any Black children. The world of literature – a world that she loved – seemed to offer no space for her, or for people like her. It was as if she didn't exist. She was nowhere, nothing, just as much of a blank as Callum. 'Without being explicitly told as much,' Blackman explains, 'my place in society – as a third-class citizen – was being constantly reinforced.'

*Noughts & Crosses* offers a vivid reimagining of the world. It's not quite a reversal of the world Blackman grew up in: it's more brutal than that, with capital punishment and public executions. But it's close. Noughts live in poorer areas of the city, with substandard housing. They are given fewer educational opportunities, and therefore end up in low-paid, low-skilled jobs, any ambition they might once have had knocked out of them by the thousands of obstacles placed in their way. They experience constant slights and microaggressions. Crosses clutch their bags tighter when a nought walks past. Security guards are on the alert whenever they enter a shop. ID cards are checked and fingerprints held on databases. Sticking plasters are dark brown, as if this is the only skin colour that can be imagined. It's a world, in short, where noughts are made to feel as if they don't belong. The messages Callum receives are clear. Make yourself unobtrusive. Don't be angry. Don't stand out. Squash down your needs and desires and make them as small as possible, and then maybe, just maybe, the Crosses will offer you a place at the table. Only don't make yourself too comfortable, and make sure you always, always show how grateful you are.

Flipping the world on its head allows Blackman to highlight difficult realities. In interviews, she has spoken of the fact that people who belong to the majority don't necessarily see these realities: they don't need to. In *Noughts & Crosses*, the character who learns the most about Albion's ingrained racism is Sephy. She is doubly privileged: not only a Cross, but also the daughter of a wealthy politician, Kamal Hadley. Through her friendship with Callum, Sephy becomes aware of the prejudices and insults to which noughts are subjected and the inequalities she could previously ignore. She notices the casual racism of her Cross friends at school, the absence of noughts from her mother's fashion magazines and the stereotyping of nought men in films as 'ignorant drunkards or womanizers or both'. In one chapter, when Sephy and Callum go for a day out, Callum is challenged on the train by a police officer who questions his right to be in a first-class carriage. Sephy intervenes, and explains that Callum is with her, but the message is clear: he wouldn't be allowed to stay there in his own right. It's deeply uncomfortable, but that's the point. Many times, when white students have read *Noughts & Crosses*, they've remarked that they hadn't realized what it must be like to be on the receiving end of all of this. Some say: isn't it a bit of an exaggeration? Their Black classmates reply: no, it's absolutely not.

Callum's situation has its counterparts – and worse – in all manner of real-life injustices. Stop and search. The strip-search by police officers, in 2020, of a fifteen-year-old Black student at a school in East London, without parental consent and without any other adult present: the student was on her period at the time, and the officers knew this, but went ahead anyway. Racism in the Metropolitan Police, as detailed in the 2023 Casey Report, published almost a quarter of a century after the Macpherson Report found that the Metropolitan Police's handling of the murder of Stephen Lawrence had been marked by professional incompetence, institutional racism and insensitivity. Racism in every fire brigade in England, as revealed by His Majesty's Inspector of Fire and Rescue Services in March 2023. Insults and bigotry dismissed as banter. Sapping, appalling ignorance. On the day I write this, two articles in the newspaper: one reporting that the Ritz told a Black job applicant that his hairstyle contravened the hotel's employee grooming policy, another describing an Essex pub landlady's indignation that her collection of golliwog dolls had been described as racist. Several years ago, one of my students, on her way to an orchestra rehearsal, was told by a bus driver that he didn't think 'her sort' could play the violin.

In the repressive society of the novel, some noughts turn to terrorism, believing it to be the only way they have of expressing their dissatisfaction. Callum's brother, Jude, and his father, Ryan, are both members of an underground organization called the Liberation Militia. When a local shopping centre is bombed, and several Crosses killed, Callum's father is arrested, found guilty and sentenced to death. In one of the novel's most chilling sequences, Sephy is forced by her father to put on her best dress and go with the rest of her family to witness the execution. It's their duty, her mother explains: her father is Home Secretary and needs his family to present a united front, to indicate that they all support the draconian policies he is putting in place. It's a barbaric scene, and the fact that Ryan is granted a last-minute reprieve doesn't do an awful lot to lessen the horror. Later, in what might well be a conscious nod to the death of Tom Robinson in *To Kill a Mockingbird*, Ryan is killed when trying to escape from prison, and Callum himself joins the Liberation Militia. He is fighting, he says, for 'a world with no more discrimination, no more prejudice, a fair police force, an equal justice system, equality of education, equality of life, a level playing field': all the things that should exist already, but don't.

*Noughts & Crosses* has enjoyed huge popularity since it was published. In 2003, it was voted into sixty-first place in the BBC's Big Read Top 100, and in 2019, it came eighty-eighth in a *Guardian* poll of the best books published since 2000. Many writers credit it for playing an important role in their own personal stories. Candice Carty-Williams says that reading *Noughts & Crosses* was 'the first time I saw myself in a book'. It has been turned into a graphic novel, and adapted for both stage and screen. The BBC's television adaptation, first broadcast in 2020, adds a visual dimension to Blackman's alternative history, with Afrocentric dress, hairstyles, architecture and interior design emphasizing the cultural dominance of the Crosses.

Malorie Blackman, meanwhile, has been name-checked in songs by Stormzy and Tinie Tempah. She was made an OBE in 2008 for her services to children's literature, held the post of Children's Laureate from 2013 to 2015, and was awarded the PEN Pinter Prize in June 2022, the first children's and Young Adult writer to receive this accolade. Ruth Borthwick, the Chair of English PEN, spoke of Blackman's creation of 'dynamic imaginary worlds', and her determination to engage young people with issues of social injustice.

There's no doubt whatsoever that *Noughts & Crosses* has been instrumental in getting a whole generation of young readers to see the world differently. It does this almost effortlessly, its central conceit both simple and clever. It's fast-paced, with a narrative that alternates between Callum and Sephy, and it's gripping, full of cliffhangers and tension. It's also a substantial read, almost five hundred pages long, giving many young readers a real sense of achievement. And it doesn't end happily. It's important that it doesn't, because the problems that exist in Callum and Sephy's world – the problems that exist in *our* world – are ones to which there are no easy answers. Students like this directness, this refusal to wave a magic wand.

Some teachers I've spoken to feel that *Noughts & Crosses* no longer possesses the punch that it did when it was first published. It has lost its capacity to shock, they say; its urgency has faded over the years. Such claims are easy to counter. No matter how many times we've taught a particular text, our students are meeting it for the first time, and having their first encounter with the way it presents the world to them. One of the challenges of teaching English is to keep these encounters fresh and link them to situations and events that students will recognize. My friend Emma, who teaches the stage adaptation of *Noughts & Crosses* to her Year Nine students, introduces the text by looking at racism in sport, exploring racist abuse in football and the symbolism of taking the knee. She also asks students to think of the ways in which patriotic feelings are often used to exclude and intimidate, using John Agard's poem 'Flag' to examine the aggressive side of nationalism. Her rural school is a much more monocultural environment than mine, just ten miles away: some people, she tells me, might think that diversity isn't an issue in a setting like this. But the lack of diversity in a student body makes it all the more important to tackle issues of bigotry and discrimination. If white teachers allow white students to think that racism is no longer an issue, or that it doesn't need to be considered because it doesn't affect their own particular lives, then they become part of the problem.

Being one of the few Black students in a school like Emma's, though, can lead to feeling that you have to act as a spokesperson, to discuss experiences that you might not feel comfortable sharing. Emma and I talk about the importance of safeguarding, and of making sure that Black students do not feel exposed or forced to speak up. In *Taking Up Space: The Black Girl's Manifesto for Change*, Ọrẹ Ogunbiyi describes the feeling of hypervisibility experienced by Black university students 'the moment a topic slightly related to black people comes up in a lecture', and the sense of being 'the unelected and unwilling representative of the whole black population'. In a situation where you already feel visible, painfully aware that some of your classmates – and their families – might question your right to be there, you need to feel that your teacher has your back. And, therefore, we need to tread carefully, remembering that what goes on beneath the surface of our classroom is just as important as the lessons that are part of the formal curriculum.

In recent years, the need to diversify the texts we study in school has, quite rightly, been the subject of much attention. Lit in Colour, a campaign organized by the Runnymede Trust and Penguin Books and launched in 2020, has worked with exam boards to broaden the range of texts on offer and to reflect the rich diversity of British society. Schools can now choose to study Winsome Pinnock's powerful and funny play *Leave Taking*, which focuses on identity and belonging, or Tanika Gupta's *The Empress*, an exploration of Queen Victoria's relationship with her Indian servants. We could opt for Chinonyerem Odimba's *Princess & The Hustler*, about a young girl's experience of growing up amidst the racial tensions of 1960s Bristol, or Lemn Sissay's stage adaptation of Benjamin Zephaniah's novel *Refugee Boy*, which traces the experiences of a boy and his father who have fled civil war in Ethiopia. We could study Kit de Waal's *My Name is Leon*, the story of two young brothers who are taken into care. Malorie Blackman is now on the set text list too: her 2010 novel, *Boys Don't Cry*, about a teenage boy who finds himself plunged into fatherhood, is now offered as an option by two different GCSE courses.

There have, predictably, been objections. When the new diverse texts were introduced, in the summer of 2022, Nadhim Zahawi, then Secretary of State for Education, challenged the removal of poems by Wilfred

Owen and Philip Larkin from one particular GCSE course. This, Zahawi argued, was an 'act of cultural vandalism': the work of Owen and Larkin should be passed on to future generations as it had been to him. From schools, there were anxieties about the cost of introducing new texts, and about the workload involved. There's often a temptation to stick with the tried-and-tested, with the texts you've taught year after year. You know the students respond well to them; you know they help your classes to get the results they need.

It's easy to push back against these concerns. Exam boards, with the help of Penguin and the Runnymede Trust, have developed resources and schemes of work to support departments who want to introduce the new texts, and will even provide free copies of the set texts to a number of qualifying schools. Teachers can still teach Owen and Larkin, if they want to: the removal of two poems from one particular GCSE course doesn't mean that these poets have been consigned to oblivion. And Zahawi's view of literature – as a collection of texts embodying some kind of set of eternal truths, to be handed down reverently from one generation to another – is one that many teachers, me included, would contest. It's a view that's influenced heavily by Matthew Arnold's definition of literature as 'the best that has been thought and said', a model that casts students as passive recipients of the glories of the past. But who decides what is 'the best' and what isn't? How are new texts admitted to this sacred canon? How do we balance the important texts of the past with those that are fresh and urgent, that represent a more diverse and plural world? Texts are not there simply to be admired. They *can* be, yes – but they should also be questioned and argued with. They should provoke debate. Sometimes, those debates will last the length of a unit of work. Sometimes, they'll stretch over years.

Diversifying the curriculum is, nevertheless, a complex issue. I raise it with my sixth-form reading group, a group of young men and women – my school has a mixed sixth form – who gather in my room after school once a term to eat cake and talk about books. They're a much more diverse bunch than people might expect in Lincolnshire, with their roots in Turkey and Poland and Singapore, South Africa and Uganda. It needs handling really carefully, they say. What the students in my reading group don't want is tokenism, the idea that any one book written by a Black writer can sum up the whole Black experience. (They touch on what Chimamanda Ngozi Adichie described in her 2009 TED talk as 'the danger of a single story', the flattening-out of complexities that can result from simplistic approaches to diversity.) They also don't want books by Black writers that focus solely on issues of exclusion and prejudice, echoing Ọrẹ Ogunbiyi's description of the problems raised by many attempts to increase representation: 'The only times you might see someone who looks like you represented in your curriculum will be at the mention of slavery, colonising, lynching and maybe political corruption in

African states – a dehumanising experience.' What they *especially* object to is a discourse around diversity that focuses purely on urban lives and urban preoccupations. 'It's totally different being in a minority in an area like this,' one girl comments. The worst way of dealing with diversity, my students say, would be to introduce one novel about gang culture and think that that's it: box ticked, job done. Assumptions about the kinds of music young people listen to, or the interests they have outside school, make them deeply uneasy. They are also very much aware of the tensions that exist locally around the area's Eastern European population. My Polish student puts this into words. 'I'm white, so I don't seem like a minority. But as soon as I speak, people know I'm not British. Where do I fit in? Am I part of the dominant group, or am I not? Some people would tell me I am, but I definitely don't feel like it.' It's important, the group agrees, to recognize that there is diversity within diversity; that the issue is much more complicated than it might initially seem.

What my students were talking about, without actually using the term, was intersectionality: the fact that our identities are constructed by a multitude of factors. I introduce the term to them, and they immediately think of the ways in which they can relate it to their own lives, taking in not only ethnicity but also religion, gender and sexuality, disability and social class. We talk about the impossibility of making generalizations and the need to reflect on the multitude of positions that we ourselves occupy. It's a lot for a Friday afternoon at the end of term, but it's important. Our young people need to encounter texts that allow them to reflect on as many of these factors as possible. They also need to read texts where diversity is incidental, as well as where it is foregrounded. Only then will diversity become the norm, rather than something signalled by a huge flashing arrow.

It's something that we're still working towards at my school. Our biggest obstacles are time and money: time to read and research new books and to plan lessons based on them; and the money to buy enough copies for whole year groups. We've invested in a range of new class readers – novels to be read and explored alongside the main curriculum – that focus not only on Black British experiences, but also on the heritage of our Eastern European students. I've made a mental rule that we're not going to add any more texts by dead white men to the curriculum. As Jeffrey Boakye notes, 'we can't share the entire culture of all our children'. But we can at least allow them to see themselves in the books they read in school, and let them know that fighting to be more inclusive is something that we care about. We can ask those shadow colleagues in the staffroom – Seamus and Charles, Philip and Geoffrey and all the Williams – to move up and stop hogging the biscuits. In doing so, we will start to bring about the kind of education that Callum, in *Noughts & Crosses*, can only dream of: one in which all students feel represented and valued, and where nobody's voice is left unheard.

# On behaving badly: *Lord of the Flies* by William Golding

September 1995. It's the first day of our teacher-training course, the Postgraduate Certificate in Education, and we've spent the morning being filled with information about school placements and the assessments we'll need to complete. We're all a bit dazed, and we've come to the canteen to recover. We're also engaged in the careful process of sussing each other out that happens in any group of people who've only just met, and the air is thick with the making of micro-judgements. There are ten of us round the table. Distinct personalities are starting to emerge: the earnest one, the obligatory joker, the one with a nervous laugh that's already starting to grate. The conversation has turned to what the course handbook describes as 'classroom management', and people are swapping stories of the most nightmarish behaviour they witnessed when they were at school. There are tales of chaos and disorder. One person tells us about swigging bottles of cider at the back of the class when the teacher wasn't looking, and another shows us the scar where he was stabbed through the hand with a pair of compasses during a particularly rowdy Maths lesson. It's oddly competitive, as if people will gain some kind of social kudos for having been at the toughest, rowdiest school imaginable. But there's also an undertone of fear. We're making the transition from being students to teachers, to becoming Miss and Sir, and we know, deep down, that one day we'll have to face a class of misbehaving teenagers ourselves.

It was a difficult time to be a trainee teacher. There's never an easy time to be a trainee teacher, but the newspapers that year seemed to be full of stories about feral kids and open rebellion. Earlier that year, Channel 4 had broadcast a drama called *Hearts & Minds*, written by Jimmy McGovern, in which an idealistic young teacher, played by Christopher Eccleston, embarks on his career in a Liverpool comprehensive. There's defiance, threats and sullenness; before one class, a teacher vomits with fear. In the news, there were reports of students carrying weapons, vandalizing classrooms and running amok on public transport. Rising numbers of primary school pupils were being permanently excluded because of their uncontrollable behaviour. In college, we tortured ourselves with thoughts of all the things that might go wrong. Which subjects, we wondered, would be the most dangerous? Science, someone opined. Think of the Bunsen burners, the acids, the glass bottles with their skull-and-crossbones warnings. No, countered another. It's got to be Woodwork. Imagine what you could do with a bandsaw or a lathe. And we did, our overactive English-teacher imaginations conjuring up all manner of horrors. At least our classrooms wouldn't contain anything that could actually maim people. Would they?

People might imagine that teacher-training courses are full of useful advice on how to manage a classful of students. Mine wasn't. It's the kind of skill you learn not in a lecture room but on the job, from observing experienced teachers and looking at how they build relationships with their classes. That year, I watched hundreds of lessons. Some left me wondering whether I'd ever be able to control a classroom in the same way, such as the debate on the ethics of boxing led by a teacher in one of the most challenging schools in Manchester, a room full of fifteen-year-old boys behaving with impeccable courtesy and hanging on her every word. In others, I could feel tension simmering just beneath the surface. There's a sense, in some lessons, that the agenda is being set not by the teacher but by the students. You can see it in the exchange of glances, the whispers, the number of times a teacher is interrupted in mid-flow and has to wait, exasperated, for silence. The smirks, the sniggers. A pen thrown across the room as soon as the teacher's back is turned. I saw several teachers reduced to tears, little hushed clusters in the staffroom reassuring them and mopping them up before they returned to class for the next round. In the school where I did my third placement, a young teacher tried to break up a fight between two girls one lunchtime, and was punched in the face for his pains.

My unofficial mentor on this placement was a teacher in her forties who was impossibly glamorous and lipsticked. I was teaching her Year Eight group, and at the end of one particularly tough day, we sat in her classroom while she lit a cigarette – this was when smoking in schools was still allowed, for staff at least – and I ran through all the things I'd done wrong so that I could write it up later in the reflective journal that we had to submit at the end of the year. 'You'll get there,' she reassured me. 'You're making progress. You just need to be tougher sometimes. There are some lessons when you just have to channel your inner bitch. Otherwise it'll be like *Lord of the Flies.*'

*Lord of the Flies.* My class hadn't studied it when I was at school, but others had, and I remember, in one of the classrooms, a lurid watercolour painting of a pig's head, its eyes and mouth dripping blood, a student copy of the illustration on the book's front cover. It's a novel that has become so ingrained in our culture that most people have a sense of what it's about: a group of children, marooned on a desert island, whose behaviour descends into savagery once the normal props of society are taken away. I'd read it while I was doing my A levels, and remembered the terrifying final chapter where Ralph, the central character, is being hunted down by the other boys. You can feel Ralph's fear as he darts from one hiding place to another, barely daring to breathe, his imagination full of the sharpened sticks that the other boys carry. I thought back to that conversation in the canteen at the beginning of my course, to those lurid tales of classroom horror. I hadn't known that I had an inner bitch, but clearly I was going to have to dig deep and find her.

I remember reading somewhere that the classrooms in which you train to be a teacher are the crucibles in which you're fired. It's an attractive metaphor, but it's a faulty one. You don't emerge from your training as the finished article: you go on learning, adapting to your circumstances, developing your teacher identity. Once you've taught somewhere for a few years, you build up a reputation, but whenever you start at a new school, you have to establish yourself all over again. It's an exhausting process.

Skilled teachers make managing a class look absolutely seamless. They have clear routines and expectations. They use countdowns before expecting silence, or some other signal like raising a hand. They have a well-honed hard stare. Often, they'll reinforce the kind of behaviour they want without anyone even noticing: they'll go and stand behind someone who is whispering, or ask a distracted student a question to bring them back on task, and thank them for their contribution. They'll have an armoury of techniques at their disposal and they'll know exactly when to deploy each one. And they'll need these wherever they teach, because teenagers are teenagers, and they are still capable of winding you up and getting under your skin, no matter what kind of background they're from. When I got my first permanent post, one of the Heads of Year warned me not to assume that students in rural Lincolnshire would be better behaved than those I'd been teaching in the city schools where I'd trained. I spent the next year developing my repertoire of classroom-management skills, remembering what I'd learned about the importance of building relationships, being firm but fair, and giving out more praise than sanctions. And then, at the start of my second year, I was given one of the toughest classes I've ever faced. They were tough because they were my very first GCSE group, and the text I was teaching them was *Lord of the Flies*.

Here's the scene. It's the start of term and I'm nervous. There are thirty pairs of expectant eyes in front of me. I'm the youngest teacher in the school and one parent has already written in to ask if her son can be moved to a different class, with a more experienced teacher. I've asserted myself by putting them in a seating plan, ostensibly to help with learning their names but also to split up combinations who I've been warned about. They're not happy with this. Who do I think I am, telling them where to sit? I go through my mental checklist of everything I need to tell them about the novel. An atomic war has broken out and a planeload of boys has been evacuated from the UK. The plane crashes and the boys find themselves on a tropical island, with no adults to supervise them. We're not told exactly how many boys there are, but they range in age from six to about twelve. To begin with, they manage. They hold meetings and allocate roles. But cracks start to appear. Arguments break out and factions emerge, and the fragile society that the boys have managed to build erupts into violence.

Boundaries are broken, and the message of the novel is that no matter how civilized we think we are, viciousness and cruelty are never very far away.

'Why do we have to read this, Miss? I mean, what's the point?'

The boy who speaks is blond and confident. He's in the top set for everything except English, and he thinks he's slumming it in my group. He's fifteen; he's clever and good-looking; he has a girlfriend and is the self-appointed King of Year Ten. Who am I, compared with him? In his eyes, I'm as low down the educational hierarchy as it's possible to be.

'Well, why? It's not as though it's going to get us a job or anything, is it? We can all read and write already. It's all pretty useless, if you ask me.'

There's a whole raft of things I could say. I could tell him that English helps you to read closely and look below the surface; that it introduces you to texts and ideas that will enrich you as a person. I could even point out that education isn't just about getting a job, and that things are sometimes worth doing even if they aren't immediately useful, but I don't think this is likely to convince him. In one of the sessions on our teacher-training course, we'd talked about the way that English should get students to question received ideas, but this particular boy is already skilled in questioning just about everything he's told. In any case, I don't think he really wants any of my careful justifications. He's challenging me for the sake of it, creating a diversion.

'We're reading it because it's an important novel. It tells us about human nature and how fragile civilization is. What Golding's telling us is that in extreme situations society can break down. Once you scratch the surface, we're all potential savages.'

'What, even you, Miss?'

There's a laugh from the class. The boy smirks.

'Yes, even me. Now. Turn to Chapter One and let's make a start.'

The first few pages of *Lord of the Flies* are a masterclass in establishing character and setting. We look at them closely. I'm learning, a year into my career, that the early stages of studying a novel or play often take a relatively long time. You need to build a relationship between the students and the text, introducing them to concepts and themes and taking time to make sure they know who's who. Golding makes this easy for us, introducing characters gradually, letting us get to know the major players. The novel starts with a fair boy clambering through creepers and broken trunks to a lagoon. He's an archetypal English schoolboy, still in uniform, his shirt sticking to him with sweat. There's a backdrop of greenery and the unsettling cries of unfamiliar birds. The heat is overwhelming. Now there's another boy, more cautious. I get the students to look at how Golding signals this second boy's inferiority. He is awkward and ungainly, and very fat. Our attention is drawn to his grubby clothes, his thick spectacles, his plump knees. Even the way he speaks marks him out as the fair boy's subordinate, his regional accent and non-standard grammar contrasting with the fair boy's Home Counties tones. We count the number of questions he asks. Where's the man with the megaphone? How many children got out of the plane? Are there any grown-ups? You can sense the fair boy's irritation: how should he know? The fat boy's constant questioning allows Golding to demonstrate his lowliness in the pecking order, and also, deftly, to give his readers some brief details about the situation the boys are in. Brief because, of course, there's a lot that the boys themselves don't know. The fat boy is worried by the absence of any grown-ups, but the fair boy is so overjoyed that he stands on his head. The fat boy, meanwhile, has eaten too much tropical fruit and has to disappear into the jungle to relieve himself. Year Ten like this detail: it's another sign of the fat boy's status as the obvious victim, another mark in the tally of his weaknesses.

William Golding was himself a schoolteacher. He apparently wasn't a very good one – he was too absorbed in his writing – but his years in the classroom gave him the ability to spot character types and sketch them with a few well-chosen details. There's not just the fair boy and the fat boy – Ralph and Piggy, the natural leader and the clear outsider – but also aggressive Jack, otherworldly Simon, the twins Sam and Eric, and Roger, furtive and sinister, capable of meting out unimaginable cruelties. There are also the innumerable small boys – the 'littluns' – who swarm and play by day and whimper in their sleep at night. One of the littluns, the splendidly named Percival Wemys Madison, comforts himself by reciting his address and telephone number over and over again, using the memory of the Vicarage, Harcourt St Anthony, to stave off the horrors of the island. I've taught many Ralphs and Jacks in my time, a few Piggys and a couple of Simons, and there's definitely something of the Percival Wemys Madison about the Year Sevens who line up outside my classroom for the first time every September, in their too-big blazers and shiny new shoes, frowning with anxiety as they contemplate the terrors of secondary school.

The way in which the boys relate to each other, sizing each other up and forming allegiances, is also completely recognizable. I'm always struck by the arrogance of Jack's assumption that he should be leader, since he is head boy and chapter chorister and can sing C sharp, and his mortification when the boys choose Ralph instead. There's the easy cruelty with which Ralph reveals Piggy's nickname, producing instant jeers and forming 'a closed circuit of sympathy with Piggy outside', a description that will resonate with anyone who's ever seen a group of children turn on somebody they want to isolate. And there's the sheer variety of boys: shy boys and giggly boys, boys who are uncertain and boys who simply want to enjoy themselves. They have found themselves in the middle of their own adventure story, and they have to decide how to manage until the grown-ups come to find them. They will have fun, but there will, nevertheless, be meetings, summoned by Ralph blowing the conch shell that he finds on the beach. People will have to put their hands up to speak, just like at school. There will be roles and responsibilities. As Jack says, 'We've got to have rules and obey them. After all, we're not savages. We're English; and the English are best at everything.'

But already, there are stirrings. A scared little boy with a birthmark on his face reports that he has seen a beastie, a snake-thing, and while Ralph tries to reassure him, uneasiness ripples through the group and threatens to take over. The older boys manage to light a fire, using Piggy's glasses, but it spreads more quickly than they imagined and threatens to take over the whole island. (The English, best at everything, I remind my students.) There are arguments. Piggy, the voice of reason, is sneered at and ignored. A tree explodes in the fire like a bomb, and the boy with the birthmark goes missing, never to be seen again.

There is brutality too. Jack and his hunters, their faces painted, manage to kill a pig. They delight in recounting how they encircled it and crept up on it, the sight of the blood. They chant. *Kill the pig. Cut her throat. Bash her in.* High on the delight of the hunt, Jack is increasingly cruel to Piggy. The littluns continue to talk of the mysterious Beast, infecting each other with their fears. The Beast comes out of the sea, one insists, like a giant squid. No, it doesn't. It's up on the mountain, with something like wings behind its head. Ralph struggles to maintain order. The rules are starting to break down.

\*

*Lord of the Flies* is as much about leadership as it is about savagery. In class, over the next few weeks, we look at how Golding draws a clear contrast between the leadership represented by Ralph on the one hand, spurred by Piggy's common sense, and Jack on the other. Ralph is driven by thoughts of rescue and shelter. He and Piggy want to build huts on the beach, and to keep the fire going on the mountain, in the hope that a passing ship might notice it. Jack offers the glamour of the hunt, and also the safety of being part of a crowd. You'd want to be one of Jack's hunters, one student comments, so that Jack wouldn't turn on you. You'd want to minimize the chance of becoming one of his victims. Looking at my students, I reflect on how much they've learned, in their fifteen years on earth, about how people work: how they spot weaknesses and exploit insecurities; how they form bonds and protect their interests; how they try to avoid drawing attention to themselves. Some of them have made connections between *Lord of the Flies* and the work they're doing on Nazi Germany in GCSE History, commenting that the boys who side with Jack could be seen as the equivalent of all those who follow orders and do as they're told because making a stand is far too risky. They make notes and underline key words. *Democracy. Dictatorship. Anarchy. Microcosm.* But one day, one of them is restless.

'Miss. Is somebody going to die? Somebody needs to die. I thought they'd be ripping each other to shreds by now.'

It's a girl. The girls in this class are divided into two groups. One group is quiet and studious, with neat exercise books and multicoloured pens. The other is confident and openly challenging. If I'd been in their class, I'd have kept my head down and tried to avoid this group, just as some of the boys do with Jack on the island, for fear of falling victim to their taunts about what I wore or the way I talked. I'm only ten years older than they are and sometimes I feel as if I'm back at school again myself, worrying whether there's anything that marks me out as easy prey. This particular girl rules her circle of friends with enviable ease. I am trying very hard to keep her on side, which I am managing – mostly – by selectively ignoring various uniform infractions and making sure I praise her as much as I can when she contributes appropriately, which essentially means without swearing, or being sarcastic, or asking me which of the teachers in the school I'd marry if I had the choice. I veer between respecting her for not being meek and conformist, for dominating classroom conversations in a way that's usually associated with boys, and being relieved to get to the end of a lesson without having my entire personality torn apart by her.

'Somebody is going to die, yes. Two people, actually.'

'Oh, brilliant! Who is it? Is it really gruesome?'

'Wait and see. It's in the next chapter. Not long now.'

The first death is that of Simon. He is an odd figure in this novel, shy and enigmatic, where other characters jockey for attention. There are hints that he has fits and that he has been bullied. He is in the habit of disappearing into the jungle on his own, and on one of these excursions he spots a pig's head that has been mounted on a stick and left, by Jack and his hunters, as an offering for the Beast. Surrounded by flies, the head becomes a nightmare vision, an obscene grinning thing, the Lord of the Flies itself. It taunts him. Fancy thinking the Beast is something you can hunt and kill, it sneers. The Beast is part of you. Later, Simon finds the body of a pilot entangled in the trees, and decides that this must be what the others thought was the Beast, its wings actually the remnants of a parachute. This beast is not terrifying and threatening, but 'harmless and horrible', and Simon decides that the others must know. But a storm is brewing, and down on the beach a frenzied scene is unfolding. The hunters have killed again. The boys are feasting on meat, and Jack is jubilant. He invites the boys to abandon Ralph and join his tribe, and he and his hunters recreate the hunt as a crazed, horrific dance. There are stamps, and chants: *Kill the beast! Cut his throat! Spill his blood!* Simon emerges from the jungle to tell them of his discovery, but he doesn't get the chance to speak. The mob descends on him, biting and kicking and tearing, and at the end of the chapter, when the storm has blown over and all has quietened down, the broken body of Simon is washed out to sea.

Poor Simon. He's often interpreted allegorically: a visionary who goes into the wilderness to meditate, a prophet who descends from a mountain to bring good news but is murdered by an unheeding crowd. His death is a study in how humans can lose themselves in the anonymous brutality of a group, how people can be swept along in the heat of the moment and carry out acts they would never otherwise contemplate. I ask the class to think of times when they've been caught up like this. I don't get them to share these experiences, recognizing that these thoughts might be uncomfortable, that sometimes students need the space to reflect quietly rather than being pushed to talk. I know, too, that some students might well have been on the receiving end of bullying and intimidation themselves; and when teaching a text like *Lord of the Flies*, it's always important to remember that some students might well identify with Simon and Piggy, the victims in the novel. (One of our discussions in college had touched on whether you'd do *Lord of the Flies* if your group contained a student who had been picked on for being overweight, and our consensus was that we absolutely wouldn't.) Students are always shocked by Simon's death, and I am glad that they are. It's an incident to dwell on, not just because of its importance in the novel but because of our own reactions to it, and it's the kind of moment when English escapes its boundaries in the curriculum and becomes something much more important, inviting us to think about those aspects of ourselves that we might rather not consider.

After the killing of Simon, life on the island can never go back to being just a game. Ralph and Piggy are increasingly isolated, their only companions now the interchangeable twins, Samneric. They worry. One significant problem: how can they possibly keep the fire alight? And another: will they ever be rescued? Elsewhere, Jack is no longer referred to as Jack but the Chief, his choir now a tribe of savages, wielding spears. The Chief, like so many dictators throughout history, uses the threat of the Beast – the Other – to instil fear into his followers. They will kill another pig, to placate the Beast, and afterwards there will be dancing, and meat to eat. But they need fire. And so they launch a raid, and Piggy's glasses are stolen.

'What's going to happen, Miss?' Year Ten are eager now. There's all the buzz of a group of children gathering after school, knowing there's going to be a fight. 'Are they going to get attacked?'

We read on. Ralph and Piggy debate what to do. They know they must challenge Jack, and head down to the grassy platform, on the edge of a cliff, where the hunters have gathered. The tribe is 'a solid mass of menace that bristled with spears'. Ralph and Jack argue. Piggy tries to make a stand, a final, futile attempt to call on the boys' better natures and the appeal of law and democracy. But Roger, high above, has found a giant boulder, and manages – with 'a sense of delirious abandonment' – to dislodge it. It crashes down the mountainside and hits Piggy a glancing blow. Golding's description of this second, appalling death is horrible in its simplicity, but my bloodthirsty Year Tens love it:

Piggy fell forty feet and landed on his back across that square, red rock in the sea. His head opened and stuff came out and turned red. Piggy's arms and legs twitched a bit, like a pig's after it has been killed. Then the sea breathed again in a long slow sigh, the water boiled white and pink over the rock; and when it went, sucking back again, the body of Piggy was gone.

For Ralph, there is panic. He is being hunted and all he can do is hide. He knows that the taboo surrounding the taking of life has been broken, that 'these painted savages would go further and further'. He can hear the tribe chanting: *Kill the beast! Cut his throat! Spill his blood!* He hides in thickets, runs when he judges it safe, listens to the ululations of the hunters. There is fire – an attempt to smoke him out – and the forest bursts into flame, sending all the boys running for the safety of the beach. Ralph's legs are weak under him. He collapses, exhausted, on to the sand, and when he opens his eyes it is to the sight of a naval officer in perfect uniform, all epaulettes and shiny buttons, who stares down at him in astonishment.

*Deus ex machina.* Year Ten write it down, the more dutiful amongst them underlining it in a different colour. They like the respectable solidity of the Latin term, something they can memorize for the exam. Its literal meaning is 'god from the machine', a plot device used to resolve the seemingly irresolvable, and it comes from ancient Greek drama, when actors playing gods were lowered on to the stage using a wooden crane. The appearance of the *deus ex machina* is supposed to be sudden, and in *Lord of the Flies* it certainly is. The savages become, instantly, 'a semicircle of little boys, their bodies streaked with coloured clay'. The officer assumes they've been playing games, pretending to be at war. He is surprised that Ralph doesn't know how many boys there are: surely a pack of British boys should have been able to put up a better show? But Ralph is dissolving into tears, weeping for 'the end of innocence, the darkness of man's heart, and the fall through the air of the true, wise friend called Piggy', and the officer turns away, embarrassed.

At the end of term, we watch the film. In 1997, this still involves wheeling in an enormous television set in a wood-effect cabinet: a big event, met with whoops of excitement. We're watching Peter Brook's 1963 adaptation of the novel, recorded on to VHS by my Head of Department and labelled in her beautiful, precise handwriting. There's a rota for borrowing it, and strict instructions to rewind the tape before putting it back. I've told the group that this particular film is a classic of British cinema, but when they watch the opening montage – which sets the scene of the war, the atom bomb and the plane crash through a series of still images – they're less than impressed. When the action begins, a howl goes up.

'Miss! This isn't going to be black and white all the way through, is it?'

I stop the tape. 'Yes. Why?'

It's an outrage, they claim. It's abuse. They demand to know if there's a colour version. There is: it was made in 1990, and diverges so far from the original that there's little point in watching it. Would they prefer to do an essay instead, I ask? The protests subside and they settle down.

Brook's film version of *Lord of the Flies* is notable for many things. It has some fantastic scenes: Jack's choir-boys, sinister in their black robes, marching along the beach; Simon contemplating a lizard in the jungle; Piggy's laborious tale of how his home town of Camberley got its name. There's the haunting Kyrie Eleison that is sung as Simon's body is washed out to sea, and of course, there's the mounting tension between Ralph and Jack. The story behind the film is also fascinating. In the spring of 1961 Brook assembled a cast of thirty-five boys and took them to the island of Vieques, off the coast of Puerto Rico, where they would spend the summer filming. None of the boys were professional actors. They were chosen because they represented particular character types: the earnest, the playful, the dominant, the aggressive. Scripting was minimal and many scenes were improvised. Perhaps inevitably, as filming continued, there was a blurring of the lines between fiction and reality. Brook acknowledged that he was getting the boys to do 'something quite alarming'. In 1996, he assembled some of the cast to see what influence the film had had on their lives. This reunion was filmed by the BBC as a documentary titled *Time Flies*, and is available on You-Tube. Some of the actors had clearly been more affected by their experiences on Vieques than others. James Aubrey, who played Ralph, described *Lord of the Flies* as the first time in his life that he had ever felt important to someone: the son of an Army officer, he had spent his childhood moving between countries and continents, always the new boy at school, picked on and insignificant. Watching him speak, listening to the tears roughening his voice, I wonder what it would have felt like to have to return to his normal life when the filming was over and he was no longer important. Simon Surtees, one of the twins who played Samneric, touches on this very issue: Brook, he says, 'plucked us from our schools and our homes, put us on the island, then cast us back to live our lives as if nothing would ever change'. It's intriguing viewing, but inconclusive, with a sense that not all of the cast had fully come to terms with the events that had taken place thirty-five years previously.

*Lord of the Flies* is increasingly interpreted, nowadays, as a satirical take on the stories of British pluck and adventure that the boys recall from their former lives, embodying in their various ways all the things a bright boy can do. Jack's comments on the English being best at everything, the officer's remark about what British boys should have been able to accomplish: we snort knowingly, now, at their windy patriotism. The teacher and broadcaster Jeffrey Boakye writes in his book *I Heard*

*What You Said: A Black Teacher, A White System* of using the novel to open a debate on hierarchy, class and empire, and to challenge contemporary myths of Black adolescent criminality, pointing out that the children it focuses on are white English public schoolboys. But *Lord of the Flies* is best known, of course, for its exploration of the darker side of humanity. Look at any review, any study guide or book blog, and you'll find the same phrases cropping up again and again. It's an examination of the wickedness that lies within all of us, shining a light on to our inherent savagery. It alerts us to the dangers of the mob and the appalling things that can happen when the rule of law breaks down. Golding's original title for it was *Strangers from Within*, and it was his attempt to present a more realistic alternative to R. M. Ballantyne's 1857 novel *The Coral Island*, which the boys refer to, excitedly, when they realize that there are no grown-ups on the island. He wanted, he explained to his wife, to write about what children would really do if they found themselves without adult supervision. It was less than ten years after the end of the Second World War and people were only too aware of humanity's potential for cruelty, of the way in which apparently civilized people could commit the most horrendous crimes.

It took some time for Golding to find a publisher. Fans of literary trivia will know that *Strangers from Within* was rejected by a number of publishing houses before it was accepted by Faber and Faber (they might also tell you of Golding's unfortunate technical slip-up: as Piggy was short-sighted, his spectacles couldn't possibly have been used to start a fire). Yet once it was rescued from the slush pile, it became a huge critical and commercial success. E. M. Forster described it as 'outstanding', and it was lauded as a modern classic, a novel for all time. When I first taught it, it had already spent decades as a staple of the school curriculum. Reading *Lord of the Flies* could be seen as an initiation into adulthood, a passing-on of vital knowledge. What could be more important than to make teenagers aware of the truth of the human condition?

But what so many people have seen as an immutable truth about human nature – that if all constraints are removed, people will return to savagery – is not necessarily as incontrovertible as it seems. In his book *Humankind: A Hopeful History*, the Dutch historian and social philosopher Rutger Bregman explores the counter-evidence. Bregman sees *Lord of the Flies* as an example of what the primatologist Frans de Waal has termed 'veneer theory': the notion that civilization is merely a thin layer that covers a morass of barbarity and will break down at the slightest provocation. It's a persuasive idea, Bregman concedes, and it underpins so many novels, films and television shows. We seem to be endlessly fascinated with tales of humans in isolated societies, forced to find ways of surviving. From *Robinson Crusoe* to *I'm a Celebrity ... Get Me Out of Here!*, from *Swiss Family Robinson* to *Big Brother*: humans in a petri dish, under the microscope, their behaviour held up for analysis. The more gruesome the behaviour, the better. Think of the Korean drama *Squid Game*, and the hugely successful *Hunger Games* trilogy, in which competitors – living in debt and poverty – play for high stakes and face death if they lose. Think of the 1993 survival drama *Alive*, based on Piers Paul Read's 1974 account of Uruguayan Air Force Flight 571, which crashed in a remote part of the Andes in October 1972: when food supplies ran out, survivors resorted to eating the bodies of their dead companions in order to stay alive. Cannibalism also features in the Emmy Award-winning drama series *Yellowjackets*, about a New Jersey high school girls' football team stranded in a Canadian wilderness after a plane crash, and in Mari-anne Wiggins's 1989 novel, *John Dollar*, a reimagining of *Lord of the Flies* that sees a group of girls abandoned on an island in the Indian Ocean after a tsunami. The only man on the island has been paralysed from the waist down, and in one horrific scene near the end of the novel, we learn that the girls have been eating the flesh from his legs, slicing it off bit by bit. People, it seems, are little more than beasts, motivated purely by self-interest and the desire to survive.

Or maybe not. Bregman cites a story that has been described as a 'real-life *Lord of the Flies*', that of six boys from Tonga who were shipwrecked on a deserted island in 1965 after a fishing trip turned to disaster. Rather than descending into savagery, the boys drew up a rota for tasks, developed a system for managing conflict, and ended each day with singing and prayer. By the time they were rescued, over a year later, the boys had created a garden for growing food, a makeshift gymnasium, a badminton court and chicken pens. One had even made a guitar, from a coconut shell and a piece of driftwood.

Why, then, do we want to believe that darkness lurks within all of us? Is it because we are fundamentally mistrustful? Does it allow us to explore the murkier corners of our own personalities, those impulses and reactions that our respectable selves manage to control? Is it simply because darkness is more interesting than light? I don't know. What I do know, though, is that it's an idea that sells. Our entertainment industry continues to return to this trope, year after year, and our exam syllabuses continue to feature Golding's most famous novel. And people continue to use *Lord of the Flies* as shorthand whenever the social contract is put under stress: food shortages, panic-buying during the Covid-19 pandemic, any time when it feels that naked selfishness is starting to kick in.

What I also know is that people want to believe that teenagers are scary, that they're dangerous and threatening and out of control. They loom large in our imaginations, just like that first GCSE class of mine did, keeping me awake at night with thoughts of what they might do and say, how many ways they could find to undermine me. But in the end, the kids were all right. They got a good set of grades, and some of them – gratifyingly – went on to do English at A level. They're in their early forties now, a good fifteen years older than

I was when I first taught them. I'm friends with several of them on Facebook and hear of others through mutual acquaintances. They've gone on to become teachers and nurses, tradespeople, a vet, an accountant, an NHS consultant. They own small businesses and run marathons for charity. Most importantly, they are people making their way through life, happy with who they've become. I played a small part in who they've turned out to be, but they did much more to shape me, with all their teenage energy and rebelliousness. They showed me, very early in my career, that the groups who are toughest to teach can also be the most important. And they helped me to make that difficult transition from being a trainee to a fully-fledged teacher: still a work in progress, because teachers always should be, but definitely one for whom the classroom held fewer fears.

# On secrets, lies and family histories: *Coram Boy* by Jamila Gavin

Britain's largest collection of eighteenth-century domestic textiles is held in a museum in Bloomsbury, midway between the bustle of King's Cross and the squirrels and plane trees of Russell Square. You'd expect such a collection to be housed in the V&A, or some other specialist centre dedicated to craft and design, but instead it lives in a very different kind of museum: the Foundling Museum, in Coram's Fields, built on the site of what was London's first Foundling Hospital. It is made up of thousands of scraps of fabric, some of them only a few centimetres square, that were cut from clothes and given to the hospital authorities by mothers leaving their babies in the hospital's care. These scraps, or tokens, could be used to identify children if their mothers were ever able to reclaim them. The tokens are a patchwork of colours, patterns and textures: stripes, spots, birds, flowers and leaves, in reds and blues, greens and browns. Some are faded and stained, others surprisingly vivid. Some of them have been embroidered or blanket-stitched, in an attempt to add a final layer of individuality, a sign of dedication to a child who might never be seen again. One piece of cream linen is adorned with a pale-blue ribbon and a red woollen heart, a decoration that would not look out of place in a contemporary shabby-chic gift shop.

Many of these tiny snippets of fabric are on display in the Foundling Museum, alongside the 'billets', or admissions records, to which they were originally attached. These records tell of each baby's gender and age, along with their 'state of grace' – whether or not they were baptized – and any distinguishing marks. In a display case fixed to the wall, there are yet more tokens: coins stamped with holes, medals, a thimble, a slender ivory fish. In another part of the room, a sound system plays recordings of the testimonies of people who grew up at the Foundling Hospital in the early twentieth century, before it relocated to Hertfordshire in 1935. The uniforms worn by the children – navy, red, tweed – stand obedient and alert on their mannequins.

The Foundling Museum is run by Coram, a charity that supports children and young people. It is named after Thomas Coram, who established the Foundling Hospital in 1739. Coram was a sea captain, born in Lyme Regis, who set out for New England in 1693 and founded a shipbuilding business in the town of Taunton, south of Boston, Massachusetts. America must have seemed, at first, a place of clear air and endless possibilities. Yet Coram quarrelled with the locals, who were suspicious of his fervent Anglicanism. His business fell into debt and his home was attacked. He returned to London and found it filthy and diseased. He was horrified by the dirt and the poverty, the open sewers, the beggars, the dead dogs. Most of all, he was horrified by the thousands of babies abandoned on the streets, by mothers who were too poor, or too alone and scared, or too addled by gin, to care for them. And so he formed a project to help them.

Coram's plan was to set up an institution to provide for these children, give them an education and prepare them for a trade so they could eventually earn their own living. They would be cared for by wet nurses until they were five years old, and would then return to the institution until they were old enough to make their own way in the world. Their upbringing would include music, the arts, fresh air and opportunities for play. With the help of a distinguished group of benefactors that included the artist William Hogarth and the composer George Handel, Coram managed to secure royal assent, and his Foundling Hospital admitted its first children in 1741. It would eventually become the United Kingdom's oldest children's charity.

The Foundling Hospital provides the backdrop for Jamila Gavin's novel *Coram Boy*, published in 2000 and winner of the Whitbread Children's Book Award. *Coram Boy* is a relative newcomer to the canon, but it is popular with schools – many of whom have brought groups of students to the Foundling Museum to explore the stories of real-life foundlings – and has recently been introduced as a GCSE set text by the Edexcel exam board in a welcome move to include the works of a more diverse range of writers in the curriculum. It is sometimes taught as a precursor to Dickens, and it's easy to see why, as it introduces students to a vividly realized world where wealth and poverty exist side by side and the trajectories of lives are subject to sudden dips and twists. In this world, villains are larger than life and children have to use their wits in order to survive. As with Dickens himself, there are improbable coincidences and chance reunions, but there are also fascinating insights into the morals of eighteenth-century society and the way it treated its more vulnerable members. And there is scope to reflect on our obsession with one of fiction's most enduring themes: children who are abandoned, fostered or adopted, and the complicated family histories that often surround them.

As an adoptive parent, I have a personal stake in this subject. My son joined our family just after his second birthday, and in the years since then, I've been struck by just how many stories feature orphaned, abandoned and adopted children. Lemn Sissay's poem 'Superman was a Foundling', on display in the Foundling Museum, lists over a hundred of them, from Anne Shirley and David Copperfield to Princess Leia, Luke Skywalker, Edward Cullen and Lisbeth Salander. Once you start looking for these children in literature, they're everywhere. Perdita in *The Winter's Tale* is a foundling, abandoned on the orders of her father, Leontes, because he mistakenly believes that his wife, Hermione, has been unfaithful to him. The story of Rome is built on that of the foundlings Romulus and Remus, abandoned on the banks of the Tiber and suckled by a she-wolf. Oedipus was a foundling, and so was Moses, concealed in a basket by the side of the river Nile. So was *The Importance of Being Earnest*'s Jack Worthing, discovered in a handbag on the Brighton Line at Victoria Station. There are anthropomorphic foundlings: Po in *Kung Fu Panda*, Moominpappa, Paddington Bear. And, of course, there's Harry Potter, left by Albus Dumbledore on the Dursleys' doorstep in suburban Privet Drive.

Why are we so fascinated with stories of the orphaned and abandoned? Part of it is, undoubtedly, due to simple human curiosity. What does it feel like to be brought up by people who aren't related to you? What would it be like to track down your biological parents, to trace your genetic roots? For some of us, there's also a lurking sense that there's something – however indefinable – that sets us apart from our own families. In Sigmund Freud's notion of the family romance, the fantasy of being adopted enables us to deal with negative feelings about our parents. We imagine that we have a different mother and father elsewhere, usually richer and definitely more sympathetic and understanding. If only we could go and live with them, all our problems would be solved.

I certainly felt this sense of difference myself as a spiky teenager, the youngest child by nine and a half years. There were many times – especially when I was doing my A levels, and at university – when I didn't seem to fit in. Would it explain everything, if I found out that

I'd come from somewhere else? But in other ways, my family and I were far too similar. Put my sisters and me in a line, with me in the middle, and you'll see the resemblance. I have my dad's eyes and my mum's mannerisms. The idea of a different past wasn't a fantasy I could have sustained for long.

Orphaned and abandoned children offer all manner of possibilities to storytellers. In some ways, they're like an extreme version of the free-range children who populate so many adventure stories: get rid of the parents and the kids are let loose to do whatever they want. But abandonment, in whatever form, also gives characters a layer of psychological complexity that they might not otherwise possess. In 2022, an exhibition at the Foundling Museum focused on the world of superheroes and the representation of orphaned, abandoned and adopted children in fiction. A panel explained that traumatic backstories give these characters a spur, a drive to transcend their difficult origins. According to the artist Woodrow Phoenix, these children need answers: 'They need justice. Perhaps they need revenge. They definitely need to build a new world to replace the one they lost.'

How do these images of adoption and abandonment, these stories of orphans and foundlings, shape our perception of their real-life equivalents? This is something I'm acutely conscious of, as both a parent and a teacher. Many of the texts we teach in school deal with adoption in some form or other: Willy Russell's play *Blood Brothers*, Susan Hill's novel *The Woman in Black*,

Jeanette Winterson's *Oranges Are Not the Only Fruit*. And so when I teach these texts, I'm careful. I'm careful because I want to counter the prejudices and misconceptions, the stereotypes that crop up again and again when adoption is discussed. And I'm careful because I don't always know the family histories of the students sitting in front of me. So many of the books that students encounter in English – especially those written primarily for young adults – touch on difficult experiences and emotions. Some students might want to talk about these, although this needs sensitive handling. Others won't, but will be listening, warily and perhaps afraid, to the things their peers might say, the assumptions they might make. Being aware of this emotional hinterland – the feelings that can be unlocked by the texts we teach – is one of the most demanding things we have to do as English teachers. It's also one of the most important.

*Coram Boy* opens one evening in 1741, with a man and a boy making their way to the city of Gloucester with their pack of mules. The man is Otis Gardner, seller of pots and pans. Otis can charm his way around anyone: today, he'd be an estate agent, a seller of used cars or promoter of pyramid schemes. The boy is his son, Meshak, clumsy and vulnerable. People call Meshak a simpleton, but he notices more than they think he does. He notices the strangeness of the shapes made by the trees against the night sky; the animals in the undergrowth; the shadows of nameless things that lurk and threaten to pounce. All of this scares him. So, too, does the secret job that he and Otis perform. For Otis collects unwanted children and takes them to new places. Some are orphans who have lived for so long under the care of their local parish that they are now considered a burden. Others have been abandoned by families who have fallen into poverty and cannot provide for all the mouths they have to feed. Otis hands them over to people who want servants or apprentices, or to the cloth mills or weaving sheds where their nimble fingers are in high demand, or to the docks, where they will be sent away to foreign lands. That's if they're old enough. Money changes hands, of course: Otis doesn't do this out of the goodness of his heart.

These older children don't know it, but they're the lucky ones. The youngest, the babies, will meet with a different fate. These babies have been born to unmarried mothers who are so desperate to conceal their existence that they entrust them to Otis. They tell themselves that they are giving them the chance of a better life, that Otis will take them to Thomas Coram's Foundling Hospital in London to be cared for and given an education. For Otis knows that the Foundling Hospital takes in not just poor children but also the 'brats of the rich'. There is money in foundlings, money paid by the wealthy to 'salve their consciences and purchase respectability'. That way, a mistake can be erased. A daughter's eligibility for marriage can be preserved; a dalliance brushed over. And so Otis, with his eye always on the main chance, has spotted an opportunity. For a fee, he will take on the unwanted babies of the upper classes and promise to deliver the infants to Coram's marvellous institution.

They won't get there. They won't actually get anywhere near London. They will be slung in panniers on the backs of Otis's mules and left to grow weak. Then they will be buried, submerged in ditches and covered over with a few shovelsful of earth. Some will have died of thirst or starvation, but others will still be alive. Their cries catch at the edges of Meshak's thoughts when he tries to sleep at night. Poor Meshak: he's just as trapped as they are. He flinches from Otis like a kicked dog, abject and terrified. He is desperate for a saviour, but nobody wants a lad like Meshak, daft in the head and prone to falling into strange trances. There are many kinds of cruelty in the world that Gavin describes, and Meshak has experienced most of them.

*Coram Boy* is divided into two parts, both of them focusing on the different fortunes of two characters. The first part of the novel introduces us to Alexander and Thomas, two choirboys at Gloucester Cathedral School. Unlike the foundlings we meet later, both Alexander and Thomas know exactly where they come from. Alexander is the oldest son of a rich man, heir to the family estate of Ashbrook. His father, Sir William, disapproves of his passion for music and wants him to leave the school. Thomas, on the other hand, has grown up in poverty, the son of a ship's carpenter. The friendship between the two allows Gavin to build a detailed picture of their contrasting homes. Thomas lives in a one-up, one-down cottage in the centre of Gloucester, a jumble of younger siblings and chickens and geese, with his father hammering and sawing and his mother smoking herrings. Alexander's family home, Ashbrook, is built from honeyed stone and set in acres of parkland, with ornamental gardens and an artificial lake. When he first goes to visit, Thomas is astounded, out of place. But he soon realizes that for all his material wealth, Alexander is deeply unhappy. He knows that his time at the cathedral school is limited: as soon as his voice breaks, he will have to leave in order to learn how to run the Ashbrook estate. Music, as far as his father is concerned, is a distraction and an indulgence. Alexander finds solace in his friendship with Thomas and his relationship with Melissa, daughter of the family governess. He waits for the inevitable to happen.

In my department, *Coram Boy* is a class reader for younger students, explored and discussed alongside the main curriculum, a few chapters at a time. Whenever I've shared it with a class, students have been gratifyingly outraged on Alexander's behalf. How dare his father crush his passion, take control of his life? We look at the hints in the text that Sir William's wealth is built on slavery, and their outrage increases. It's a brilliant opportunity to teach them about the legacy of the slave trade and the concealed histories of many British stately homes, of streets and statues and institutions.

Like so many other texts, *Coram Boy* helps students to develop their understanding of the practices and beliefs of the past, giving them an insight into how things used to be. It also opens up wider debates. One of these concerns the work of Alexander's mother, Lady Ashbrook, who wants to establish a local orphanage. She is appalled – just as Thomas Coram had been – by the scale of child abandonment, by the desperation of mothers who are unable to support their own children. Other wealthy locals disagree. Funding orphanages, they say, encourages immorality. People should take responsibility for their own offspring and not expect to live on charity. I tell the students that these arguments don't just exist in fiction; that they were raised back in the eighteenth century when Coram was trying to establish the Foundling Hospital, by real people, who could have done something to help but didn't. I think ahead to when my students will read *An Inspector Calls*, for GCSE, and to Mr Birling's bluster about the cranks who believe that everyone has to look after everyone else, all mixed up together like bees in a hive. And I think about the vilification of the poor in certain strands of contemporary media, and reflect that what we do in English often borders on an act of resistance, an attempt to make students think more carefully not just about the texts we read but about the world we live in.

Alexander's voice is late in breaking, but when it does, he returns to Ashbrook to find that his father has removed every trace of music: every instrument, every score. Devastated, he leaves, renouncing his inheritance and vowing to make music his life. Shortly afterwards, Melissa finds that she is pregnant. There are lessons here, too, especially in the all-boys school where I teach, about male responsibility, about the fact that men throughout history have been able to walk away without even realizing what they have done while women are left behind to cope with the consequences: lessons that we try to capitalize on, especially with students who are lairier and more laddish, and for whom relationships with girls are starting to loom large in the world beyond school. When the baby is born, it is handed over – you probably saw this coming – to the Coram Man. Melissa is told that it is dead.

The second half of the novel, set nine years later, focuses again on two young boys, Aaron and Toby. They are growing up at the Foundling Hospital. Toby was brought to the Hospital as a baby. He is the son of an African woman who was being sent to the New World on a slave ship; he was rescued by a rich man, a Mr Gaddarn, who is now his benefactor. Toby's story gives us an insight into the lives of Black foundlings in eighteenth-century London. On his regular visits to Mr Gaddarn, he is treated as exotic, dressed as a miniature prince in silks and a turban. Wealthy women pull at his clothes and run their fingers through his hair. Toby knows that when he leaves the Hospital, he is destined for a life as a servant, a curiosity in a London where he is still very much in the minority. His best friend, Aaron, arrived at the Hospital in the care of a strange man called Mish, a child in a man's body, who turned up one day with a baby boy tucked under his jacket and has remained there ever since, taken on out of charity to work on the Hospital's land. Aaron has been identified by the Hospital's choirmaster as having an unusual talent for music. He is to be apprenticed to a composer, Charles Burney, where his abilities can be nurtured.

It's here that we start to find out the connections between the two halves of the novel. Mish, of course, is Meshak, and Aaron is the son of Alexander and Melissa. The choirmaster at the Foundling Hospital is Thomas. Alexander – in one of those fabulous coincidences beloved by eighteenth- and nineteenth-century novelists – is himself working with Charles Burney, and pieces together the clues that tell him that Burney's new apprentice is his own son. Mr Gaddarn, meanwhile, is none other than Otis Gardner, who has given up his old life and changed his identity. People back in Gloucester believe that Otis was hanged, for crimes including murder and blackmail, but no. That was just a cover story. He is still child-trafficking, still preying on the innocent. These days, he's procuring girls from the Foundling Hospital on the pretext of sending them to America as servants; in reality, they're being shipped to the harems of North Africa and the Middle East. He's involved in just about every kind of slavery imaginable, and the proceeds are keeping him in a life of luxury.

What of Melissa? She is still living at Ashbrook,

trapped in her past, alone with her grief. Her mother will not speak to her about her child. Her situation echoes that of so many women throughout history who have been coerced into giving up their babies shortly after birth, told that a fresh start was best for everyone. The stigma of illegitimacy, the cruel morality of the past. My students will meet this in Year Nine, when they study *The Woman in Black*, and explore Susan Hill's story of the pain of a young woman forced to hand over her son for adoption. Melissa longs to see Alexander again. He has written to her: she knows he is well, and living in London, and making a name for himself as a composer. Thomas is trying to bring about a reconciliation between Alexander and his father. Melissa must be patient, and wait. In the meantime, she works at Lady Ashbrook's orphanage, teaching lost and abandoned children to read and write, pouring on to them the love and care that she is unable to lavish on her own son.

One day, Thomas brings a group of six Coram boys to Ashbrook to sing anthems from the *Messiah* at a benefit concert in aid of the Ashbrook orphanage. One of the boys is Aaron. His treble voice, pure and angelic, reminds everyone of Alexander. There are twists and turns, peril and sword fights, and a few pages where it seems that Aaron, Toby and Mish are about to be sent to America on one of Mr Gaddarn's slave ships. But, eventually, the story is pieced together. Aaron, Melissa and Alexander are reunited, and my students breathe a sigh of relief.

*

We love a reunion. Who doesn't? There's a neatness, a tying-up of loose ends. We especially love reunions in stories of lost and adopted children. Think of the popularity of television shows like *Long Lost Family*, with their tears and drama. Blood calls to blood. Strangers realize that they have something in common – a shared passion, a quirk of the eyebrow, a way of gesticulating when they talk – and then, gradually, work out the connections that unite them. We love the romance of affinity, the pulling-back of the curtain, the hug that resolves a lifetime of separation.

Part of this, I think, is driven by a desire for tidiness. It's the satisfaction of putting that last piece in the jigsaw: nobody likes a puzzle that's left unfinished. It also, undoubtedly, reflects our interest in our own roots. Genealogy, once the preserve of people with lots of time on their hands and a penchant for exploring long-forgotten archives and parish records, is now a multi-billion-dollar industry. Users of Ancestry.com, the world's biggest genealogy company, have created over 125 million family trees between them, and the site holds the DNA records of over twenty-two million people. We like to know where we come from: the idea of not knowing who your parents are, who your ancestors were, seems utterly alien to us.

I've been seduced by this too. I'm one of over three million paying subscribers to Ancestry.com. My family tree is a bit uneven – I've got back as far as 1720, though some branches are stronger and leafier than others – but

I've found out some important things. Many of these concern my Irish roots, which I'd always known about in vague terms, but which I was able to flesh out with names and dates and places. I found out, too, about my great-grandfather James Brady, who was killed during the First World War when my grandmother was a baby, and about whom she knew very little, as her mother would never speak of him. James Brady was a reservist who had fought in South Africa; in the summer of 1914, at the age of thirty-seven, he was recalled, and went over to Belgium with the Loyal North Lancashire Regiment. My grandmother, who was born in July 1914, would have been just a few weeks old when he left. He never got to see her grow up. He was killed outside Ypres on 31 October 1914 and his body was never recovered.

James Brady is commemorated, along with thousands of other men, on the Menin Gate in Ypres, and a few years ago, my husband and son and I went to find his name, along with that of my husband's great-uncle, Daniel Hindmarsh, who fought with the Lincolnshire Regiment and died in Flanders in July 1917. It was a crisp autumn day, with leaves bright on the ground, and it didn't take long to find them. Their names were about six metres apart. They could have been drinking in the same bar, have raised a glass to each other and had a chat.

I can't read Philip Larkin's poem 'MCMXIV', now, without imagining my great-grandfather and the thousands of men like him, standing in lines that August, thinking it would all be over by Christmas. Sometimes, when I teach the poetry of the First World War, I show my students a photograph of James Brady's name on the Menin Gate, and tell them the story of this man who died over a hundred years ago, before my grandmother had the chance to get to know him, a piece of my family's history put into place through the wonders of the internet. But I'm aware, at the same time, that this knowledge is a privilege. Family histories are complicated things, and even if you do know where you come from, it's not necessarily a source of pride. We want to learn about our roots, but we also hope they don't bring any unpleasant surprises.

It's only right at the end of *Coram Boy* that Aaron meets his birth parents, so we never get to know what happens next. And this is something I always wonder about, with stories of search and reunion. How do things work out? In narrative terms, there's a sense of closure, of justice. The missing child has been restored to his family. What was lost has now been found. It's there, too, in the language that's widely used about adoption. People speak of 'real parents', of 'real families'. We look for similarities between birth parents and their lost children, for shared preferences and odd coincidences. It's proof, if any were needed, that they were meant to be together, and that any other arrangement is merely a temporary interruption.

But neat narrative solutions don't necessarily reflect reality. I think of the many accounts I've read that describe the difficulty of reunion, the challenge each person has of replacing the imaginary version of the other with the actual human being in front of them. The broadcaster Nicky Campbell writes in his memoir *Blue-Eyed Son* of his image of his birth mother as an 'independent, forthright, empowered figure', commenting that this image 'was intrinsic to my sense of self and I had cherished it in a special place at the back of my mind for as long as I could remember'. The real woman, however, was very different. Campbell 'wasn't able to accept a mother whose image was so dissonant with the fantasy figure of my imagination'. This most complex of situations can bring great joy, but it can also bring conflict, and anger, and grief. Finding someone can, paradoxically, involve losing them.

Growing up in a family that is not genetically yours is difficult, for all manner of reasons. It's especially difficult when the narratives that surround families that contain adopted and care-experienced children – and the children themselves – are often simplistic. It's another example of Chimamanda Ngozi Adichie's notion of the danger of the single story, where one set of tropes is allowed to prevail, skimming over the complexities and lodging itself blithely in people's minds.

The contrast between fictional stories of adoption, fostering and reunion – those stories that crop up, almost without being noticed, in so many of our school set texts – and the lived experiences of fostered and adopted children are stark. In schools, we need to be aware of these contrasts. The ways in which adoption is represented in the texts we teach, and the ways in which teachers mediate these representations, can be crucial to young people testing out their sense of identity and navigating their relationships with both birth and adoptive families. Adoption, and experience of the care system, don't feature on our teaching radar in the way that – for example – gender and ethnicity do. But they should, because adopted and care-experienced children face many kinds of disadvantage. Research on the long-term effects of developmental trauma indicates that neglect and abuse can have a negative impact on those areas of the brain that are responsible for impulse control, self-regulation, planning and reasoning, and these problems do not disappear, magically, once a child has been adopted. Adopted children are more likely to require involvement from educational psychology services and child and adolescent mental health services than their non-adopted peers, and Department for Education statistics indicate that outcomes for adopted children are still lower than those for their cohort as a whole. Yet anecdotes shared by adoptive parents suggest that many schools remain ignorant of the consequences of early trauma, and adoption forums overflow with stories of children who find the demands of the classroom desperately hard to negotiate.

So, as with Pip's missing years in Cairo, as with so many of the gaps in the texts we read, I'm curious. There's an untold story at the end of *Coram Boy*, of lives that need to reassess and settle themselves into new patterns, just as the lives on the TV reunion shows need to do, away from the attention of the cameras. These stories will complicate what our society likes to believe about separation and reunion. They won't be easy to tell. But they need to be told.

Because stories, as we've seen so many times, are important. On her website, Jamila Gavin writes of the role stories play in helping children to learn

> about values and roles, about good and evil, about fun and silliness, about happiness and sadness – about life and death. It is through stories that children can make sense of a confused world and learn to over-come the obstacles they will inevitably meet.

When you're trying to make sense of your own life story – a story that contains gaps, and questions, and things you don't quite understand – you need books that acknowledge these complexities. You need stories that are written with you in mind. And you need to feel that your teachers will be careful when they choose books about situations like yours, that they don't let those simple narratives go unquestioned.

At the Foundling Museum, I buy a book of poems, *Tokens for the Foundlings*. It's an anthology of poems about children and parents, about love and loss. One poem, 'What Typesetters Call Them' by Katy Giebenhain, plays on the printing terms 'widow' and 'orphan', used to refer to isolated lines at the beginning or end of a page.

Orphans, declares Giebenhain, 'aren't alone the way widows are alone'. They are a symbol not of loss, but of hope: 'We like orphans to be hopeful, plucky, gifted / With a clean slate'. But these expectations must weigh heavily. There's the pressure to be brave, the pressure to be heroic. Fictional foundlings, like Aaron and Toby and so many of their companions from page and screen, are indeed plucky and gifted, blazing a trail and inspiring millions. Yet for their real-life equivalents, the world is a much more complicated place.

# On relationships, longings and female desire: *Of Mice and Men* by John Steinbeck

Teachers are not always aware of what their students are learning in school. This is a sobering thought, but nevertheless it's one that every teacher needs to accept. While we spend time planning lessons and worrying about grades, our students are engaging in a different kind of education, one that consumes far more of their energy and imagination than the formal curriculum. The knowledge they absorb is urgent and complicated. It focuses on how to stay alive in the dangerous ecosystem of the school, on remaining fully alert to the shifting criteria that set the parameters of acceptability and dictate your place in the social hierarchy. It encompasses such vital matters as how to behave and what to wear, who to make friends with and who to avoid, what kinds of hobbies and tastes in music you should have. It takes in the complexities of relationships and all their different stages. And a lot of it, inevitably, is about sex.

Picture the scene. I'm thirteen years old, and it's ten to nine on a Monday morning. We're waiting for our form tutor, Miss Harrison, to arrive, and in the meantime, we're being introduced to Ralph. There's a little gaggle of us – Jennifer, Lisa, Angela, Claire, a roll-call of the names that thirteen-year-old girls had back in 1985 – and we're all giggly and intrigued. This mixture of emotions is because Ralph is not a person, but a penis. A fictional penis, but a penis nonetheless. He belongs to Michael, the boyfriend of seventeen-year-old Katherine, narrator of Judy Blume's novel *Forever*, and things are about to get very serious.

It feels a bit weird, reading about all of this on a Monday morning. There's a sense that we're doing something we shouldn't. But we can't tear ourselves away. It's Jennifer's book, but Angela is reading it out loud, and we all hold our breath as she gets to the bit where Katherine finally *touches* Ralph and – well, you can imagine. (I once read a description of *Forever* as 'seminal', a queasily appropriate adjective for a novel that contains its fair share of teenage ejaculations.) And then Miss Harrison finally appears, and we have to wait until breaktime for the next instalment.

Over the following weeks, *Forever* is passed around most of the girls in our form. Other people elsewhere in the year get to know about it, and before long several have bought their own copies. There's a rumour that one girl's mum has made her tippex over the more explicit bits, which renders the book pretty much redundant: there are other things in *Forever* as well, like college applications and learning to ski, but nobody's really interested in those. We follow Katherine and Michael's relationship from first kiss to actual sex, through all the different bases in between. All of this feels as though it's something we need to keep hidden. We're not sure if we're supposed to be learning the lessons that *Forever* is teaching us. But we're finding out a lot: not only about the physical side of things, but about doubts and insecurities, health checks and awkwardness, and the complex and confusing nature of desire. It might all be a long time in the future, for most of us, but it's best to be prepared.

We needed *Forever*, and Judy Blume's other books about navigating the tricky landscape of growing up, because sex education at my Catholic comprehensive school was distinctly lacking in any discussion of feelings. We had a much-anticipated series of lessons on human reproduction, drawing carefully labelled diagrams of sexual organs and watching a video of a woman giving birth. The girls were whisked away for a talk about periods from a nurse who told us how to use tampons and reminded us – in a bit of an embarrassed afterthought – that when we eventually got a boyfriend we needed to be on our guard in case things went a bit too far. Kissing was fine, but even then we needed to be careful. (A friend of mine, who went to school in Northern Ireland, remembers being told that if she ever sat on a boy's lap, she should put a telephone directory down first, *just in case*.) The overall message was pretty simple. Sex was about creating babies and therefore we should wait until we were married. But there was nothing about the emotions that surrounded it, no sense in which any of this helped us to cope with our emerging sexuality and what it would mean. Fear and indecision, longing and inadequacy, excitement and risk-taking and the complicated thrill of what our changing bodies represented: all of this was up to us to learn about, in whatever ways we could.

As we grow up, we receive all manner of messages about being in a relationship and what it involves: how people in relationships should behave, how they should treat their partners, what the ideal relationship should look like. Some of these messages are confused and outdated; others are narrow-minded and misleading. In some cases, they're downright offensive. Messages about attractiveness and how it's measured; about finding your soulmate and winning someone's heart. Messages that tell you it's impossible to be truly happy and fulfilled if you're not in a relationship, that you should make sacrifices and suppress your own needs – even make yourself into a different kind of person entirely – rather than risk being rejected. They hit us from every direction imaginable, from our families and friends and acquaintances, and via every possible medium. There's television, music and film; today, there's obviously the internet. And then there are books and the values they reinforce.

When they focus on relationships, the kinds of books we read in school tend to concentrate on love and marriage, rather than actual desire. There's flirtation, the complicated dance of courtship, but characters like Elizabeth Bennet and Jane Eyre are hardly sexual beings.

Yet sexuality and desire do find their way into some of our set texts. Think of Juliet, musing on 'every other part belonging to a man': Claire Danes, in Baz Luhrmann's 1996 *Romeo + Juliet*, makes it absolutely clear which part she has in mind. Think of Catherine in Arthur Miller's *A View from the Bridge*, slowly recognizing the power she has not just over Rodolpho but, catastrophically, over her uncle, Eddie. And then there's Curley's wife, in *Of Mice and Men*, and from the moment she first appears – her rouged lips and polished nails trumpeting a warning from the doorway of the barn – the idea of desire is never very far away.

Curley's wife is the only female character who actually appears in *Of Mice and Men*. Others are mentioned. There's Lennie's Aunt Clara, a woman called Susy who runs the local brothel, and the girl in the red dress in the unfortunately named town of Weed. (*Miss! It says Weed!* Thanks, Steinbeck.) But we never meet them, never get to hear them speak, and so Curley's wife stands out. She's young and newly married, and she's also dissatisfied with her life. And over the years, she's been studied by so many teenagers around the world that it's worth examining what she teaches us about being a young woman – about desire, about longing, and about the limitations within which you have to exist.

*Of Mice and Men* is primarily a novel about loneliness. It's set in the Salinas Valley in California in the 1930s, a time when migrant workers headed west to escape the effects of the Great Depression and the Wall Street Crash. Its two main characters lodge themselves in our minds as soon as they appear, stepping out into a clearing by the river, its banks shaded by sycamores and printed with the tracks of rabbits and raccoons. There's George, the smaller man, wiry and sharp-eyed. And then there's Lennie, a huge, shambling hulk of a guy, as happy and innocent as George is cautious and watchful. They have found work on a ranch, but they know this is only temporary. They're used to packing up their belongings and moving on, rarely making friends and never putting down roots. The men they meet on the ranch are also outsiders. They've been driven west by bankruptcies and foreclosures, by the drought and the Dust Bowl, ravaging the farmlands of the Midwest and the Great Plains. When I've taught *Of Mice and Men* in the past, I've begun by showing students Dorothea Lange's famous images of migrant workers and their families, living in tents and cars, their clothes patched and ragged, their faces etched with exhaustion and hunger. Lange's photographs capture a breadline in San Francisco and deserted farms in Oklahoma, highways heading into the distance, an advert offering cotton pickers a wage of seventy-five cents. In one image, *Toward Los Angeles*, two men walk along a long, straight, dusty road. Both are in jeans, dark shirts, wide-brimmed hats. One, the taller, carries a battered suitcase; his smaller companion has a holdall slung over one shoulder. The taller man could be Lennie. The smaller one could be George. They are passing an advertising hoarding for Southern Pacific Railways, in which a suited businessman reclines in a seat. The slogan exhorts: 'Next time, try the train. Relax.'

On this ranch full of lonely men there is one young woman. She's married to Curley. And that's important, because Curley, unlike all the other men, *does* belong. His father owns the ranch, and therefore he struts around, cocky and swaggering. His high-heeled boots tell us – as every hardworking student knows – that he does not need to do any physical work. Instead, he picks fights, throws his weight around and tries to intimidate Lennie. Like George, he is small, but unlike George, he is the kind of little guy who, in Candy's words, 'hates big guys . . . Kind of like he's mad at 'em because he ain't a big guy'. And he has a wife. We're told that he wears 'a glove fulla Vaseline' on his left hand, to keep it soft for her, and if you've ever had to explain that reference to a class of fourteen-year-old boys you'll know that you've definitely earned your teaching stripes. The fact that he has a wife at all, in this intensely male world populated by drifters and outsiders, elevates him above everyone else on the ranch. His wife is both a possession and a trophy, known to us only by her status. As many a teenage girl has observed in disgust, we never even get to know her name.

We hear about Curley's wife before we actually meet her. We learn that she's pretty – 'purty' – but she's only been married for a fortnight and she's already giving other men the eye. According to Candy – who confides in George in a whisper, checking to see if anyone is listening – she's a tart. When she first appears, she's like an exercise in symbolism, with her rouged lips, red nails and red mules with ostrich feathers (highly unsuitable, you'd think, if you live on a ranch). She stands in the doorway, cutting off the sunshine, drawing attention to her body and giving the men an arch, playful smile. Steinbeck definitely lays the warnings on thick: she might as well have a giant flashing danger sign on her head. Lennie is fascinated by her. George tells him to keep away – she's poison, a bitch, a tramp. You know, somehow, that we haven't seen the last of her.

But Curley's wife is also a lesson for teenagers in looking beyond the surface. What Steinbeck also wants us to know about Curley's wife is that she's just as lonely as everyone else in the novel. She's constantly begging for attention. She always seems to be trying to find out where Curley is, but we don't feel that she actually wants to know: she just wants to have a reason to go into the barn and talk to people. The second time we meet her, it's a Saturday evening. Lennie and Candy are in Crooks's room. All the other men have gone into town – they're visiting the local brothel, old Susy's place – and, as Curley's wife scornfully puts it, 'they left all the weak ones behind': innocent Lennie with the mind of a child, elderly Candy with his missing hand and proud Crooks with his aching back and pain-tightened face. She is in an odd mood, restless. She sneers and picks arguments. At one point, horribly, she threatens to have Crooks lynched. Candy accuses her of wanting to make trouble, saying that she has 'no call foolin' aroun'' with other guys'. Yet Steinbeck makes it clear that if Curley's wife wasn't there in Crooks's room with the three remaining men, she'd be completely on her own, knowing that her husband of just two weeks has gone off to Susy's brothel with the others and left her behind. It's hardly surprising that she's desperate for company.

*Of Mice and Men* was an instant hit with readers. The first stage production of the novel opened less than three months after it was first published, with the first film version following two years later. Steinbeck always intended the novel to be performed, as well as read, and he had definite ideas as to how the characters should be portrayed. In 1938 he wrote to Claire Luce, who was starring as Curley's wife in an adaptation of the novel at the Music Box Theatre on Broadway, with his thoughts about the character's backstory. She had grown up, Steinbeck said, in 'an atmosphere of fighting and suspicion', learning very early to trust nobody. She had also learned that her sexuality was to be both put on display and jealously guarded. On the one hand, she 'knows instinctively that if she is to be noticed at all, it will be because someone finds her sexually desirable'. On the other, she has been told 'over and over that she must remain a virgin because that was the only way she could get a husband. This was harped on so often that it became a fixation.'

Steinbeck's words sum up, very neatly, the situation that so many young women find themselves in: told that they need to make themselves attractive, to present themselves in a particular way, but warned at the same time about the judgements that will be made about their appearance and behaviour, especially if they act on their desires. Just like the Duchess in Robert Browning's poem, Curley's wife is subject to constant scrutiny. She's more defiant and more willing to hit out. But she still exists in an environment that is deeply restrictive and must walk a difficult tightrope, aware of the perils that attend on any slip.

How do teenage girls learn how to be in the world, how to behave? You spend a lot of time, as an adolescent girl, being told what you should look like and how you should act. Do this, but don't do that. Behave like this, but don't behave like that, because if you do, this is what people will think of you. At the same time, you're trying to disentangle what *you* want, and what you want to be, from what you're told you should want and want to be. And the voices telling you what to do are often so insistent that it's hard to work out whether you actually want to listen to them at all.

When I was growing up, our guide to life was *Jackie*, the weekly magazine published by D. C. Thomson between 1964 and 1993. My introduction to *Jackie* came early, via my two older sisters. Their copy of *Jackie* dropped through the letterbox on a Thursday morning along with the *Daily Express* and my copy of *Twinkle*, 'the picture paper specially for little girls'. They'd pore over photo stories and beauty tips; I'd immerse myself in the adventures of Nurse Nancy, repairing toys at her dolls' hospital. But the lure of *Jackie* was too great. Spying my chance, I'd sneak it away and hide in a corner, trying not to crinkle the thin, shiny pages. I found out about spots and friendship traumas; how to style your hair and discover your personality type. I read quizzes and interviews, careers advice and Cathy and Claire's problem page. And I learned about boys. Getting a boyfriend, it seemed, was what being a teenage girl was all about.

I was only six years old at the time, but for my sisters, boyfriends were very much in the present. They were fifteen and seventeen, and I'd got used to various teenage boys hanging round the house. Sometimes, on a Sunday morning if Mum was busy, my sisters would be told to take me to church. These were some of my favourite times, growing up. We'd head off in the right direction, me trotting along to try to keep up, and make our way to the local newsagent, where we'd spend the collection money on crisps and sweets. Then we'd go to the park. There was a huge concrete pipe there, graffiti-scarred and sun-warmed. We'd sit on top of it and my sisters would talk about whoever they were going out with at the time, who they fancied, what the gossip was at school. I'd drink lemonade and munch Toffos and listen, entranced. Over time, I heard about their wedding plans and where they wanted to live; how they'd decorate their houses and what they'd call their children. They had it all worked out. They just had to find the right boy.

A few years later, when I reached secondary school, it felt as if someone had turned up the heat on life. Almost overnight, boys had become an obsession. All the talk was of who fancied whom, how you could tell if a boy was interested in you, how to flirt without seeming too obvious. There was a way of working out if you were destined to be with someone that involved writing both of your names and then calculating how many times the letters of the word 'LOVE' appeared in them. You added the numbers together until you had a two-digit number left, and whatever number this was corresponded to how compatible you were. Ninety-seven per cent! It must be love. All you had to do was get him to notice you first.

And all of this mattered, because having a boyfriend was a marker of status. It meant that you were more of a person, a step further along the road to becoming an adult. The optimum was to have a boyfriend who was maybe a year or two older than you, possibly even at a different school for added glamour. If your boyfriend was in your year, he should be someone who other girls fancied (putting you ahead of the pack: he'd chosen *you*, not them) but not someone who played around. He should also be someone who other boys respected and perhaps even looked up to. You didn't want someone who was too low down the teenage food chain, after all.

He shouldn't be either too clever or too stupid. He should preferably have an air of not trying, being a little bit of an underachiever, as if he'd made a conscious decision not to exert himself too much. All these minute calibrations of who was acceptable and who wasn't; the careful weighing-up of cool.

Reading *Jackie* now is both intriguing and alarming. It's a glimpse into an age that seems in many ways more innocent than today, its pages filled with drawings of doe-eyed girls showing off the latest fashions. They're the kinds of images that I can imagine Curley's wife poring over, and perhaps modelling herself on, a glimpse into a world of glamour and possibilities, far removed from her own. But *Jackie*'s insistent focus on boys asserts a kind of compulsory sameness, a feeling that being in a relationship is the only thing a teenage girl should ever want. Articles tell you how to find your ideal boy and capture his heart, offer advice on flirting and first dates. There's a constant sense of agonizing over what to do and what to think. Having a boyfriend – when you finally achieve this goal – is not so much about desire as about fitting in, being able to take part in a public show of dates and red roses and huge satin Valentine's cards. It's a complex world, as coded and elaborate as a medieval courtly romance. You need to be desirable, but not too available; flirtatious and friendly, but not desperate. That tightrope, again.

Curiously, though, I don't remember *Jackie* ever addressing the topic of sex. Physical desire – once it went beyond kissing – was neatly avoided, as if it was too complicated and dangerous to deal with. And the idea of being anything other than heterosexual was never entertained. What if the person you gazed at across a crowded classroom was not a boy, but another girl? What if you were scared of being different and didn't know what to do? What if you didn't want to be in a relationship at all? *Jackie* wasn't going to help. You'd have to find your own ways of coping.

Teenage girls in the UK would have to wait until the late 1980s for anything more explicit. In 1988, the magazine *More!* was launched, with its Position of the Fortnight and advice that was far franker than anything Cathy and Claire ever offered. We gathered round it at breaktime, just as intrigued as we had been by *Forever*. How can you . . . ? How does that . . . ? *Oh.* We read about talking to your partner. We read about finding out what turns you on, about exploring yourself (exploring yourself!) and about the fact that sex wasn't just about pleasing boys. It was also about pleasing yourself and being able to take control. And if this felt revolutionary back in the late 1980s, it would perhaps be even more so today, in an era when exposure to pornography – often violent and coercive – has become an uncomfortable part of many young people's lives, creating its own norms as to what relationships should consist of and setting up expectations that teenagers often feel pressurized to fulfil.

Curley's wife never gets the chance to please herself. She's perpetually all dressed up with nowhere to go, and there doesn't seem to be any possibility of anything better. She tells Lennie that she could have made something of herself, that she dreamed of being in the movies. People said they'd help her – an actor who promised to let her join his show, a guy who told her she was a natural – but things didn't work out. Her mother wouldn't let her go with the first man because she was only fifteen, and the second promised he'd write but she never got a letter. So she married Curley, not because she loved him or even because she liked him, but just to get away. She's scathing about Curley, who 'spends all his time sayin' what he's gonna do to guys he don't like'. She's actually quite pleased about the fact that Lennie has crushed Curley's hand, commenting that 'sometimes I'd like to bust him myself'. We get the sense that she's never had much of a chance to decide what she wants from life, as opposed to what other people think she should want. We're not told how old she is, but it seems she's still in her late teens. It's a pretty bleak existence.

I've heard plenty of teenage readers over the years argue that Curley's wife is responsible for what happens to her in the novel's catastrophic fifth chapter. She goes into the barn, knowing that Lennie will be there. She tells him that she is lonely, consoles him over the death of his puppy and confides in him about her longings and dissatisfactions. She invites him to stroke her hair, knowing that he is naive and susceptible, that he will be flattered by the attention she pays him. But then, things escape from her control. She's afraid that Lennie will mess up her hair, so she tells him to let go, but he's scared. He puts his hand over her mouth, to quieten her down, but she struggles. He shakes her. And then she lies still. Lennie has broken her neck. In death, Steinbeck writes, 'all the meanness and the planning and the discontent and the ache for attention were all gone from her face'. It's as if death is a cleansing, a bringer of peace.

But hang on. How can we expect Curley's wife to be anything other than discontented and desperate for attention, given the life she leads? Is it fair to think she could have been otherwise? She was stuck somewhere that she didn't exactly choose, married to a man who seemed like her only chance of escape. Lennie was a distraction, someone who would give her – even just for a few minutes – the feeling that someone liked her and was interested in her. He possibly doesn't even understand what it is that she tells him, the yearnings and dreams that nobody else cares about. But just the fact that he is there, and will listen, is important.

I've taught *Of Mice and Men* in both mixed and single-sex schools. Girls tend to be more sympathetic to Curley's wife, and certainly understand why she feels so trapped, so desperate for any kind of outlet. Boys can, on the surface, be more judgemental. But often their jeering is purely performative, an act that helps them to stay on the right side of those complicated criteria of social acceptability. The things they might say in front of their peers, in whole-class discussion, can be very different from the observations they make when I speak to them individually, going round the classroom, looking at their work. It's these one-to-one conversations, enabling me to tease out half-formed thoughts and draw attention to specific pieces of evidence, that frequently elicit the most thoughtful responses.

I don't know how many essays, around the world, have been written about Curley's wife, how many character analyses, how much ink and paper. One worksheet I was given early on in my career – and found, again, while I was writing this chapter – began with the question 'Curley's Wife: Miss Dynamite or innocent victim?' Of course, the correct answer is that she's neither. She's a complicated mixture: unhappy and unfulfilled, and very definitely misunderstood. She's bored and therefore acts out in order to get attention. People *think* they know her, but what they think they know is based on the surface. The way the men describe her – as jailbait, a rat trap – tells us an awful lot about them and their ability to control themselves, as if the very presence of this one young woman is enough to taunt and tantalize them. It's as though all their self-loathing has been transferred on to her, making her the focus for all their inadequacies and their sense of what they don't have.

Many schools, nowadays, have chosen not to teach *Of Mice and Men*. The novel's demise was hastened in England and Wales in 2014 by the decision of the then Secretary of State for Education, Michael Gove, to prohibit texts by non-British writers for study at GCSE. *Of*

*Mice and Men* became synonymous with a lack of adventurousness and ambition, the kind of thinking that led teachers to rely on the tried-and-tested, on whatever happened to be in their stock cupboard. Some schools decided to use the novel with younger students instead. But many teachers have found it increasingly uncomfortable to teach a novel that contains so much racist language, where the character of Crooks is subject to open insult and prejudice. So *Of Mice and Men* has been taken outside, like Candy's poor old dog, and put out of its misery. Even curriculum staples can reach their use-by date. It seems that Curley's wife is going to be left to rest in peace at last, with her dreams of stardom and her hopes for a different kind of future. And other characters will come to take her place, to be the misunderstood young women who teenagers analyse and write essays about.

Meanwhile, teenagers will continue to learn those unofficial lessons, about fitting in and being judged, about working out what you want, and about the whole minefield of sex and relationships. These lessons have always been hard, but they are perhaps even harder nowadays, with the advent of social media. All those fumbling mistakes, all those gauche attempts at presenting yourself in a particular way: they're now shared and Snapchatted and turned into memes, plastered across the internet for evermore. Imagine being perpetually confronted with all those moments you'd like to forget, or finding that someone has sent intimate photographs of you to half of your year group. Let's not forget, though, that the internet has also made spaces for teen-agers to be themselves, to find that other people share their doubts and insecurities, and to recognize that it's okay not to want the things that the mainstream holds up as objects of desire. The world is more various than it ever seemed back in the 1980s, incorrigibly plural. And that has brought negatives, but it has its good sides too.

The internet brought about the demise of *Jackie* and its counterparts, *Patches* and *Blue Jeans* and *My Guy*, with their photo stories and endless insistence on romance as the be-all and end-all. *Forever*, though, is still in print. In 2019, it was chosen by a group of critics as one of the hundred novels that had had the biggest impact on their lives. Amazon describes it as 'the bravest, freshest, fruiti-est and most honest account of first love, first sex and first heartbreak ever written for teens'. The cover of its latest edition features a large, ripe cherry.

I imagine Curley's wife, nowadays. She'd be on Insta-gram, definitely. She'd think very carefully about how she wanted to appear: fully made-up, the right angles and lighting, airbrushed and filtered. She'd wear her best clothes and practise her pout. People would undoubt-edly judge her, because – it seems – people always will judge young women for doing what they want to do, working out who they want to be. But I hope she'd be less lonely, less desperate for attention. Maybe she'd have her own YouTube channel; maybe she'd be an influencer. And maybe she wouldn't even be Curley's wife at all. Because for all the messages that teenage girls receive, one of the most important should be that they don't need to bow to pressure and settle down; that relationships and marriage aren't the be-all and end-all.

There's a creative writing activity that I used to get students to do. It involved imagining that you were Curley's wife, writing from beyond the grave about your life on the ranch and your need for something else from your existence. It was a task that unlocked all kinds of things that a straightforward essay just wouldn't allow for, an exercise in empathy and subtlety. Students wrote about thwarted ambitions, about restlessness, about recognizing that you'd made the wrong choice and now had to live with it. Girls often drew on their own anger at being judged by appearances, knowing that no matter what they looked like or how they dressed, it would be interpreted in ways that weren't theirs to control. Boys who had hooted and catcalled when Curley's wife first appeared learned a lot about having to see the world through her eyes. Many students looked at the people around them – including their own families – and thought about what it would be like to be stuck in a marriage with someone you didn't love but couldn't get away from. And in doing this, they grew. Because this is one of the things that books do. They get you to think about characters and to think about them carefully, tactfully, reading between the lines. They ask: what would this feel like, to be in this world and faced with these choices? And then, having drawn you into whichever character you're studying, they invite you to look back outwards, at the people around you in the real world, and open up the possibility of seeing them in a new light.

The one thing I never liked to do, though, was to give Curley's wife – this famously nameless character – a name. Some of my students loved to speculate about what she might be called. They looked up the most popular girls' names in the USA at the time she might have been born; they drew up shortlists and argued over possibilities. But I prefer it if she's left anonymous. That way, she can be everywoman. She can be every teenage girl who's ever been judged by her appearance, told one moment that she needs to dress to impress and warned the next that she's 'asking for it'. She can be every young woman who's ticked the boxes life sets out for her but still feels unsettled and restricted. She can be everyone who's ever felt that ache of a different kind of life pulling at them, a desire that they might never get the chance to fulfil. And if she wants a name, she can choose one for herself.

# On rising, like air: *I Know Why the Caged Bird Sings* by Maya Angelou

We need books for different reasons. Sometimes, we need them to offer us an escape, an alternative world in which we can lose ourselves. Sometimes we need them to stir us up and open our eyes to injustice. Sometimes we need them to comfort us and wrap us in their warmth. And sometimes we need them to put iron in our spines, to help us to square our shoulders and face a world that seems unbearably difficult.

When my dad died suddenly, when I had just turned twenty-one, the book that kept me putting one foot in front of the other was an unexpected one: *An Evil Cradling*, the Northern Irish writer Brian Keenan's account of the years he spent as a hostage in Beirut in the late 1980s. It was a deliberate choice. I didn't want to read about loss, and I absolutely didn't want to read self-help books or collections of maudlin poems. I wanted to read about humans who had found themselves, suddenly, in appalling circumstances, and had to dig down to their very core in order to survive. Keenan's book was full of fire and anger and humanity. It raged and blazed and was also unexpectedly funny, with flashes of the kind of black, bleak humour that was helping my mum and me to get through each day. It didn't matter that

Keenan wasn't writing about bereavement. It was enough, for me, that he had done the hard yards and wasn't afraid of the difficult emotions involved. When people offered platitudes, I gritted my teeth and turned again to Brian, stuck in his filthy cell, his situation an unexpected but somehow fitting parallel to mine.

There have been times, during my career, when I've been aware that students have responded to particular texts in a similar way. Again, they're not always the texts you'd expect. Years ago, my A-level students were exploring Matthew Arnold's poem 'Dover Beach'. The poem, written in the mid nineteenth century, describes the breakdown of faith and the indifference of the natural world to human suffering. Depressing, the class concluded: why do poets never write anything *cheerful*? But one girl, whose mother was terminally ill, said that she thought Arnold's message was pretty true, actually. The poem's astringent honesty spoke to her far more clearly than any attempt at consolation could have done. Life's hard, but that's just the way it is, Arnold seemed to be saying. Take a deep breath. You can do this. A text can become a talisman, bracing us against difficulties; a silent friend at our shoulder whose presence is enough to help us carry on.

In his book *Empireland: How Imperialism Has Shaped Modern Britain*, Sathnam Sanghera describes a mural of Rudyard Kipling's poem 'If' at the University of Manchester. The poem had been painted over by students who objected to Kipling's imperialism, and had been partly replaced by a mural of Maya Angelou's poem 'Still I Rise'. Significantly, the students had not obliterated 'If' entirely. It remained visible underneath, creating what Sanghera describes as 'a quietly profound piece of work': a palimpsest of resistance, not just the fight but what was being fought against. Angelou's poem is one of defiance and self-determination. There are questions: 'Did you want to see me broken? Bowed head and lowered eyes?' And, threading its way through the stanzas, a steady insistent pulse: 'But still, like air, I'll rise.'

You don't have to look hard to find examples of people for whom Maya Angelou shines as a beacon. Paying tribute to Angelou on her death in 2014, Barack Obama said that she had 'helped generations of Americans find their rainbow amidst the clouds, and inspired the rest of us to be our best selves'. Michelle Obama described her words as 'so powerful they carried a little black girl from the south side of Chicago all the way to the White House'. Malorie Blackman credits Angelou as a huge influence on her own career, with 'Still I Rise' carrying an important message 'about having courage, as a person, as a woman, and as a Black woman'. People write of Angelou's work helping them to survive abusive relationships, to rise above poverty and realize that their lives didn't have to be ordinary. In her obituary of Angelou, the writer and broadcaster Afua Hirsch describes her own younger self, 'growing up in a suburban corner of England, clinging fiercely to her books and even when not reading them, inhaling the spirit of her struggle from the titles alone'. Angelou's words can be found emblazoned across walls, engraved on jewellery, worn on T-shirts and badges. If the words themselves aren't enough, you can buy a Maya Angelou bust, or a pair of socks depicting a jaunty Angelou in a red two-piece suit, dancing.

I first heard of Maya Angelou when I was nineteen, when a friend a couple of years younger than me studied *I Know Why the Caged Bird Sings* for A level. It was felt, at the time, to be a daring addition to the syllabus: not just a text by a woman, but a text by a Black woman, recounting her experiences of growing up in the USA during a time of segregation and prejudice. I didn't actually read it until many years later. It was one of those books I always intended to get round to sometime, a book that, for some reason, never quite made its way to the top of my to-be-read pile. Part of the issue was my own stubbornness. So many people had told me to read it; so many people said it would change my life. I was sceptical. I had my own list of books that had changed my life, and they'd all been ones that I'd found out about for myself. I didn't need anyone else's ideas about what might be life-changing.

When I finally got round to reading Angelou's most famous book, though, I found its message – of bravery and grace, of digging deep and never giving in – a hugely powerful one, and I could see why so many people have drawn so much strength from it. It is narrated with warmth and generosity. Reading it, and exploring the role Angelou has played in the lives of millions, reminds us of the capacity books have to help people feel less alone: to feel that someone, somewhere, has felt similar feelings of trauma and exclusion, and survived.

*I Know Why the Caged Bird Sings* doesn't appear on any current exam syllabuses in the United Kingdom, but it is a popular choice for coursework at A level, which accounts for a fifth of students' overall grade and allows them to select the texts they write about. It's also popular as a book to recommend for private reading outside of school. In some ways, this perhaps makes it more powerful. Someone – an English teacher or a school librarian or another student – mentions it because they think there might be something in it that speaks to you. Maybe they've picked up, in the way people do, that you're struggling and need the kind of comfort that a book can give. Maybe they recognize your anger and your need to know that someone else has trodden the same path. In my experience, it's the kind of book that works best this way, as a careful suggestion rather than an imperative must-read, passing from one person to another when it's the right time for it to do so. It needs to be read in a quiet corner, on the kind of day when you can lose yourself in it for as long as you like without being disturbed. When you finally uncurl yourself, several hours later, your limbs will be stiff and it might have gone dark outside without you realizing. You'll feel as if centuries have gone by.

There are other reasons, too, why Angelou's memoir is possibly better read alone, rather than taught as part of the formal curriculum. Many of the events it deals with are so traumatic that to impose it on whole classes, to pick it apart and analyse it in the way that the discipline of English often demands, raises all manner of ethical issues. These concern not only our duty to our own students but also our duty to Angelou herself. As readers, we owe it to writers to read sensitively. This is especially the case when writing is autobiographical, and when it acts – as Angelou's writing does – as a testimony of pain.

*I Know Why the Caged Bird Sings* is the story of Maya Angelou's life from her birth to the age of seventeen. As such, it speaks very powerfully to teenage readers. I discussed it with my sixth-form reading group, away from the structures and constraints of the formal curriculum. In this context, conversation could be more exploratory and questioning than it might have been in a taught lesson with objectives to fulfil and an exam to aim towards. The students all commented on the hugeness of the struggles faced by someone who was of a similar age to them: Angelou experienced enough in her first seventeen years, they felt, to fill several lifetimes. She was born in April 1928 as Marguerite Johnson ('Maya' came from a childhood nickname) in St Louis. When she was just three years old, she and her older brother, Bailey, were sent to live with their paternal grandmother, known as Momma, and their uncle, Willie, in the town of Stamps, Arkansas. In telling the story of her early childhood, Angelou gives a vivid picture of what it was to grow up in a society that was deeply segregated. From the very first chapter, we are aware of the gap between the young Angelou's perception of herself and what she would have liked to be. 'Sweet little white girls,' she comments, were 'everybody's dream of what was right with the world.' As a young child, she would dream of waking up with blue eyes and long blonde hair, rather than being a skinny Black girl with 'nappy black hair, broad feet and a space between her teeth that would hold a number-two pencil', wearing a dress cut down from a white woman's cast-offs. Growing up with this persistent sense of inadequacy, of wrongness, was painful. As Angelou said in one of her most frequently quoted statements, for the Southern Black girl, 'being aware of her displacement is the rust on the razor that threatens the throat'.

The rhythms of everyday life in Stamps are depicted in detail. Angelou is brilliant at evoking the sensory memories of childhood: the soft light of early mornings; the smells of fruit and vegetables and kerosene in Momma's store; the conversations of the customers, laughing and joking and passing the time of day. There are rhymes and songs, games with Bailey in the yard, stealing pickles and listening to gossip. There are local characters, such as Mr McElroy in his brown three-piece suit, Sister Monroe with her gold-crowned tooth, and the Reverend Howard Thomas, who laughs 'like a hog with the colic' and eats the best parts of the chicken at dinner whenever he comes to visit. And annual rituals: the canning of vegetables and making of sausages, the fish fry with its mounds of potato salad and fried chicken, the passing-on of notes on Valentine's Day.

But there is also, of course, the harshness of life in the Deep South, its poverty and its ingrained racism. Many of Momma's customers work in the cotton fields, carrying out exhausting physical work for a wage that barely allows them to make ends meet. There are taunts and insults and the ever-present threat of the Ku Klux Klan. In one early chapter, a visitor arrives with a message for Uncle Willie. A Black man has 'messed with a white lady', and 'some of the boys' will be coming over later. The young Marguerite knows that they are not 'boys' at all, but Klansmen, intent on violence. She and Bailey are sent to take the potatoes and onions out of their storage bin, and Uncle Willie climbs in. 'Then we covered him with potatoes and onions, layer upon layer, like a casserole.' It's the best way the family knows of keeping Willie safe. The description has a matter-of-fact tone, but for my sixth-formers, this was just the first in a series of shocking incidents. One commented: 'You can read about segregation in History, but this is different, because it's first-person, it's real.' Another agreed: 'You know it's autobiographical, but at the same time, it's so awful that you want it to be fiction. You don't want it to have actually happened.'

Another disturbing early incident concerns a group of

white girls, described by Angelou as 'powhitetrash', who attempt to humiliate Momma. Momma is standing in front of her store, singing. The girls mimic her behaviour, pull hideous faces, and try at length to provoke a reaction. Finally, their leader does a handstand, revealing that under her dress, she is completely naked. Marguerite is angry and tearful, but Momma does not react. She simply carries on singing, and bids the girls goodbye when they decide to leave. Angelou observes that 'Whatever the contest had been out front, I knew Momma had won.'

Reading the early part of Angelou's memoir, I'm reminded in many ways of Harper Lee's evocation of a Southern childhood in *To Kill a Mockingbird*, with its dares and escapades, sibling loyalties, admonitions about disobedience and the need to be seen and not heard. Except, of course, that the spaces inhabited by the young Marguerite and Bailey would have been very different to those occupied by Scout and Jem. In Stamps, Angelou recalls, 'the segregation was so complete that most Black children didn't really, absolutely, know what whites looked like. Other than that they were different, to be dreaded.' In my head, I transplant Scout to Stamps, and imagine her musing idly about the little Black girl sent on errands by her grandmother, crossing the white part of town quickly, to avoid trouble. One day, their eyes meet. But then, things being as they are, the little Black girl looks away, shyly, and carries on her way.

The relative safety of Marguerite's early childhood comes to an end when she is seven years old. This is when her father comes to visit, and when, as Angelou puts it, her world 'humpty-dumptied, never to be put back together again'. She and Bailey are taken to St Louis to live with their mother and her partner, Mr Freeman, amidst a swirl of violent, swaggering uncles and hot city streets. They learn about the local racketeers and whiskey salesmen, the flashy-suited gamblers, the local taverns and blues bars. It's a different kind of life. It's also where Marguerite experiences the trauma that will define her, and that stands out, for many readers, as one of the most shocking sequences of events they have ever read about. For Mr Freeman – described as a quiet man who moves gracefully, apparently devoted to Marguerite's mother – sexually assaults Marguerite early one morning, and makes her promise not to tell, saying that if she ever reveals what has happened, he will have to kill her beloved brother. A few weeks later, he rapes her. She is just eight years old. When the rape is discovered, Mr Freeman is arrested and put on trial, and found guilty. He is sentenced to a year and a day in prison, but is released the next day. Later that evening, a policeman arrives with news. Mr Freeman has been found beaten to death.

The details of what happens to Marguerite in St Louis are horrific. I warned my students before they read the book that parts of it would be harrowing. In our reading group meeting, in my bright, safe classroom at the end of school one quiet Friday, they talked about their feelings of revulsion and anger at Mr Freeman's actions. They spoke of feeling sickened, of having to put the book down and take some time away from it. There were things that they had found particularly difficult to read, such as Marguerite's own desire for attention, and her sense – before the rape occurs – of feeling wanted and special. There was also the knowledge that she was an eight-year-old child who had been made to suffer something utterly sickening. Some hadn't wanted to read on, but had done so out of a sense of duty to Angelou, feeling that they owed it to her to accompany her on the rest of her journey.

It's because Angelou's writing evokes such powerful feelings that I am deeply conflicted about using it as a set text. Look on the internet and you can find a host of study guides to *I Know Why the Caged Bird Sings*, with quiz questions, infographics and even revision videos. Does this sanitize it, flatten it out, reduce its power? And what about students who might themselves have suffered abuse and rape? How might they be affected by not only having to study a text that deals with these themes, but by having to answer questions on it, listen to other students discussing it, revise it for an exam?

In our reading group meeting, we discussed the concept of trigger warnings and whether Angelou's memoir should be accompanied by one. The students' views were mixed. One remarked that a specific warning – telling readers exactly what happened to the young Angelou, rather than just the general warning that I'd given them beforehand – might have put him off reading the book. It had definitely been a difficult read, he said, but the experience had been an important one. 'It was really sobering.

I've never read anything like it before.' Another was surprised that schools might use it as a set text, as his reaction
had been so visceral that he felt it needed to be read, and
processed, in private. A third had been warned by her
mother, beforehand, that she might find the book upset-
ting, but had continued nevertheless. 'I kind of felt I
should. You can't hide from the fact that things like that
happen, and if other people have to experience them
then it's not fair for me to be able to choose not to read
about them.' Their responses were thoughtful, mature,
deeply respectful of Angelou's experiences and her desire
to share them. But I'd still think very carefully about recommending the book to younger students. I would want
to be absolutely sure they were aware of its themes. And
I would want them to know it was okay to stop reading if
they needed to go no further.

The most traumatic work I encountered at school was
not a book, but a film: *Threads*, the 1984 nuclear war
drama written by Barry Hines, author of *A Kestrel for a
Knave*. We watched it as part of our compulsory GCSE
Religious Studies course, during the summer of Year
Ten. Looking back, I'm not sure how *Threads* actually
fitted in with the syllabus. Maybe it didn't: maybe, it
being the end of the summer term, it was something we
were shown to fill in a few stray lessons when everyone
was tired and the exams still a year away. What I do
remember is that for three consecutive afternoons a
huge television set was wheeled into our classroom and

we watched, with a mixture of horror and fascination, as the tensions of the Cold War reached their peak and a confrontation between the Soviet Union and the USA led to warnings of an imminent attack on the UK. The four-minute warning was sounded: in Sheffield, where the film was set, city-centre shoppers froze and a woman wet herself in terror. The stories of ordinary citizens were interwoven with sequences from Protect and Survive public information films and news broadcasts charting the death toll. It was all much too real. It could have been us. My imagination – far too active already – went into overdrive. Where would I be if the sirens ever went off? If we managed to build a shelter in the cupboard under the stairs, could we possibly survive? How many of us would die? I lay awake at night, my mind replaying images of hideous burns and people reduced to eating rats in order to stay alive. I still can't contemplate watching *Threads* again, because I know exactly what it will do to me, and the idea of showing it to a class of fifteen-year-olds seems appalling. Were I to consider screening it nowadays, I'd expect, at the very least, to have to talk it through with my line manager, to send a letter home warning parents of its content and to give students the right not to watch it. Back in the 1980s, we were just expected to cope.

There are other books, nowadays, that I would be very hesitant about teaching. There are some excellent Young Adult novels, for example, about teenagers facing terminal illness or the loss of a parent: powerful and deeply moving stories about confronting nightmares and facing darkness. I have put them on reading lists and recommended them to many students. But when I see them being taught as part of the formal curriculum, I always wonder what it would be like to be a student going through a similar experience, sitting in lessons where you have to read about something that cuts through to the most painful parts of your being. How would it feel to have to sit and listen to your classmates discussing characters and situations that you understood only too well? When I recommend novels about difficult subjects, I make sure students know what they're about, and warn them that parts of the story might be hard to read. It is absolutely vital that teenagers know that these books exist. However, the emotions they deal with are so big and so raw that the cluttered, public world of the classroom is not the best place for them. They need to be experienced in a different and more private setting.

In *I Know Why the Caged Bird Sings*, the young Marguerite's response to the trauma of her sexual assault and rape is to stop talking. She blames herself for Mr Freeman's death, and for the next five years, the only person she speaks to is her brother, Bailey. For the first few weeks, her relatives in St Louis are sympathetic, but as time goes on, her refusal to speak is seen as impudence. She is punished for being 'uppity', beaten 'by any relative who felt himself offended'. Eventually, she and Bailey are sent back to live with Momma in Stamps.

The person who finally manages to coax Marguerite out of her silence is Mrs Flowers. Described as 'the aristocrat of Black Stamps', Mrs Flowers is gracious, educated and highly respected. She shows Marguerite a glimpse of a different world, a world where people are 'like people in English novels'. She knows that Marguerite needs someone to bring her out of herself, and does this through her kindness, through making her lemonade and cookies, and lending her books. She also teaches Marguerite that words are more than marks on a page. It takes the human voice, she says, 'to infuse them with the shades of deeper meaning'.

But there are still hurdles to be overcome, injustices to withstand. In our reading group, we pore over the incidents recounted by Angelou, the episodes where Marguerite faces overt, unashamed racism. In one of these, Marguerite's first employer, a rich white woman called Mrs Cullinan, refuses to call her by her real name, altering it to Margaret. Then, one day, one of Mrs Cullinan's friends remarks that even this is too long a name for a young Black girl: 'I'd never bother myself. I'd call her Mary if I were you.' Being called by a name that is not your own is, as Angelou describes it, an act that induces 'a hellish horror', the legacy, for Black people, of centuries of being called whatever white people have seen fit to call them. In another incident, a white dentist refuses to treat Marguerite when she has excruciating toothache. His policy, he says, is not to treat Black people: sickeningly, he declares that he would rather stick his hand in a dog's mouth. There's also the occasion when the white speaker at Marguerite's high school graduation, a school-board official and politician, speaks of the improvements being made to the local white school, which will have a visiting artist and new laboratory equipment. To encourage them, Marguerite and her fellow students are reminded of the talented football and basketball players who have come from their school. Marguerite, her pride at graduating turning to ashes, is enraged: 'The white kids were going to have a chance to become Galileos and Madame Curies and Edisons and Gaugins, and our boys (the girls weren't even in on it) would try to be Jesse Owenses and Joe Louises.'

Lurking behind all of these events is the threat of violence. This is most clearly apparent in two incidents involving Bailey. The first sees him late home from the cinema one night. Anxiety turns to fear: Momma's movements are jumpy and uncertain. As Angelou comments, 'The Black woman in the south who raises sons, grandsons and nephews had her heartstrings tied to a hanging noose. Any break from routine may herald for them unbearable news.' In the second, Bailey is traumatized by seeing the body of a Black man who has been lynched. The rest of the family offer what comfort they can, but Bailey is 'away in a mystery, locked in the enigma that young Southern Black boys start to unravel, start to *try* to unravel, from seven years old to death. The humourless puzzle of inequality and hate.'

'But it's not over,' one of my sixth-formers points

out. 'That's what's really shocking. She's writing about something that happened in the 1940s and it's still going on.'

We're silent. Just a few days before our meeting, a sixteen-year-old Black boy, Ralph Yarl, was shot in Kansas City by a white homeowner. Yarl had been collecting his younger brothers from a playdate, and had rung his assailant's doorbell by mistake: he was shot in the head without a single word being exchanged. George Floyd, Trayvon Martin, Eric Garner. Names upon names and a sense, for some of my students, that if they were growing up several thousand miles away then they, too, would be fearful; they, too, would need to watch where they walked and what they did. Keep your head down. Speak only when you're spoken to. Lives made small; lives restricted and hemmed in.

Marguerite's response to the restrictions imposed on her life is one of stubborn determination. She and Bailey go to live with their mother once again, this time in California. She decides to get a job working on the San Francisco streetcars, but is told that she is unable to do so because of her colour. Obstacles are put in her way. It's a situation 'stale with familiarity'. But she persists. And one day, she succeeds. It's hardly surprising, Angelou observes, that Black American women emerge as such formidable characters. 'The Black female is assaulted in her tender years by all those common forces of nature at the same time that she is caught in the tripartite crossfire of masculine prejudice, white illogical hate and Black lack of power.' It's a grounding that led the young Angelou to emerge indomitable, adamant that no artificial barriers would ever get in her way.

At the end of our reading group meeting, we discuss the book's title. We look at Angelou's poem 'Caged Bird', and explore ideas of entrapment and protest. The caged bird, Angelou says, opens his throat to sing because his wings are clipped and his feet are tied. I think of other images of caged birds: of Jane Eyre, declaring that no net ensnares her; of William Blake, protesting in his poem 'The School Boy' that the bird that is born for joy cannot sit in a cage and sing. Angelou's caged bird sings because it's the only thing he can do. My students recall the times when both Marguerite and Bailey are reduced to silence by trauma, and see the song of the caged bird as reflecting Angelou's defiant refusal to let the silence win. 'She's singing on behalf of the whole Black community,' one boy points out. 'All that control that's been denied to them – she's taking it all back. She's singing on their behalf.'

As *I Know Why the Caged Bird Sings* comes to a close, the seventeen-year-old Marguerite becomes a mother. She gets pregnant as the result of a brief relationship that she instigates, conceals the pregnancy from everyone except Bailey until she is three weeks away from giving birth, and declares that she does not want to marry the father. She will go it alone. It's the ultimate assertion of control, and my seventeen-year-old students – juggling schoolwork and part-time jobs, and nervously contemplating their university applications – are in awe of how much bravery this must have taken.

I think back to our conversation about triggers and reflect on their opposite: glimmers, a term coined by the clinical social worker Deb Dana to refer to small moments of joy or peace that help us to feel safe and give us a sense of connectedness. Readers have found glimmers aplenty in Angelou's work, and in the sense she has given them of not having to bear their struggles alone. I wonder whether we pay enough attention to the glimmers in the texts we teach, whether they are so fleeting and fragile that they are almost too precious to analyse. The points of loveliness, the glimpses of something that lifts our hearts when, again, the books we read in school escape from their boundaries in the curriculum and soar.

Years after *I Know Why the Caged Bird Sings* was published, Angelou would say that she had given birth to one son, but that she also had thousands of daughters: 'black and white and Spanish-speaking and Native American . . . fat and thin and pretty and plain, some gay and some straight'. There are, indeed, many women who count themselves amongst these daughters. There are men, too, who see Angelou as a mother, an iconic and inspirational figure. And both men and women have learned a huge amount from her memoirs, from her political activism and public speaking. Her works offer comfort, but it's comfort with an edge of steel, the kind of comfort that sets you back on your feet and gives you a gentle push in the small of your back. *You can do this*, it says. *Don't give up*. And, because Angelou knew what it was to have to pick yourself up, dust yourself down and keep going in the face of all that assails you, you take a deep breath and do as she says.

# On emptiness and desperation: *Macbeth* by William Shakespeare

There are some literary texts that we think we know. We pore over them at school and write down important facts and quotations. If we're diligent, we make flash cards and colour-coded notes. Back in the past, we'd have bought the study guide; these days, we'd watch tutorials on YouTube and chart our progress on our phones using the latest revision app. We learn what we need to, testing ourselves until we've got it right, cramming our brains full of knowledge and then scribbling it all down against the clock in the final exam, half an eye on the time. We think we've got these texts sussed.

*Macbeth* is one of these. We all know something about *Macbeth*, even if we haven't actually studied it. It's the Scottish play, the one whose name is so unlucky it can't be uttered aloud in a theatre. Key lines have worked their way into our consciousness. *Double, double, toil and trouble. By the pricking of my thumbs. Out, damned spot! When shall we three meet again?* It's the one with the witches, the ghost at the banquet, the sleepwalking. The scene where Lady Macbeth tries to wash her hands is so well known that it was used as a meme alongside the World Health Organization's advice on hand hygiene in the early days of the Covid-19 pandemic. As with so many of the texts we've

looked at, there's merch: an apron from the Globe Theatre featuring a large bottle of a lurid green substance
with the label 'Eye of Newt'; a bar of Lady Macbeth
guest soap, all wrapped up in a neat tartan package.

I did *Macbeth* myself for GCSE. I've got such a strong
visual memory of it that I can remember the notes made
on my hardbacked school copy by the person who had
the book the year before me. We had to learn Macbeth's
'Tomorrow, and tomorrow, and tomorrow' speech off
by heart, and I can still reel it off for my Year Elevens
when they whinge about having to learn quotations for
their exam, my English-teacher party piece. I've taught
the play nearly every year since I started teaching, and
one year, when I moved schools and took over a group
in mid-course, I taught it twice. People sometimes ask
whether English teachers get bored, teaching the same
texts over and over again, and my standard answer is to
point out that teachers in other subjects teach the same
things over and over again too – coastal landforms, for
example, or Pythagoras's theorem – and nobody seems
to ask *them* whether they get bored. Personally, I'd far
rather have repeated encounters with complex examples
of flawed humanity than with the lengths of the sides in
a triangle, but each to their own. Besides, one of the best
things about teaching English is the fact that every time
I teach a text, it's slightly different from the time before.
I might try a new approach or read a piece of criticism
that highlights an angle I hadn't previously considered.
And, crucially, the class in front of me is also different.

Teaching English isn't a matter of simply handing on a body of knowledge. It's the careful shaping of an encounter, the chairing of a conversation. We introduce and orchestrate; we clarify and explain. But we also ask questions that get our students to explore texts, and because the best questions are open-ended, we can never be quite sure of what answers we will get. It's like planning an expedition in territory we think we know, while being ready, all the time, for the unexpected to happen.

There are times, though, when something happens to make you look at a text, or a character, in a completely different way. As we saw with *To Kill a Mockingbird*, this can stem from a shaking-up of orthodoxies, a challenge to established views. But it can also be the result of something more personal. This is what has happened for me with *Macbeth*, and as a result, this GCSE staple has become a much more complex play.

It's easy to summarize *Macbeth*. From its opening scene, with its haunting, incantatory language, to the final confrontation between Macbeth and Macduff, the play follows a clear and bloody trajectory. There's the wounded captain, recounting his story of the traitor Macdonwald being unseamed from the nave to the chaps by Macbeth, whose sword steams with the blood of so many enemies. (My students, the bloodthirsty lot, are particularly fond of this bit.) There's that fateful encounter with the witches when Macbeth is hailed with titles he never dreamed of having; the scenes where

Macbeth agonizes over whether to murder King Duncan; the descent of a once proud and loyal warrior into a deluded shadow. Along the way, there are the markers of a mind that's becoming increasingly disturbed: floating daggers, the ghost of Banquo, hands that will never be clean again. There's the Porter, with his quips about drunkenness and its effects. (This is another perennial favourite, especially the bit about drink being an equivocator with lechery: it provokes the desire, as the Porter comments, but it takes away the performance, and I remind the boys I teach that they can indeed find lessons for life in Shakespeare's plays, four hundred years after they were written.) In class, we discuss the Divine Right of Kings and beliefs about witchcraft in Shakespeare's England. We look at doom paintings from medieval churches to see how Shakespeare's audiences might have envisioned the hell to which Macbeth would be condemned, and gaze with grim fascination at images of sinners being suspended by their ears over fiery pits, leering demons on either side. Students sometimes complain that Shakespeare didn't write his plays so that they could be pulled apart in a classroom and written about in an exam, but if Shakespeare *had* been writing his plays to be studied by teenagers, he got it absolutely right with *Macbeth*. Blood and guts, witches and intrigue, a rich historical context and even a couple of knob jokes: it's the perfect text for fifteen- and sixteen-year-olds.

And it's got Lady Macbeth too. Lady Macbeth is one of those characters we think we can sum up easily. If

Macbeth is the butcher, she's the fiend-like queen. She can certainly appear more demon than human. Look at the way she's introduced, in Act 1 Scene 5, communing with the evil spirits and asking them to take away her femininity. I point out to my students, here, that she's given the first soliloquy in the whole play. Imagine that: a female character, making her first appearance alone on stage, commanding everyone's attention. Even though she'd originally have been played by a boy actor, it's still an important moment. Her witchiness is accentuated by the way she's often dressed: all in black, as when played by Judi Dench in Trevor Nunn's 1976 production for the Royal Shakespeare Company, or in the shimmering greens worn by Ellen Terry in 1888, depicted in oils the following year by John Singer Sargent. (What Sargent's painting doesn't quite capture is that Terry's dress was embellished with the wing cases of thousands of tiny beetles. When my students find this out, they shudder: *ooh, itchy.*) As with Macbeth himself, it's easy to list the milestones along her journey to destruction, the lines that allow us to calibrate her malevolence. You can have a go yourself. *Take my milk for gall, you murdering ministers. Screw your courage to the sticking-place, and we'll not fail.* There's the bit about dashing her baby's brains out, the way she needles Macbeth and taunts him with not being enough of a man. After the slaying of Duncan, there's her impatient insistence that Macbeth just needs to wash his hands and stop whinging. But then, the guilt is too much and she goes mad, sleepwalking through her castle while

Macbeth strides around repeating the witches' prophecies to himself, convinced he cannot be beaten. When she throws herself from the battlements, he complains that he doesn't have time to grieve.

It would be easy, given all of this, to teach *Macbeth* as a play about ambition and corruption, evil and paranoia. You can turn up the other-worldliness, reduce the central characters to pantomime figures and add in a few extra toads for good measure: job done. There are plenty of precedents, after all. But I'm going to do something different. I'm going to argue that *Macbeth* is also about babies.

There's a speech near the beginning of Act 3 that is absolutely crucial to this interpretation. Macbeth is reflecting on what has happened since that fateful journey home from the battle. He is now King of Scotland, but he still isn't happy. For it is Banquo's descendants who will succeed to the throne, not Macbeth's. Macbeth has no children. He tortures himself with the thought that he has committed regicide and condemned himself to hell in order to make 'the seed of Banquo kings'. The witches have given him a 'fruitless crown' and a 'barren sceptre'. Images of emptiness, infertility. In class, I point them out and, dutifully, my students highlight them and make a note in the margin.

Sometimes, when we teach, words make us flinch. *Fruitless. Barren.* I know about those words. In May 2004, when I was thirty-one and after eighteen months of trying to get pregnant, I found out it was unlikely that I'd ever be able to conceive. I had premature ovarian failure, meaning that my eggs – the eggs I'd been born with – were essentially useless. It was an unlucky quirk of biology and something that reproductive medicine was unable to solve. My husband and I picked ourselves up, took a deep breath and applied to adopt, and ever since then, I've looked at the Macbeths in a very different way: less as a pair of power-crazed maniacs and more as a couple who are facing the emptiness of having no children. They have a numbness in their lives and will do anything to make themselves feel. They exist in a society where lineage and inheritance are everything. Looking at the Macbeths from this perspective can make us think, in turn, about how society marginalizes the experiences of those who do not have children. And this is something that teenagers need to be aware of. (The texts we teach in schools aren't good at dealing with infertility. Mrs Lyons, the infertile adoptive mother in Willy Russell's play *Blood Brothers*, is depicted as a grasping baby-snatcher. It's a stereotype that nobody seems to have tackled, yet.)

Babies and young children haunt the edges of *Macbeth*. There's the bloody child that appears to Macbeth to tell him to beware Macduff, followed by the child that tells him that he shall never be defeated until Birnam Wood has moved to Dunsinane. Pity is personified in one of Macbeth's soliloquies as a 'naked newborn babe'. The Macduffs' children – described by their father as 'all my pretty chickens' – are slaughtered on Macbeth's orders.

The witches add the finger of a 'birth-strangled babe' to their cauldron. Macduff, crucially, was 'untimely ripped' from his mother's womb. Many of these images are associated with violence and horror. The most horrific image of all, of course, occurs in the words of Lady Macbeth, who vows that she would rather dash out her own baby's brain than break a promise to her husband. If she'd do this for him, she reasons, then why isn't he prepared to kill Duncan, the one thing she wants him to do?

The baby that Lady Macbeth refers to is one of the biggest puzzles in the play. It's not a theoretical baby. It did exist. 'I have given suck,' declares Lady Macbeth. She has had a baby, and has fed a baby. But Macbeth has no children. What has happened to this baby? My students are always curious about this. The play itself doesn't tell us.

History does give us an answer, for the character of Lady Macbeth is based on a real person. Her name was Gruoch, and she was born sometime before 1015. She was married twice: first, to Gille Coemgáin, the Earl of Moray, and then, after his death, to Macbeth, whose actual name was MacBethad mac Findláich. Gruoch had at least one child from her first marriage. The one we know about is a son, Lulach, who himself ruled Scotland very briefly, between August 1057 and March 1058, before Duncan's son Malcolm became king. Shakespeare dispenses with Lulach, and I can see why, as it is tidier, dramatically, for the Macbeths to be a self-contained couple rather than having a stepson hanging round like a grumpy medieval Kevin the teenager. It's also more dramatically satisfying to have the usurper Macbeth replaced as king by Malcolm, the rightful heir to the throne: there's a sense of order being restored, a colossal breach in nature being mended. Raphael Holinshed, whose revised *Chronicles of England, Scotland, and Ireland* (1587) was Shakespeare's main historical source, does not mention Lulach either, but he does tell us that Scottish women did not give their babies to wet nurses to be fed, but 'gave them sucke themselves'. So it's probable that Gruoch did indeed 'give suck', just like her fictional counterpart.

The horrific description of what Lady Macbeth would do to her baby comes from Act 1 Scene 7, when Macbeth announces that he will 'proceed no further' with the plan to kill Duncan, and brings upon himself a volley of scorn. Students enjoy this part of the play. It's so easy to analyse the way Shakespeare manipulates language here, the way he shows Lady Macbeth's influence over her husband. I get my classes to count how many lines there are between Macbeth's initial declaration that he's not going to kill Duncan after all, and the point when it's clear that Lady Macbeth has managed to change his mind. I do this partly because they like things that they can count and quantify, but mostly because it helps to drive home just how dominant she is. Lady Macbeth takes fewer than fifty lines to convince her husband to commit murder, just a couple of minutes of stage time. She calls him a coward. ('She says he's a pussy!' said one of my students, delightedly, seizing on the reference to 'the poor cat i'th'adage'.) She claims he doesn't love her. She tells him, repeatedly, that he's not a real man, even though he's a warrior who was unseaming traitors on the battlefield just a couple of days ago. We look at the barrage of questions she barks at him, the way she needles him and gets in his face, barely giving him the chance to reply. When he finally does manage to get a word in edgewise, it's to beg her to leave him alone: 'Prithee, peace.' But she doesn't let up. Look, I tell the class. Look at the way Shakespeare conjures up an image of love and tenderness, and then destroys it. It's masterly, but it's also appalling.

> I have given suck, and know
> How tender 'tis to love the babe that milks me.
> I would, while it was smiling in my face,
> Have plucked my nipple from his boneless gums
> And dashed the brains out, had I so sworn
> As you have done to this.

'Boneless gums', I point out. How old would this baby have been? Not old enough to have any teeth: a few months, at most. Tiny and vulnerable. It should be safe in its mother's arms, but instead it's being used as a bargaining chip. *I'd kill my own baby for you*, Lady Macbeth is saying, *but you won't murder the king for me*.

I show my students a series of short videos on *Macbeth* made for the BBC's *English File* in 2012. The actor Louise Lombard talks us through interpretations that depict Lady Macbeth as some kind of 'pantomime witch', like the BBC's own 1970 production for its 'Play of the Month' series, starring Eric Porter and Janet Suzman. Lombard argues that it's more interesting to try to understand Lady Macbeth, rather than to condemn her. Her words about the baby, says Lombard, 'can be played as pure evil – as if she doesn't care. But I think the Macbeths cared deeply about this baby. And I think understanding this baby helps me to understand Lady Macbeth.' In Lombard's version, Lady Macbeth sees herself as the victim of some kind of cosmic injustice: in a society where the main role of a woman was to produce children, she has been unable to give her husband any living descendants.

Other productions have explored the Macbeths' childlessness too. Julia Ford's depiction of Lady Macbeth in the 2011 production for the Liverpool Everyman was described by Alfred Hickling in the *Guardian* as expressing 'a despairing hope that an empty throne might compensate for a barren womb'. The 2015 film version, starring Michael Fassbender and Marion Cotillard, begins with the funeral of the Macbeths' child, and sees Lady Macbeth talking to the ghost of her dead child during the sleepwalking scene. In such interpretations, the Macbeths become less an embodiment of evil and more a couple whose reactions to the world have been distorted by grief.

But wait. If Lady Macbeth has had a child, like the historical Gruoch, then why are we seeing her as the one with the problem? What about Macbeth himself? Maybe – as one of my more daring students once pointed out – all his prowess with his sword is just a displacement activity. It's certainly true that Macbeth has something to distract him. He's a warrior, in a country threatened by invaders and riven with treachery: he's so busy carving up his opponents that he doesn't have time to mourn. He has other ways of demonstrating just how masculine he is. Lady Macbeth has no such outlet. Moreover, societies have, historically, seen childlessness largely as a female problem. And this, in turn, gives us another way of understanding Lady Macbeth: why she has been depicted in the way she has, and why so many sources, throughout history, have been keen to portray her as deviant and threatening.

Exploring Lady Macbeth in her historical context allows students to examine a range of beliefs about gendered bodies, relationships and women's role in society. We look, for instance, at how Lady Macbeth's hectoring can be linked to cultural stereotypes of the shrew and the scold, those nagging women who underscore society's hatred of females who speak out of turn. And we look at the idea of the wandering womb. This concept comes ultimately from ancient Greece, but its most prominent exponent in Shakespeare's day was the physician Edward Jorden, whose treatise *A Briefe Discourse of a Disease called the Suffocation of the Mother* was published in 1603. In this belief, the womb – the 'mother' – has a clear purpose. Its job, pure and simple, is to gestate babies. If it's not doing this, it goes looking for mischief. It can roam throughout the body and cause all manner of problems; it can also cause psychological disorders, hence the term 'hysteria', from *hystera*, the Greek word for the uterus. There's a powerful reference to the wandering womb in *King Lear*, when Lear, acutely aware of his increasingly tenuous grip on sanity, cries out

> O, how this mother swells up toward my heart!
> *Hysterica passio*, down, thou climbing sorrow,
> Thy element's below!

Get back in your place, Lear is saying. When things step out of line, all manner of problems can happen.

Lady Macbeth, of course, is a woman whose womb isn't doing what it's supposed to. This childless woman is a threat. She destabilizes Scotland by persuading her husband to commit regicide. She schemes and dissembles; she looks like the innocent flower but really she's the serpent under it, her false face hiding what her false heart knows only too well. She asks the evil spirits to unsex her, to thicken her blood so that 'no compunctious visitings of nature' can get in her way – a reference that can be interpreted as wanting the spirits to stop her menstrual cycle, that most compunctious of natural visitings. She wants her milk – a substance that Shakespeare's audience would have seen as the very essence of femininity – to be turned to gall. She's so callous and unfeeling that when her agitated husband returns from killing Duncan, daggers in hand and burbling like a madman, all she does is to tell him to shut up and wash his hands. *What's done cannot be undone.* Go and change into a clean nightshirt, she insists, before anybody comes along. Just don't come to me looking for sympathy.

So Lady Macbeth is trouble, a woman who is not only *not* performing her womanly duties, but seeking to cast off her womanliness itself. Why does she do this? Ambition comes into it, certainly. But I keep coming back, again and again, to that sense of emptiness, to the feeling that there is very little else in Lady Macbeth's life. She's filling a void.

Look at the interactions Lady Macbeth has with other characters. Most of them, as you'd expect, are with her husband. She gives orders to various servants. She greets Duncan – who, of course, she's plotting to kill – and has some brief interchanges with the Scottish noblemen in the aftermath of Duncan's murder. She tries to smooth things over at the banquet when Macbeth is beside himself with terror at the sight of Banquo's ghost. And she talks to herself, in her sleep, in front of the shocked doctor and serving woman. That's it. For such a dominant character, you'd be surprised at how little she actually speaks. She has 59 speeches altogether, far less than Shakespeare's most voluble female characters, Cleopatra from *Antony and Cleopatra* with 204 and Rosalind from *As You Like It* with 201. She's absent from a huge chunk of the play, making no appearances at all between Act 3 Scene 4 and the sleepwalking scene at the beginning of Act 5. Even Macbeth brushes her off when he's plotting the murder of Banquo: *Be innocent of the knowledge, dearest chuck.* You don't need to know. I have an image of her, pacing the draughty corridors of her castle as she waits for Macbeth to return, spending far too much time tangled up in the twists and turns of her own mind.

Infertility is a horribly isolating experience. It's surrounded by shame and brings you face to face with your own failure to do something that we often assume we'll be able to do as soon as we decide that the time is right. If you tell people what's going on, then you'll be on the receiving end of countless pieces of advice about eating grapefruit or trying Reiki or going on holiday and trying to forget about it all. People will tell you about their cousin's neighbour's workmate who was trying for years and then got pregnant with twins when she started taking herbal supplements. In the meantime, everyone around you will be having babies. Our friends and relatives and colleagues produced twenty-seven of them in the time that we were trying – and failing – to conceive. I know, because I counted. It got to the stage where news of other people's pregnancies felt like a personal affront. It was as if there were a finite number of babies that could be conceived and everyone else's good news diminished the chance that we would ever succeed. I had a simmering conviction that the universe had it in for me. I stomped around darkly, glowering, muttering bitterly about the normal world where people didn't have a clue.

There were times, during those difficult few years,

when I felt sidelined by life, fed up with being told that I should just relax. There are messages that society gives you if you're in your early thirties and don't have children. You're incomplete: hadn't you better get on with it? You're not a proper adult: you haven't yet made the transition to being a real grown-up with real responsibilities. You're not a real·woman, or a real man. There's something wrong with you. If you do what I tried to do, and evade questions about when you're going to start a family by pretending that you're not really interested, people will see you as a bit odd. (This, of course, is often the fate of those who have chosen not to have children, as if it's weird not to want to reproduce.) You're on the edge, looking on, while the rest of the world gets on with the important business of producing the next generation.

The idea of a Lady Macbeth consumed by her child-lessness puts an interesting spin on her reference to the one character in the play who is actually a mother: Lady Macduff. 'The Thane of Fife had a wife; where is she now?' I imagine a Lady Macbeth twisted by her inability to give Macbeth a living son; a totally unhistorically accurate and un-Shakespearean Lady Macbeth who has spent a lot of time at family gatherings surrounded by women who have done what they're supposed to and produced brood after brood of pretty chickens. She's there, on the edge of things, consumed by failure. I can sympathize with this Lady Macbeth, because I know that sense of wanting to rage at the cosmic unfairness of what you've been unable to do. Her sleepwalking words carry the dark spite of someone who feels vindicated. You thought you had it all, down there in Fife with your perfect family, and look where it got you.

Of course, some people would argue that to look at the Macbeths in this way is to treat them as something they're not. In 1933, the literary critic L. C. Knights published an essay titled 'How many children had Lady Macbeth?' This would become a classic of Shakespeare criticism, and when I first heard of it – when I was a GCSE student – I thought, as so many other people must have done, that Knights was offering the solution to a puzzle, that he had somehow managed to work out this hidden detail of the Macbeths' family life. Knights was actually doing no such thing. Instead, he was challenging the idea that Shakespeare's characters can be viewed as real people. For Knights, Shakespeare's plays should be seen as dramatic poems: he had no time for what a fellow academic would later refer to as 'the critical game of constructing a world outside the given material of the play'. The Macbeths are just words on the page. The answer to the question is that Lady Macbeth has no children, because she does not actually exist.

But the fact that Knights didn't want to play this particular game doesn't mean that it can't be played; and the mystery over what happened to Lady Macbeth's child is an intriguing one, one of the spaces in Shakespeare's plays where the drama opens up and gives us the chance to experiment with potential interpretations. Emma

Smith, Professor of Shakespeare Studies at the University of Oxford and author of the wonderful *This is
Shakespeare: How to Read the World's Greatest Playwright*,
describes this, brilliantly, as Shakespeare's 'sheer permissive gappiness', and over the centuries it has given rise to
all manner of reimaginings and rewritings, many of
them opening up Shakespeare's works to audiences who
might have thought that Shakespeare had little to do
with their own lives. *West Side Story, The Lion King, 10
Things I Hate About You, Kiss Me Kate, Romeo + Juliet, Ros-
encrantz and Guildenstern are Dead, Warm Bodies* . . . This
gappiness also offers the scope for students to consider
what might be going on beyond the words themselves.
We get students to think about set design, costume and
sound effects; we show them examples of different stage
and screen interpretations and make use of the insights
offered by actors and directors. And in doing so, we take
them much further than we could by sticking to the
words on the page.

Take Caliban, for instance, in *The Tempest*. In some
productions, he's played as hideously deformed, half-
human and half-sea creature, an object of fear. In others,
he is scarred and traumatized. Villain or victim? In class,
my Year Eight students and I examine images from different productions and consider these alongside the
play's historical context, its backdrop of exploration and
colonialism. One student says, 'If you present Caliban as
a monster, you're kind of justifying why Prospero treats
him in the way he does, because Prospero wants to bring

him under control. But if you present him as human, it makes Prospero seem worse. Prospero's more of a monster than he is.' The images that have the most impact on them are of a Caliban who is exhausted by Prospero's demands, by his insults, his constant degradation. 'It makes you think,' says one boy, 'that Shakespeare was saying that colonialism was wrong, because this is what it did to people. It wasn't just a physical thing, it was a mental thing as well. You never think of Shakespeare as being about things like that.'

We don't think of Shakespeare as being about lots of things. We certainly don't think of *Macbeth* as being, potentially, a play about childlessness. Ambition, corruption, paranoia, guilt – but not a couple's private tragedy. But that lovely permissive gappiness certainly allows us to see it that way. And Shakespeare was, himself, a master of finding a gap in a story and exploiting it. The character of Lady Macbeth, with all her haranguing and manipulation, her sleepwalking and hand-washing, is based on just a very brief reference in Holinshed's *Chronicles*. Holinshed tells us that when Macbeth began to seek advice on how to usurp Scotland, 'his wife lay sore upon him to attempt the thing, as that she was verie ambitious, burning in unquenchable desire to beare the name of a queene'. And that's it. This single sentence gave Shakespeare enough inspiration, and enough scope, to create the Lady Macbeth we're familiar with today.

I wouldn't necessarily spend too much time in class

on this reading of *Macbeth*. For one thing, there isn't time; for another, it's the conventional interpretation that students really need to know, the one where Lady Macbeth is driven by evil and ambition, and I don't want to confuse students who might already be finding Shakespeare demanding. But if I think my class can cope with it, I'll certainly get them to consider the Macbeths' childlessness and why it might be significant: the lack of an heir, the hints of unnaturalness. We'll look at how you might introduce alternative readings, how you deal with tentativeness and provisionality. *Lady Macbeth could potentially be seen as . . . Another way of interpreting this is . . . We might also infer that . . .* Exercises like this help students to develop their critical vocabulary, building subtlety and flexibility. They're difficult. But they're a vital part of developing the intellectual agility that will enable students, later, to play off competing arguments against each other, to appreciate complexity rather than trying to flatten it out.

This interpretation of *Macbeth* is also ripe for the kind of creative rewriting that I've touched on when exploring *To Kill a Mockingbird* and *Great Expectations*, giving a voice to experiences that are sidelined from the text itself. Previous incarnations of the GCSE syllabus gave us far more scope for this type of activity, which often led to stunningly thoughtful work with a real freshness of engagement. Exploring a text creatively, using Peter Bazalgette's skill of 'cognitive empathy', often allows teenagers to express insights that they wouldn't necessarily be able to articulate in a conventional essay. It gets them to engage with experiences beyond their immediate situations and brings them face to face with the difficult realities of human existence, fostering the kind of understanding that Bazalgette sees as crucial to the development of a humane society. And you've only got to think of novels like J. R. Thorp's *Learwife*, or Jane Smiley's *A Thousand Acres*, or indeed Isabelle Schuler's *Lady MacBethad* – further exploitations of Shakespeare's marvellous gappiness – to see what these imaginative interventions might lead to.

One creative activity I often use in class asks students to imagine Lady Macbeth as a user of social media. We ring the changes on the question 'How many children had Lady Macbeth?' and ask, instead, 'How many Facebook friends had Lady Macbeth?' How does she interact with these Facebook friends, or Instagram followers, or YouTube subscribers? Does she present different aspects of herself on different platforms? Teenagers have an extensive knowledge of the ways in which social media allows users to present curated versions of themselves to the world, and relish using it to explore a character who is such a staunch advocate of concealing reality behind a series of false faces. Our version of Lady Macbeth is completely anachronistic and ahistorical, and purists would be horrified, but once you've started to speculate about the online lives of Shakespeare's characters, it's difficult to stop. How would Lady Macbeth respond to other people's posts? What might she share on the Relationships board on Mumsnet? Other characters and issues can be brought in too. What might the Scottish thanes discuss on their private group chat? In a Scotland ruled by a paranoid tyrant, would social media exist as a genuinely free space or would spies be set to snoop and catfish?

Exercises like this might seem like a distraction from the business of writing essays and preparing for exams. But they have a serious purpose. They often allow students to make very subtle observations about character and motivation that can then be brought into more formal essays. Considering Lady Macbeth as a user of the internet helps my students to understand Lady Macbeth's insistence on the management of appearances, and to think about how she might manipulate the public's view of her husband's kingship. It also encourages them to think about what might lie behind these heavily edited selves. We talk about the fears and insecurities that lurk not just beyond the surface of our imagined Lady Macbeth, but also behind all of the images which we see on social media, and to which we ourselves contribute. Again, it's the kind of lesson that takes us into the world beyond the confines of the syllabus, into issues that are bigger, and more insistent, and much more likely to stay in students' minds.

So, alongside all the Lady Macbeths who are fuelled by venom, I think there's room for a Lady Macbeth who is desolate, consumed by her apparent redundancy, desperate to do anything that will give herself a sense of purpose. Let's take her back to before that fateful letter arrives from Macbeth to tell her of his encounter with the witches. Let's pause to think about her grief, to imagine those voices in her head that remind her, constantly, that she hasn't been able to manage what other women have achieved quite easily. Let's remember that loss can make people feel sidelined and excluded. And let's remember, always, that we have no idea what might be going on beneath the surface of someone's life.

# On not being enough: *Death of a Salesman* by Arthur Miller

I'm wide awake. It's 3.26 in the morning and I wish there was some way of switching off my thoughts. I know I should try to get some sleep, but too many things are speeding through my brain, crashing into each other and bouncing off in different directions. At the weekend, or in the holidays, I'd go downstairs and read, stealing time from the night, but it's a Tuesday during term and my alarm will go off in just over two hours. I lie on my back, watching the lights of the occasional cars outside as they slide across the ceiling. I try to remember everything I've read about relaxation techniques and sleep hygiene, but my mind is too busy and none of it works. I try to pick just one set of ideas to focus on, but inevitably the things I set aside jostle for my attention, their voices rising. They want to be allowed back in and I'm powerless to stop them.

They feel like weasels, these things in my mind. There's a whole colony of them, their claws skittering as if on a polished floor, squeaking and demanding. Sometimes, they bother me about whatever I'm going to be teaching next day. *Are you sure that's the best way of doing it? Wouldn't it be better if you approached it like this instead?* They twine themselves around each other and sometimes the noise they make rises to a cacophony, filling me with doubts, making me question my judgement. When they're at their most sinister – creatures from a nightmare world, their eyes glinting with malice – they sneer at me about the things I've done in my life and the choices I've made. *Didn't make much of yourself, did you? Look at all the things you could have done, if you hadn't been a teacher. All those chances. Other people managed it. Why didn't you?*

There are certain things that set them off. News of a former colleague who's scored a big promotion; the annual magazine from my old college, listing glittering prizes and lifetime achievements. The social media feed of the latest educational superstar. A story leaping up from a newspaper, an interview with someone on the radio: people I knew when they were in their late teens and early twenties, lounging around the common room watching Australian soaps and putting off going back to the library to do some work, now in positions of power and influence. The weasels snicker. *See. They're doing well for themselves, aren't they?*

At other times, it'll be a question from one of my current students. 'Miss,' they'll ask, 'if you went to Oxford and got a PhD, why are you just a teacher?' It's an innocent question, and it gives me the chance to unpick lots of things with them, starting with the fact that I love teaching and think it's an immensely important job. I talk about the reasons why people choose particular careers, and the belief that money and status aren't everything. I also point out that there's no such thing as 'just' a teacher, and that teachers in the UK are criminally undervalued and underpaid for what we do. But it sets the weasels going. *Just a teacher. You could have been anything, and you're just a teacher. You know what they say about teachers, don't you? Those who can, do; those who can't, teach* ... I know only too well what they'll say, and I know, too, that once their words are in my mind, I won't be able to dislodge them.

I turn over in bed, hoping that the movement will scatter the weasels temporarily. It's 4.08. What are the chances of being able to get an hour's sleep, just one hour, before the alarm clock sounds? I think of all the literary insomniacs I know. Gerard Manley Hopkins, waking to what he described as 'the fell of dark'; Philip Larkin in 'Aubade', his last great poem, rising in the soundless dawn to the knowledge that death was another day nearer. At some point, I doze off, and jolt awake when my alarm finally rings. Tuesday, and a whole day of teaching before I can even try to go to sleep again.

The weasels in my head are easier to deal with during the day. I can't control them completely, but I can distract myself from them. I go for long walks, or pound a treadmill at the gym. I talk to my teacher friends, and we console ourselves with wine and black humour. We tell ourselves that the roads we didn't travel in life aren't the ones we would have wanted to go down anyway. Not for us, the worlds of corporate law or hedge-fund management; not for us, the six-figure bonuses and business-class travel. We remind each other that what we do is vital. We're teaching the future, we point out. We nurture and build confidence; we open minds and set young people off on their own pathways through life. Today's students are tomorrow's barristers and politicians, doctors and nurses, journalists and policymakers and shapers and influencers and a whole host of other important things (including, of course, teachers: I've sent a fair few of them out into the world). It's our responsibility to ask the questions and introduce the counter-narratives, to help instil the values that people in power should be guided by. What could possibly be more important than that?

But I think everyone, unless they're exceptionally lucky, will be visited by headweasels like mine at some point. Most people have hopes and dreams, a plan for the future, and most people will, at some point, have to confront the fact that not all of these plans will come to fruition. There are compromises that have to be made; shortcomings that have to be accommodated. We realize that we're not necessarily up to the tasks we set ourselves. We might be hampered by glass ceilings or by doors that slam unequivocally shut in our faces. Events might dent our confidence and leave us wary of making our next move. On the one hand, there's Pip from *Great Expectations*, bright-eyed and looking forward to the promise of becoming a gentleman; and on the other, there's Willy Loman from Arthur Miller's 1949 play, *Death of a Salesman*, arriving home from work exhausted, looking back over the long years of his career and seeing only the bleakness of a life that didn't turn out the way he wanted it to.

*

Some texts have a quality that I think of as being eminently teacherly. They take teenage readers by the hand and say, look: this is what can happen if you use language in this way, if you play around with this particular form or genre. Many of the teacherly texts I know are poems. Wilfred Owen's 'Exposure', describing soldiers in a freezing-cold trench, waiting for an attack to break the numbness: here's how half-rhyme works, how it creates a sense of restlessness and unease. Walt Whitman's 'Patrolling Barnegat', with its overlong, unspooling lines conjuring the uncontrolled energy of a storm at sea: here's what you can do if you take the sonnet form and push it to its limits. Thomas Hardy's 'The Voice', his haunting poem of love and regret: here's how you use rhyme and metre to create a feeling of wistfulness and hope (and how you break it, devastatingly, in your final stanza). *Death of a Salesman* is one of these teacherly texts. I teach it as part of an A-level unit on tragedy, and it demonstrates, brilliantly, how the features of a genre with its roots in ancient Greece can be adapted for the modern era. In the process, it also opens up conversations about success and failure, and about the way work shapes our lives and identities. At a point when students are making decisions that will affect their futures, it acts as a cautionary tale. Another teacherly function, albeit of a different kind. *Be careful*, it says. *Things might not turn out the way you want them to.*

Willy Loman, the low man, the ordinary person. The significance of his name is obvious. So is the difference in scale between Willy and New York, the city in which he lives. He is a low man in a city of skyscrapers and big dreams, a city that towers above him. When I introduce the play we begin by looking at the way New York is represented in Frank Sinatra's 'New York, New York' and Jay-Z and Alicia Keys's 'Empire State of Mind', weaving the lyrics of both songs together to create a rich symbolic landscape. It's a city full of potential: the city that never sleeps, a concrete jungle, a place dreams are made of. Its streets will make you feel brand new. If you can make it there, you'll make it anywhere. New York appears as a place of reinvention and possibility, where everything is yours for the taking. There's nothing you can't do. You only have to make the most of it.

The problem is that the streets of New York don't make Willy feel brand new at all. Quite the opposite. Our first view of him is of a man in his sixties with two heavy suitcases, telling his wife, Linda, that he is 'tired to death'. He has spent his career as a travelling salesman and the years on the road have taken their toll. He admits to Linda that he is struggling to concentrate when driving, that his car keeps veering off the road. In Miller's lengthy description of the set at the start of the play, even the house Willy lives in seems fragile, overshadowed by towering apartment buildings, its walls partly transparent. Linda soothes him, offering to bring him an aspirin and make him a sandwich. He is vulnerable, worn out.

The A-level unit on tragedy is one of my absolute favourite courses to teach. We begin by studying *King*

*Lear*, Shakespeare's meatiest tragedy. We explore Aristotle's writings on tragedy and look at the journey the tragic protagonist makes. It's a neat, highly structured path with a number of key elements. The protagonist is initially a person of high status, held in great esteem. He commits an error that sets in motion a sequence of events that lead to his inevitable downfall. Along the way, he experiences moments of insight into the errors he has made, and emerges with the potential to be a much better person. However, his downfall cannot be halted, and the play ends with his death. Students love the simplicity of this journey, and the transliterated Greek terms for the different stages it involves. *Hamartia*, the tragic error. *Peripeteia*, the reversal of fortune that concludes with the protagonist's inevitable demise. *Anagnorisis*, the moment of insight when the tragic protagonist recognizes his failings and becomes a morally greater person as a result. And *catharsis*, the hardest for students to grasp: the process by which the dramatist elicits pity and fear for the protagonist, bringing the audience to an emotional pitch that will leave them feeling exhausted but ultimately cleansed and rebalanced, with a sense that the events of the play have restored order to the world.

Many tragic protagonists also possess a sense of hubris, an overblown belief in their own importance. It's an inflated sense of pride, a conviction that one has the right to demand the respect and esteem of others. In class, we discuss examples from wider life. Reality TV stars feature heavily, especially contestants from *The Apprentice*. So, too, do politicians. (A theatrical poster by the Hungarian designer István Orosz, created in 1999, features a King Lear in profile who looks uncannily, presciently, like Donald Trump.) Lear's own hubris is apparent right from the start of the play. He wants to divest himself of the cares of monarchy while retaining 'the name and all th'addition to a king'. In the very first scene, Lear stages a ceremonial trial where his daughters must make public declarations of their love for him in order to receive a share of his kingdom. The trial, how- ever, is entirely false, as he has already decided which daughter is going to receive which part of his territory. His youngest daughter, Cordelia, refuses to play along, and is disowned by Lear as a result. He is enraged when his other daughters refuse to go along with his plan to stay with each of them for a month at a time, with his retinue of a hundred unruly knights in tow. He spends a lot of time telling people what to do and expecting to be obeyed, even trying to order the gods to do his bidding. At the height of his fury, shut out on the heath on the wildest night anyone can remember, he commands the storm to 'strike flat the thick rotundity of the world' – to destroy the whole planet, to start again, as a way of assuaging his sense of despair.

*King Lear* embodies beautifully Arthur Miller's belief that one of the defining features of the tragic protagon- ist is his struggle to gain – or retain – what he considers to be his rightful place in society. Lear has a particular vision of his relationship with the world and demands that others treat him accordingly. In *Death of a Salesman*, Willy Loman has a view of himself as a prominent businessman, admired by many. Through a series of flashbacks, Miller shows us the stories that Willy tells about himself, making his sense of hubris abundantly clear. Willy boasts to his family that he is 'vital in New England', that he can park his car in any street 'and the cops protect it like their own'. He has drunk coffee with the Mayor of Providence. He is known everywhere and welcomed with open arms. His teenage sons, Biff and Happy, vie with each other for his praise and approval. Biff polishes his car; Happy lies on his back and pedals with his feet to show him how much weight he has lost. Willy is not a low man at all, but a New York success story: king of the hill, top of the heap.

Except he isn't. Willy's life is built on a web of lies and, before long, gaps start to appear between the claims he makes about himself and the reality of his very ordinary career. In one early flashback, Willy tells Linda that he was 'sellin' thousands and thousands', but then amends this to 'five hundred gross in Providence and seven hundred gross in Boston'. Less than a minute later, he downsizes this again: 'Well, I – I did – about a hundred and eighty gross in Providence. Well, no – it came to – roughly two hundred gross on the whole trip.' Reality weighs heavily on him. There is money owing on the washing machine, the vacuum cleaner, repairs to the roof and the car. People don't seem to like him. There are mocking voices just out of earshot. The doors that used to open for him are emphatically shut.

It might be easy for students to scorn Willy. Miller certainly gives them plenty of ammunition, filling his central character with many unattractive characteristics. Willy is impatient with his wife, Linda, despite her concern for his well-being. In the flashbacks, he insults Bernard, the studious teenage son of his neighbour Charley, calling him 'anaemic', a pest, a worm. (His own sons, meanwhile, are 'Adonises', pumped dangerously full of self-confidence.) He has an affair with a nameless woman in a hotel in Boston. His pettiness and cruelties are there for everyone to see.

And yet we cannot dislike him entirely. Miller's masterstroke was to introduce Willy not as a boastful man in his prime but as an object of sympathy, approaching old age, exhausted. In his essay 'Tragedy and the Common Man', published in the same year as *Death of a Salesman*, Miller argued that the tragic protagonist was 'a character who is ready to lay down his life, if need be, to secure one thing – his sense of personal dignity'. We see Willy's dignity slipping, and in these moments he emerges as a character of great pathos. One of the best examples of this is when he goes to ask his boss, Howard Wagner, for a job in New York that will allow him to continue working without having to travel. Willy has worked for the Wagner Company since he was in his twenties: surely this must count for something? But Howard isn't interested. He is absorbed in his new wire-recording machine, on which he has been able to capture the voices of his wife and children, and insists on showing this off to Willy. It's clear that for Howard, Willy is a bit of an embarrassment. He has hung around for too long. Not only is there no New York job for Willy, there isn't a job at all. Howard doesn't want him to represent the company any more. Left alone in Howard's office, Willy accidentally sets the wire-recorder working and tries frantically to get the machine to stop while the voice of Howard's son spools out solemnly, reciting the names of states and their capitals. It's a moment that captures, brilliantly, the anguish of many a person who feels that the world has moved on and left them behind, and often makes students think of their own older relatives, struggling to cope with new technology. I tell them of my mum's fear of using cash machines, of the panic induced by a simple trip to the ATM to withdraw money, and we're quiet for a little while, imagining what kind of device it might eventually be that brings about our own feelings of exile and inadequacy.

Tragic drama needs an antagonist, and my students decide, quite early on, that the biggest antagonist in *Death of a Salesman* is America itself. The American dream – the belief that America is a place designed to nurture the ambitious, where anyone can prosper – seduces Willy with its glamour and false promises. For Willy, the key quality one needs in order to succeed in this environment is to be charismatic, 'well liked'. (He has a fine eye for the distinction between being merely 'liked' and being 'well liked': his neighbour Charley is the former, Willy himself is very definitely the latter.) It's all about who you know and the smile on your face. The wonder of America, he declares, is that it's a country where 'a man can end with diamonds . . . on the basis of being liked'. Yet Willy does not end with diamonds. He has built his life around the belief that selling is the greatest career a man could ever want, but is reduced to accepting handouts from Charley and passing them off to Linda as his salary. He comes to recognize that American capitalist society no longer has any use for him. At one point, he exclaims, anguished, 'You can't eat the orange and throw the peel away – a man is not a piece of fruit!' But America can do whatever it likes, and the city that never sleeps is oblivious to the cries of a tired old man.

Lurking behind this is the concept of meritocracy, the idea that our status in life is a reflection of our own hard work and our drive to succeed. In a meritocratic society, we are the captains of our fate: there is no limit to how high we can rise. If we apply ourselves, we will get what we deserve. Yet this rhetoric – on the surface, so inspiring and empowering – papers over all manner of inequalities of birth and health and ability and circumstance, all of which prevent people from rising as far as the meritocratic ideal might suggest is possible. In his book *The Tyranny of Merit: What's Become of the Common Good?*, the philosopher Michael J. Sandel explores the impact of living in a meritocracy on those who do not find themselves rising to the top. If the winners in a meritocratic society believe, as Sandel puts it, that 'they have earned their success through their own talent and hard work', what does this mean for those who do not achieve this kind of success? What about those who, in Sandel's words, are 'equally hardworking but less endowed with the gifts a market society happens to prize'? Meritocracy offers little to those whose jobs are seen to be of low status, but are nevertheless essential to the functioning of society: those who care for the vulnerable and cope with emergencies and keep our streets and hospitals clean; those who put food on the shelves of our supermarkets and ensure the safe running of our public transport. It also offers little to those like Willy, who have slogged hard all their lives but do not receive the prizes that society has held out as an incentive. No wonder Willy feels let down.

I ask my students what they think about the idea of meritocracy. Dream big. The sky's the limit. They find it stressful, the idea that they should always strive for something better. They are very conscious of all the targets in their lives, particularly the target grades they have in school, generated on the basis of their GCSE results and used to measure their progress throughout their two years of A-level study. They feel they should constantly be setting their sights high: which universities to apply to, which careers they should aim for. Some of them talk about the pressure of juggling extracurricular activities and part-time jobs, all the things they are told to do in order to make themselves stand out from other candidates for those coveted university places. And there are the inevitable stresses of being a teenager in an age so dominated by social media, the feeling of always having to be aware of the self you are presenting to the world. They have weasels in their heads too, telling them what they should look like, how they should behave, what kind of social life they should be having, how much they should be able to lift at the gym, how long it should take them to pass their driving test. *Not doing as well as you should be, are you? Look what everyone else is up to. They're making a success of things. Why aren't you?*

Discussing all of these issues in class takes the lesson off on a bit of a tangent, but it's another of those unplanned conversations that so often turn out to be the most valuable. They're part of the emotional hinterland that lies behind the curriculum, revolving around the big topics that the characters we're studying have to grapple with: relationships, injustice, loyalty, ambition. In *Death of a Salesman*, it's how you judge yourself, and how you cope when you realize that your life hasn't turned out how you intended it to. One of the students observes that this is a really scary idea. 'I mean, how do people make all these decisions about their lives? How do you decide when you want to apply for promotions and have children and things like that?'

I agree. It *is* scary. I tell them that sometimes you can't plan. There are stretches of your life when everything goes smoothly, and then there are wobbles and bumps in the road and you just have to manage.

'What about you?' one of them asks. 'Did you always plan to go into teaching?'

No, I say. I didn't. And I didn't plan to spend my entire life as a teacher, either. I give them the potted history. When I made that move to Lincolnshire, when I got my first teaching job, I told myself that I'd give teaching a couple of years, and then think about going back to university. But getting funding to do a PhD in the arts and humanities, then as now, was incredibly difficult. Making a career in academia would be even harder: friends who'd already embarked on that route were chasing one temporary contract after another, never knowing where they'd be from one year to the next. The precariousness of this kind of life was alarming. Could I really give up a full-time job for something so uncertain? I was living with my partner by then, and knew that whatever decision I made would affect him too. I'd heard so many stories of long-distance relationships, of people commuting between Brighton and Lancaster or Reading and Sheffield, trying to make the best of a difficult situation. It wasn't what either of us really wanted.

Then, at the start of my second year as a teacher, my mum died, of an undetected and unsurvivable aortic aneurysm. I was twenty-four and I'd lost both parents in just over three years. What I desperately needed, at that point, was stability. There are some times in your life when you need to challenge yourself and leave your comfort zone behind, and others when you need to put down roots.

I think it helps teenagers to know how complicated these journeys can be and how the plans you start out with can be influenced by factors you never envisage when you set off. It normalizes the fact that lives are shaped by chance and contingency, not simply by our own striving. We are not responsible for everything that happens to us. Recognizing this helps us to be kinder to ourselves, to help silence those weasels. It also, as Sandel argues, encourages us to be kinder in our attitude to others. If we see our successes as simply a reflection of how fortunate we have been in life's many and various lotteries, then we are also more likely to see other people's failures as a reflection of their misfortune, rather than their lack of merit. It's not that they didn't work hard enough. It's just that things didn't work out. And kindness – especially the kindness to let people just be, rather than constantly feeling that they have to prove their worth – is a quality that often seems in short supply. I think of Mary Oliver's poem 'The Wild Geese', reassuring people that they do not have to be good, that they do not have to walk on their knees for a hundred miles through the desert repenting. I think of the slogan I saw on a postcard in a gift shop: *You are enough*. I repeat this to myself when the weasels start squeaking, a mantra to calm myself in the early hours.

Willy is unable to believe that he is enough. He hasn't been the kind of success he wanted to be and is painfully aware of the gap between his fantasy life and the reality. He looks to his older brother, Ben, for help. Ben is a self-made man who went to Africa at the age of seventeen and earned his fortune from diamond mines. There's something deeply unsavoury about Ben, both in the source of his wealth and in the way he challenges his nephew Biff to a fight in order to assert his superiority over him, but to Willy he is a replacement for the father he never really knew. He wants Ben to be impressed by what he has achieved, but is also desperate for his advice. 'I still feel – kind of temporary about myself,' he admits, but Ben has a train to catch and cannot – or will not – stop to listen.

I still feel kind of temporary about myself too. I think most people do. And I'm tired, as well, because teaching – like being a travelling salesman, like most professions really – drains the life out of you. It leaves you longing for someone to take your shoes off and fix you a sandwich at the end of a hard day's work, like Linda does for Willy. There's a particular kind of exhaustion that sets in when it's been too long since the last holiday, when you are so blunted and worn out that you can barely remember what you're supposed to be doing, when any unexpected demands can make you feel physically sick. I can think of any number of similes that I could use to describe my job. There are the obvious ones, the clichéd ones, like spinning plates and herding cats, but the one I like best comes from the children's game Buckaroo, where players take it in turns to load a plastic mule with all manner of items – saddlebags, frying pans, cowboy hats, lanterns – until the mule has had enough and kicks its heels skywards, sending everything crashing to the ground. All teachers will know those Buckaroo moments, the feeling of having reached your absolute limit.

It all takes its toll. Over the years, I've known so many people who've left the profession sad and broken, their mental reserves sapped. For some, it's because of the relentlessness of student behaviour. This doesn't have to be anything dramatic. The continual drip-drip of low-level disruption erodes your patience and wastes countless hours of everyone's time. You develop ways of coping with it – stopping and waiting, looking meaningfully at your watch, a significant raised eyebrow – but there are days when your tolerance can feel dangerously thin. For other people, it's the constant cycle of new initiatives, new buzzwords and acronyms, leaving them feeling oddly detached from the profession to which they've devoted decades of their lives. They're no longer at the cutting edge, no longer up to date with whatever is considered shiny and innovative: they used to be a safe pair of hands, but now they're an educational dinosaur, a barrier to progress. And for some, the thing that brings them to the edge is simply tiredness. Tiredness with the piles of marking, the admin, the meetings; tiredness with the perception that teachers clock off at 3.30 and have thirteen weeks' holiday a year; tiredness with juggling work and family responsibilities and feeling that you're spread far too thinly; tiredness with a job that leaves you with the perpetual sense that you could be doing something different, something else, something more. Like Willy, there are days when I drive home close to burnout, running on empty, desperate for a proper night's sleep.

My teacher friends and I talk about what we'll do when we finally leave. We'll get out while we're still ahead. We'll get part-time jobs and learn new languages and find absorbing hobbies, like making cheese or restoring antiques. We'll do some voluntary work, for a foodbank or community garden, or for the local wildlife trust, clearing footpaths and restoring habitats. Quiet features heavily in these plans, as do the natural world and animals. We need a sense of restoration and renewal.

Both Willy and his son Biff share this desire for fresh air and the feeling of earth between their fingers. Biff tells Happy, wistfully, of springtime in Texas, on the ranch where he used to work, where there are newborn colts and a sense of freshness and promise. The city holds very little for Biff, who would rather be out in the countryside, if it were not for the fact that he feels he should be making his future – building a career, paying off a mortgage, getting married, all the conventional markers of success. Willy laments the lack of open space in the neighbourhood and the two elm trees that were cut down by developers. He remembers the scent of lilacs and wisteria. Nothing will grow, he says. In the depths of his breakdown, he tries to plant seeds, carrots and lettuce and beets. He exclaims, desperately, that he doesn't have a thing in the ground. It's ironic, given the meritocratic focus on rising and reaching for the skies, that in the end, Willy's concern is for the soil beneath his feet.

Willy is ultimately unable to silence the weasels in his mind. He tries to shush them, whirling in anguish, terrified. But he can only stop their chittering by doing something drastic. He gets into his car, ignoring Linda and Biff as they try to stop him. There is a crash. And then Linda, Biff and Happy, and Charley and Bernard, walk solemnly downstage to place flowers at his grave.

A review of *Death of a Salesman* on Goodreads comments that the play should not be taught in high schools, because the play's concerns – 'decline in later life, vanquished dreams, worrying about losing a job and not being able to pay the mortgage' – do not resonate with adolescent readers. But the fact that a subject doesn't immediately appeal to teenagers should never be a reason to avoid teaching it. And, in any case, my experience of the play is different. My students find Willy's situation deeply absorbing. They are frustrated by his stubbornness and angered by the way he treats Linda. They can also see how his belief in the importance of personal charisma has affected his sons, who are both directionless and dissatisfied, having learned that being 'well liked' is not everything that Willy claimed it to be. Biff, at thirty-four, has worked a series of jobs and is unable to settle: 'Shipping clerk, salesman, business of one kind or another. And it's a measly manner of existence.' He complains to Willy that 'I never got anywhere because you blew me so full of hot air I could never stand taking orders from anybody.' Happy has his own apartment, a car and 'plenty of women', but is still lonely. The 'anaemic' Bernard, on the other hand, is a successful lawyer, married with two children, and about to fight a case in the Supreme Court.

I have only ever seen one stage production of *Death of a Salesman*, but it was at one of my favourite theatres, the Royal Exchange Theatre in Manchester. I'd gone there on school trips as a teenager, and now, in the winter of 2018, I was taking my own students, arriving at Piccadilly Station after a long train journey from Peterborough and threading our way through drizzly streets, past shops and buskers and market stalls, to the theatre in St Ann's Square. The Royal Exchange is set in the Great Hall of the building that once housed the city's commodities market, and a board showing the closing figures on the last day of trade in 1968 is still on display, high up above the bustle of the Hall with its café and craft shop. There are coloured lights, classical columns, a magnificent sense of size and space. The theatre itself is a theatre in the round, a massive, seven-sided pod, made from steel and glass and suspended inside the Great Hall. It was the perfect venue for *Death of a Salesman*, with an intensity that heightened Willy's sense of being hemmed in and unable to breathe. 'I thought I knew what catharsis was, but it was always in the abstract before,' one of the students remarked as we headed back to the station. 'Now I really know. You have to feel it.' Wrung out and exhausted, none of us spoke much on the way home. We needed to sit with our own thoughts, letting it all sink in.

Every time I've taught *Death of a Salesman*, we've needed to pause, at the end, to reflect on the journey it has taken us on. We've thought about the long distance between the students, at seventeen, and Willy, at sixty-three, with me somewhere in the middle, all of us trying in our own ways to come to terms with the messages we absorb about the value of who we are and what we do. I'm closer now in age to Willy than I am to my students, and that's quite a frightening thought. I can help them to think not just about the society Willy lives in, but also the one in which they are just about to reach adulthood, full of its own insistent clamour. I can help them to push back against what this society tells them about the kinds of lives that are worthy of attention, the kinds of jobs they should be aiming for, the ways in which they should judge themselves and others. *You are enough*. We sit, and we are quiet. And then the bell rings for the next lesson and the noise of the world seeps back in, again.

# On the purpose of education: *The History Boys* by Alan Bennett

A debate about education is unfolding on the internet, and the participants are arguing energetically. On one side are advocates of what's known as 'direct instruction', where the teacher is the fount of all knowledge, the expert in the room, and lessons are mini-lectures, with little student participation. On the other are supporters of groupwork and discussion, of flexibility and freedom of interpretation. Positions are becoming entrenched and people have started to reduce their opponents' arguments to extremes: teachers are either control freaks or woolly liberals, their students compliant automata or rowdy savages. It's clear that this is going to run and run. Someone has already posted a GIF of a man with an enormous bucket of popcorn, his hand moving from the bucket to his mouth as he watches, mesmerized.

People who've been teaching for any length of time will know that these debates crop up on a regular basis. Ideas and initiatives cycle through; trends come and go. The subject of English is a particularly contested one. Opinions about the texts we teach and how we should approach them, how we should teach students to read and write and spell and even talk: the stuff of our curriculum is so fundamental to everyday life that it sometimes feels as though everyone wants to weigh in. During the time I've been a teacher, actors, journalists, members of the Royal Family and endless politicians have all had their say. These arguments have been going on for decades. When I was researching the history of English Literature as an academic discipline for my PhD, I found that the debates being played out in the early twentieth century, when the subject was in its infancy, were remarkably similar to those taking place in the present. Some commentators back then felt that English Literature was unsuitable for academic study, as it lacked the rigour and precision of mathematics and the sciences. One professor reduced it, sniffily, to 'chatter about Shelley': shades, here, of all those who deride English as a Mickey Mouse subject, a mere indulgence. Others believed that literature was too special to be picked apart and analysed. There were comments about the dangers posed to the 'delicate flowers' of English literature, and Virginia Woolf – who had her own complaints against the world of academia – warned of reducing literature into 'ABC; one, two, three' and losing 'all sense of what it's about'.

You wouldn't necessarily think that debates about education would be a fruitful topic for drama, let alone a drama that would win multiple awards on both sides of the Atlantic and be made into a BAFTA-winning film. But this is what Alan Bennett's 2004 play, *The History Boys*, managed to achieve. It explores the fundamental question of what education is for: whether its main emphasis should be exams and results, or whether it has a broader responsibility. In doing so, it also examines the influence teachers have over their students and vice versa. It looks, ultimately, to what is left over when the last lesson has finished and the last exam has been taken: when the corridors are quiet and the dust motes hover in the air, and there is time to reflect on what all of this has been for.

*The History Boys* is set in 1983, and focuses on a bright group of teenage boys at a fictional grammar school in Sheffield. The boys have got their A-level results and are now applying to read History at Oxford and Cambridge. Coming from a state school in Sheffield, this is a big thing for them. Back in the early 1980s, fewer than 50 per cent of Oxbridge students were from state schools. The general public's mental image of Oxbridge was still dominated by Granada Television's 1981 adaptation of *Brideshead Revisited*: privileged undergraduates quoting poetry against a backdrop of honeyed stone; Sebastian Flyte with his teddy bear. The boys in Bennett's play are about as far away from Evelyn Waugh as it's possible to be. They are, in their headmaster's words, 'clever, but crass', all untucked shirts and adolescent awkwardness. They're not even sure why they want to apply to Oxbridge. It's just because it's there.

Their headmaster, an odious man, knows exactly why he wants the boys to apply. He wants a place at the top of the league tables: results, scholarships, all the glittering prizes. The boys, he knows, have had a thorough grounding. But something else is needed. Think charm, he remarks to one of his staff. Think polish. Think Renaissance Man. As it stands, the boys are a little too ordinary. Something else will be needed if they are to succeed.

The boys in Bennett's play are being guided in their preparation by two members of staff. One is Hector, played in the 2006 film and the original National Theatre production by Richard Griffiths, a larger-than-life English teacher approaching retirement. The other is Irwin, played by Stephen Campbell Moore, a young History graduate who has been appointed by the headmaster to give the boys the required edge. The two couldn't be more of a physical contrast – Hector flamboyant in tweeds with a red bow tie, Irwin pale and unassuming – and this contrast continues into their teaching styles. Hector's lessons are deeply unorthodox. He is the Lord of Misrule, teaching behind a locked door, the curriculum made up of whatever takes his fancy: a bit of Auden or Larkin, some Edith Piaf, a rendition of 'When I'm Cleaning Windows'. Irwin's lessons, meanwhile, are focused and disciplined. He gets his students to approach their subject from unexpected angles, finding tangential ways in. Irwin makes it clear that the study of history is not about facts, but about arguments, interpretations. It's a performance, he says. 'It's entertainment. And if it isn't, make it so.'

The boys themselves are sketched deftly, with typical Bennett humour. Some are developed more fully than others, but we're given a clear sense of individual personalities. There's Timms, mouthy and coarse, played in the National Theatre production and in the film adaptation by James Corden. Down-to-earth Rudge, dismissed as a no-hoper by the headmaster. Sporty Crowther. Lockwood, with his mop of hair, and Akthar, the future magistrate. Thoughtful Scripps, the voice of reason. Dakin, sharp-witted and sexually mature. And Posner, the boy Bennett identified with his own younger self, eager and sensitive and hopelessly in love with Dakin. There are many memorable lines in the play, and one of the best is Posner's summary of his situation in life: 'I'm a Jew. I'm small. I'm homosexual. And I live in *Sheffield.* I'm fucked.'

Posner and Dakin, Scripps and Crowther, Akthar and Lockwood and Timms: all face a significant hurdle. They will have to sit an entrance exam and be interviewed by a panel of academics. It's a process that Bennett himself went through in the early 1950s, and he describes it, in detail, in his Introduction to *The History Boys*, writing of the daunting experience of going to Cambridge for his interview and the embarrassment he suffered over not having a proper dressing gown (his mother assured him that nobody would mind if he wore his raincoat). For Bennett, who won a place at Cambridge but eventually went to Oxford after National Service, applying to Oxbridge was a mysterious process. It still is today, and perhaps always will be, although the universities have worked hard to dispel the myths that surround their admissions procedures. Applicants still wonder nervously if they'll be judged on their extracurricular activities, and if so, whether playing hockey for their county will be considered more or less impressive than having Grade 8 violin or captaining their school's debating team or building toilets in Nepal on their gap year. And there are the same old rumours about the interview, probably the scariest part of the whole process. There's the story about the candidate who, on being told by the interviewer to 'surprise me', set fire to the newspaper that the interviewer was reading, and was promptly offered a place. There's also the one about being thrown a rugby ball by the interviewer as soon as you walk into the room: if you catch it, you're in; if you catch it and throw it back, you've got a scholarship.

All of this, of course, is nonsense. The universities are very open about the fact that all they are interested in is academic potential, intellectual curiosity and a willingness to work hard and think on your feet. No rugby balls; no ordeals involving how to use a fish knife or which way to pass a decanter of port. Entrance exams still exist, but the type of exam that the boys take, in the term after their A levels, was abolished in the late 1980s, as it gave an unfair advantage to candidates whose schools were able to provide the necessary extra term of teaching. Nevertheless, the mystique of Oxbridge entrance is ripe with dramatic potential, and Bennett exploits it to its maximum. There's the obvious will-they-won't-they about whether the boys will succeed; there's the soul-searching and keenness to impress. But most of all, there's the clash between Hector and Irwin, and the two different approaches to education that they embody. And it soon becomes clear that Irwin will emerge the victor.

*The History Boys* is a fantastic play to teach. Part of this, of course, is because of the film adaptation. It has a cast of familiar faces, a cracking soundtrack – the Cure, New Order, Echo and the Bunnymen – and offers a beautifully evocative portrayal of a secondary school in the 1980s, with its roll-top blackboards and piles of fading textbooks, its staff car park full of Vauxhall Chevettes and Morris Marinas. Students sometimes struggle to 'see' a play in their mind's eye, to lift the lines off the page, and if you can't see an actual production of whichever play you're studying, a screen version is the next best thing. But it's also a brilliant play to teach because its subject matter is so close to students' own experiences. Everyone has a take on what makes a good teacher, and, in class, we discuss these opinions at length. Should a teacher be an entertainer? How strict should they be? Should teachers be judged purely on the results their students get or on how much their students enjoy their lessons? The students always want to give examples, and I tell them to make these anonymous: it's not fair to let them name names, although I've usually got a good idea who they're talking about. They're pretty clear on what makes a bad teacher: somebody who doesn't seem to care about their students, who doesn't even bother to learn your name. As for good: somebody who helps you to make progress, who praises you and makes you think. Somebody who takes the time to explain things. All the effort spent on research into educational methods, all the furious back-and-forth on the internet, and the students have got it sussed.

We look at Hector and Irwin, and the different philosophies they represent. Hector takes the long view. You don't need to understand the poems you read, he tells the boys: just learn them now, commit them to memory, and they'll be there when you need them. Irwin is more organized, more goal-orientated. Which is better? We think about the way the play positions us as the audience, the stance it expects us to take. It seems, initially, that we're supposed to be on Hector's side. After all, it's Hector who offers the laughs. There are the songs, the acting-out of scenes from classic films; there's the very funny sequence where the boys improvise an encounter in a French brothel. Nevertheless, it quickly becomes clear that the boys see Hector's charms as relatively limited. They are bored with his endless quotations and frustrated with lessons that seem to go nowhere. They sigh, slump on the desks, roll their eyes. Irwin, in contrast, fires them up. It's not about knowing more than the other candidates, he says. It's about not being dull. His teaching is invigorating. He sends them rushing to the library to find out more, vying with each other for his rare words of praise. As Rudge comments, 'It's cutting edge.' If the boys want to get into Oxbridge, it's Irwin's lessons that will help them to succeed, not Hector's.

Yet Irwin, too, is flawed. We find out, later, that he has lied about being an Oxford graduate, telling two different stories about which college he attended. In the play, he becomes a television historian: when we first meet him, he is advising a panel of MPs on how to pass a bill that will limit trial by jury and the presumption of innocence. It's all about spin and surface, appropriate for a play written at the height of Tony Blair's leadership. It's playing the system. But, ultimately, it gets results.

If we want *The History Boys* to have a moral centre, we have to look to Mrs Lintott, the fourth member of staff we meet and the play's only significant female presence. Like Hector, Mrs Lintott is approaching retirement. Unlike him, she is thorough and meticulous. She has given the boys an excellent grounding in clearly marshalled facts and, arguably, the intellectual agility they gain from Irwin rests on the foundations she has helped them to lay. I imagine her being very much in favour of a well-organized lever-arch file, properly sectioned up with dividers and plastic wallets, the headings neatly underlined. She also has another of the play's best lines, telling Hector where she went to university: 'Durham. It's where I had my first pizza. Other things, too, of course, but it's the pizza that stands out.' Mrs Lintott is the kind of person who'd look after you in your first few weeks as a rookie teacher, making sure you knew how the coffee rota worked and whose chair you shouldn't sit in. She'd dispense wisdom and offer suggestions on how to approach particular students. It was the Mrs Lintotts of my first school who gave me the pieces of advice that have stayed with me all my career. *Don't try to be their friend. Be kind, but make sure they know where the boundaries are. If you expect to make a meaningful connection with every student you teach, you'll burn yourself out.* We never see the contents of Mrs Lintott's desk drawer, but I bet she's got a box of tissues and a packet of digestives in there, because she's the kind of person who'd know just when you need them. A school without at least one Mrs Lintott is a very poor thing.

Mrs Lintott acts as a confidante to both Hector and Irwin. She listens to both, without taking sides. She can see that Irwin's star is rising, while Hector's is on the wane. But even though she has known Hector for many years, she is ultimately unable to help him. This is because Hector is convinced that he is right. Like his classical namesake, he holds fast: to his ideals, and to a way of teaching that is increasingly outmoded.

When I taught *The History Boys* in a previous iteration of the A-level course, I taught it not as comedy, but as tragedy. We looked at how Hector is depicted at the start of the play as the master of revels, his status amplified by the ways the boys help him to divest himself of his motorcycle gear, presenting each item to the audience with a flourish. His hubris, in clinging to his idiosyncratic methods, assuming that he is so well established and well loved that he will be allowed to continue unimpeded. His fatal error, of groping the boys on the back of his bike when he gives them lifts home. His fall from grace and his death. The headmaster, and Irwin, are his obvious antagonists, but there's also the fact that the world of education is moving on and leaving him behind. As Irwin says, at the end of the play, 'I do not think there is time for his kind of teaching any more.'

Hector is a complex character, and one of the reasons for his complexity is those lifts home and what he does on them. It's indefensible – of course it is – and it's absolutely right that there are consequences. Nowadays, he'd be suspended with immediate effect, pending an investigation that would inevitably lead to his dismissal and possibly to criminal charges. In the play, his retirement is brought forward, although he is allowed to continue teaching until the end of term. Some critics have argued that Bennett does not treat Hector's actions seriously enough, that he lets the character off the hook by making him such a lovable figure. However, as my students point out, it's also significant that the boys themselves minimize the nature of what he does. When Hector offers a lift at the end of the day, they sigh theatrically and make their excuses – computer club, running, heading into town – until one of them, resignedly, volunteers, grinning at the others and raising his middle finger. Scripps uses his school bag as a barrier: 'I think he thought he'd got me going. In fact it was my *Tudor Economic Documents, Volume Two.*' Dakin is more afraid of the next roundabout than of anything Hector might do to him. The only boy Hector refuses to take is Posner, and this is significant too, since gentle Posner, with his spaniel-hearted love for Dakin, is the boy who would be most damaged by Hector's actions, and Hector knows this.

Hector also recognizes his own scars. He warns Irwin, who is himself falling for Dakin's dark-eyed charms, against getting involved with any of the boys. 'See it as an inoculation . . . Briefly painful but providing immunity for however long it takes.' He argues against Irwin's flashy approach to the teaching of history, seeing it – especially when applied to the Holocaust – as immoral. His view of literature is profoundly humanist, and humane. In one of the play's most moving sequences, he talks to a forlorn Posner about Thomas Hardy's use of compound adjectives, speaking of 'a sense of not sharing, of being out of it . . . a holding back. Not being in the swim. Can you see that?' Posner admits that he can, that this is how he feels, and Hector describes for him the power of books to help one feel less alone. The best moments in reading, he says, are

> when you come across something – a thought, a feeling, a way of looking at things – which you had thought special and particular to you. Now here it is, set down by someone else, a person you have never met, someone even who is long dead. And it is as if a hand has come out and taken yours.

It's a speech that adorns thousands of classroom walls – including mine – and, as a summary of the power of reading and writing, I'm not sure it can be bettered.

One of the many strengths of *The History Boys* is that

it does not offer us any easy answers. Instead, as with so many of the books we study in school, it sets out a debate, and invites us to take part. It contains many laughs, but also moments that are desperately sad. One of the saddest is when a broken Hector, his hours in the timetable reduced and his boys openly mocking his teaching methods, puts his head down on the desk and cries. The boys think it's an act, at first, but then they realize it's serious. There are uneasy nudges and glances. Scripps says, afterwards, 'I was the nearest. I ought to have been the one to reach out and touch him. But I just watched.' In the end, it's Posner who goes up to Hector and pats him awkwardly on the back. And then the moment passes. The boys act out another scene from another film. As Mrs Lintott comments: 'One of the hardest things for boys to learn is that a teacher is human. One of the hardest things for a teacher to learn is not to try and tell them.'

Teaching *The History Boys* always, inevitably, makes me think back to the time when I was applying to Oxford, not a History boy but an English Literature girl, seven years after the boys and sixty miles away. I had extra lessons after school and would walk home with a head full of ideas. That December, I got on a train at Liverpool Lime Street, bound for Oxford and my interview to read English at St Edmund Hall. The train was full of sixth-formers from various parts of the north-west, all rucksacks and excited apprehension, and before long we were swapping names and experiences. *Which college are you applying to? What A levels are you doing? What are you going to wear for your interview?* The most vocal bunch on the train were the independent-school students, who all seemed very confident and opinionated, helping themselves to information about everyone in our little part of the train. Sitting opposite me was a quiet girl from the Wirral who was trying to keep herself to herself. Next to her was a girl called Vicky, who was also applying for English and wanted to know what preparation I'd done. Which Shakespeare plays had I studied? Had I read any Dickens? What about Jane Austen? It was as if there was some kind of literary exchange rate going on, in which one Shakespeare equalled one Dickens novel or two Austens, unless the Dickens was a short one like *Hard Times*. Vicky was reading David Lodge's *Nice Work*, which of course I'd already read. I was reading Antonia White's *Frost in May*, which Vicky had never heard of. I began to feel quite optimistic.

I shared a taxi from the station with a few other people and tumbled into a cold front quad to register at the lodge and find my room. The next morning, I met the other English candidates, and in the afternoon, it was my interview. I was given a poem to read beforehand, and then knocked on the white-painted wooden door, prepared for a thorough grilling.

It was nothing like I'd expected. It was essentially a nice chat with two English tutors who got me to discuss the poem I'd read and asked me about what I was reading outside my A-level course. I talked about Charlotte Brontë and about historical contexts and the need to understand how writers felt about the society they lived in. And that was that. No inquisition; nothing I hadn't been able to handle. After so many months of preparation, it was a huge anticlimax. They must have already made up their minds that I wasn't going to get in, I thought. They'd decided to let me down gently rather than getting me to show what I really knew. Deflated, I found one of my fellow candidates and we went off to a coffee shop on the High Street for huge slabs of chocolate gateau. If I couldn't drown my sorrows, then at least I could smother them in cake.

I recognized a few people from the train – half-remembered faces across a lecture room or crowded street – when I started at Oxford the following year. I looked out for Vicky and the quiet girl from the Wirral, but I didn't find either of them. But we were all there in the same place for a little while, held together – like the newlyweds in Philip Larkin's 'The Whitsun Weddings' – by the frail travelling coincidence of being on the same train for the same reason, heading for a place so bound up in myth that it can feel difficult to experience it for yourself. I warn my aspiring Oxbridge candidates nowadays that one of the toughest things to negotiate is not the workload or the social life, but the process of disentangling what you want from Oxbridge from what all those other voices say you should want. Other universities, without Oxbridge's layers of association, are easier spaces to inhabit. Bennett's Introduction is shot through with his ambivalence about his own Oxford experience, his characteristic sense of not quite fitting in, and for me, one of the most salient moments in *The History Boys* is its final sequence, which sets out what happens to the boys in the future. The film differs from the play here – Posner's future is more hopeful, Lockwood's much sadder – but the overall message is that a place at Oxford or Cambridge is not necessarily a ticket to happiness and success.

Most importantly, *The History Boys* also makes me think back across the long years I've spent in schools, as both a pupil and a teacher. All schools have their own quirks and characteristics, but there's a sense in which they're all fundamentally similar. The smells. The hessian-backed display boards; the spider plants in the library that someone might remember to water, one day. The mixture of personalities. The sense of people coming and going, one generation after another passing through those doors. The small dramas being played out, over and over again. And the lessons learned there, which aren't always the ones you expect to learn or the ones you think are going to be the most important.

I think of those moments when students see you not as a teacher, but, as Mrs Lintott says, as human. A couple of weeks after I first saw the film of *The History Boys*, back in October 2006, I broke the news to my A-level students that I wouldn't be teaching them for the rest of their course, as they'd expected. Instead, I'd be going on adoption leave. My voice was shaky as I told them about the process that my husband and I had been through in order to adopt, and how, after months of waiting, everything had happened very quickly, in the end. I showed them photos of the little boy who was soon to become my son. A few days later, when it was our last lesson, they presented me with a card and a teddy bear that they'd clubbed together to buy, and eventually, when he'd settled in, I took my son to visit them. He caused chaos with his beloved blue tractor and his magnetic fishing game, a ginger-haired whirlwind, and over the years I had a steady stream of volunteer babysitters, several of whom are now teachers themselves.

We share parts of ourselves when we teach. We make known who we are and what we believe in. For some of us, this is more significant – even riskier – than others. Teachers who are open about their sexuality, acting as a point of security for children who feel vulnerable and sending out an important message that the world is not as straight as some people would like it to be. Teachers who share experiences of injustice and racism, who act as role models and help their students to stand tall. Teachers who use wheelchairs or communication devices, and by doing so, make it clear that these are a normal and empowering part of everyday life. Teachers who have diabetes, and talk their students through what to do if Miss or Sir goes wobbly and needs some sugar. Teachers who display posters supporting different causes and let their classrooms be used at lunchtimes as a safe haven for children who need a quiet place. Teachers who show young people what it is to be human; teachers who, just by being themselves, make the world of schools more plural and inclusive.

We're important. Outside of family, we're the most significant adult influence in many of our students' lives. Some might actually see more of us than they do of their own parents. We mop up tears and share joys. We have secret stashes of cereal bars for children who don't get breakfast at home and make sure, as best we can, that these children don't go without in other ways too: arranging funding for school trips, providing sanitary products, giving them a pound to donate to the charity collection so they can take part along with everyone else, organizing clothes exchanges so they've got something to wear for the end-of-year prom. We're a voice of calm, a point of stability in a bewildering world. We're there for the frustrations and the triumphs. None of this could be captured in a job description, but we do it anyway, because it matters. We see young people through the most complicated years of their lives, and then we watch them go off into the world, ready to become who-ever they want to be.

Schools act as witnesses to life, but they also, some-times, act as witnesses to death. I think of the funerals I've attended over the years, for both staff and students, including one, unbearably bleak, for a boy who ended his own life, and one shocked and sudden, for a colleague who died unexpectedly at the end of the Christmas term.

And the memorial services, like Hector's, with everyone in the school hall, unusually silent, a little bit embarrassed by the solemn music and the unfamiliar circumstances. I remember one memorial service when a deputy head spoke to the assembled school about death, and about the fact that a death within a school community is also part of learning: learning what to do and what to say, about the finality of death, and about the member of staff who had died, who was not just a teacher but a husband and father and friend. Occasions like this, she said, remind us that we are all mortal, that we, too, will die. It was an education in the bleak reality of life, in something bigger than any exam syllabus, and everyone was quieter and more careful for the rest of that day.

I think of the moments in my own school career that shaped me the most, the people who had the greatest influence on who I have become. Miss Spelman, the headmistress of my infants' school, who set her standards high and commanded an assembly hall full of four-to-seven-year-olds with admirable ease. Mrs McGrath, who taught me in my final year of primary school and helped my class to make the transition to a bigger and scarier world. Patient Mr Wilson, with his Fair Isle sweaters and air of bewildered amusement, without whom I'd never have passed my Maths GCSE. Ms Nevin, the Head of English who got me through sixth form and spent endless hours letting me talk about books, and who is still a friend, over thirty years later.

*

It's the end of Year Thirteen, the last lesson before study leave, and my A-level group and I are having our own bit of calculated silliness. I've brought in a box of ginger-bread people, tubes of coloured icing, cake decorations and pots of sugar sprinkles. Everyone has a gingerbread person on a paper plate, and our task is to turn it into a character from one of our set texts, *King Lear*, *Death of a Salesman* and *Tess of the d'Urbervilles*. We set to work. The concentration in the room is immense. We swap different-coloured icing, exchange one set of sprinkles for another, and cast surreptitious glances at each other's plates. At the end of the lesson, we have to guess which characters everyone has made. There are several Gloucesters, with smudges of red icing where the eyes should be, a Tess Durbeyfield on a multicoloured blighted star, and a Willy Loman, accompanied by two suitcases made from spare bits of gingerbread. It's a marvel of creativity at the end of two years of hard work. They've had a tough time, this particular year group. They had a fractured experi-ence of GCSE, because of the Covid-19 pandemic: they found themselves plunged into A levels having missed out on so many teenage rites of passage, and still have a lot to catch up on. It's been a difficult journey. But they've got there.

A week later, it's their final assembly. I say goodbye to my tutor group, some of whom I've known since they were in Year Seven, just eleven years old. Here they are now, ready for university and apprenticeships and employment. Seeing young people grow up and grow into themselves is one of the biggest privileges of my job, and now, amidst the hugs and handshakes, I've got a lump in my throat.

'Hey, Miss!'

It's the boy who, amongst all of his year group, has had one of the rockiest rides. There have been times when we weren't sure he'd make it to the end of A levels; we've had meetings with parents, difficult conversations, targets to meet. I'm still not convinced how much revision he's done. He shouldn't actually be in school today: he was told to stay at home, as the result of some end-of-term high spirits that went a bit too far. But his mates have smuggled him in somehow, and now he's here, larky and excited. 'Miss. You didn't think I'd make it, did you?'

I didn't, I tell him. But I was wrong, and I'm glad I was. He's learned a lot from the last two years, and I have too. It never stops. And this, *this*, is what it's all about.

# Afterword

In Celeste Ng's 2022 novel, *Our Missing Hearts*, the sharing of stories is an act of resistance. Children have been taken away from parents whose political views have been deemed insufficiently patriotic. Censorship is rife and citizens are encouraged to spy on their neighbours. Families depend on a network of librarians to carry hidden messages that are tucked into books and slipped into a pocket or a drawer. A poet, Margaret Miu, manages to gather accounts from parents whose children have been lost to the authorities, placed in foster care far from home. She writes down their memories, a witness to their quiet griefs. They want her to pass on their experiences and tell the world what is happening. But Margaret has to do this in secret. And so she forms a plan, involving tiny speakers, concealed in plastic bottle tops and hidden throughout the city. One night, she broadcasts her collection of stories. Her voice emerges from litter bins, from trees, from gutters and fire hydrants. People stop in their tracks, transfixed. Margaret speaks of the seemingly unimportant events, the tender human moments that make up family life: playing peekaboo, cutting the crusts off sandwiches, a day out at the pier that ends with ice cream for dinner. She does not know if any of this will make a difference. But she hopes. She hopes.

*Our Missing Hearts* is a story of love and rage and pro-test, and of the appalling acts that governments can carry out when they decide to exploit social divisions. As such, it's a warning. In her Author's Note, Ng says that the world of the novel 'isn't exactly our world, but it isn't *not* ours, either'. It's a novel that reminds us to be scep-tical, to question the messages we're fed by those in power. I'd love to teach it. I know exactly how I'd do it: not as an exam text, to be picked apart and made the subject of meticulous notes, but as a class reader, a bit every lesson, to maintain the pace and keep students intrigued. Much as I love the process of analysing texts, teenage readers need their initial encounters with novels to be different. There's a time for that deeper, more detailed exploration, but it's not on first reading.

There are other texts, too, that I want to add to my list. Elizabeth Acevedo's Carnegie Medal-winning verse novel, *The Poet X*, whose narrator, fifteen-year-old Xio-mara, pours out her anger and passion in spoken-word poetry. Dean Atta's *The Black Flamingo*, which explores themes of race and sexuality, and sees its protagonist find-ing a new identity as a drag queen. And some that I've started to teach recently, and want to get to know further.

Last year, my department introduced a new set text in Year Seven: Zana Fraillon's *The Bone Sparrow*, set in a deten-tion centre for Rohingya Muslims in Australia. It's a novel that explores friendship, family, the importance of stories, and what it is to grow up without a home. We examined narrative methods and analysed the creation of character;

we researched the situation of the Rohingya people and the UN Convention on the Rights of the Child. And we also talked about being an outsider, about feeling strange and unwelcome. One of my students contacted Zana Fraillon, via her website, to ask some questions about the novel, and was beside himself with excitement when she replied, less than twelve hours later. Another student said, 'It's really weird, when you think about it. We've read a book, but we've learned about so many things I'd never have expected to learn about.'

In Year Eight, we explore Robert Macfarlane and Jackie Morris's *The Lost Words*, a beautifully illustrated collection of poetry that was inspired by a decision made by the Oxford University Press, in 2008, to remove certain words from its *Junior Dictionary*. These words, so the OUP claimed, were 'no longer relevant' to today's young people. *The Lost Words* begins by inviting us to imagine a world where words begin to vanish from the language of children. Words such as 'otter' and 'dandelion', 'conker' and 'hare': the very words removed from the *Oxford Junior Dictionary*. My students pore over the images and talk about the creatures they see: a barn owl's ashy wings, the sudden flash of a kingfisher. We write poems of our own based on Morris's illustrations, and then listen to each other as we read out loud, describing the acrobatic tumble of an otter, the blue sheen on a magpie's feathers, the gawky unfolding of a heron.

One of my favourite books to explore in class is a book that doesn't actually contain any words. This is

Shaun Tan's 2006 graphic novel, *The Arrival*. It's a story of exile, of a man who has to leave his family and home and travel to a different country. We don't know why, but we're given hints. There's a tentacled creature that twines itself around the rooftops of the city and lurks menacingly round corners, its shadows haunting the town at night. We discuss whether the creature is real or metaphorical, and decide on the latter. It could be war or disease or prejudice: anything, in fact, that makes people feel that they're no longer safe. The illustrations are in sepia tones. Some – the man's tearful wife saying goodbye, a steam train disappearing into the distance, a crowd of people on a ship – carry echoes of particular historical situations, most notably the Second World War, and migration to the USA in the nineteenth and early twentieth centuries. But the country that the man eventually arrives in is like no other. The writing system, the buildings, the vehicles, even the animals, are all utterly estranging. And that's the point. No matter who you are, no matter which language you speak or what kind of background you're from, this new country will be alien to you. Tan does not privilege any of his readers: nobody will find this strange world easier to navigate than anyone else. We are all equally disorientated.

Books and books and books. Books that prompt teenagers to look inwards, at themselves and their developing identities, and out, at the messy world they are inheriting from us. Books that are reassuring and books that are angry and spiky and difficult. Books that ask questions. Books that young people might not like or understand at first, but that will needle themselves into their minds and stay there until they finally make sense. Hundreds of them, all wanting our attention and our time. And time spent reading, as Hugh Hewitt of the *Washington Post* writes in an article about the importance of fiction in a period of difficulty and unrest, is never time wasted. Instead, 'it is time, and the lessons of time, brought into focus'.

I used to be able to make more creative choices about the books my students read. At GCSE, as long as we ticked certain boxes, we had a lot more freedom to select texts that would speak to the young people we had in front of us. We could study film and television alongside plays, novels and poems. Our students could respond imaginatively, rewriting part of a text from the point of view of a minor character, producing a playscript or staging a discussion.

Things have changed, and not for the better. Our teenagers have to write, under exam conditions, about a nineteenth-century novel and a Shakespeare play, a collection of poems and a text that is supposedly modern but could have been written as long ago as 1945. The answers they have to produce are conventional literary essays that analyse authorial methods and comment on historical context. There is little room for creativity.

I'm sometimes asked what I would change about our current education system, if I could. There are many things on my wish list, but one of the biggest is this scope to be creative. I want my students to be able to dig into the books they read and find threads they can pick away at and explore. That character who's always silent, always on the outside: what are they thinking? That person who misses out so that the protagonist can get what he or she wants: what's it like to be them? What's going on in the minds and lives of Joe Gargery, or Mr Farthing in *A Kestrel for a Knave*, or Edna, the maid in *An Inspector Calls*? How do Ralph and Jack behave towards each other after their rescue? How do Helen Robinson and her children cope after Tom's death? What does Lady Macbeth think about, in her castle in the cold north of Scotland, when she realizes that her husband does not need her any longer?

I want all of this because one of the most important things our young people need is to be able to position themselves elsewhere. The biggest change I have seen during my years in the classroom is, of course, the rise of the internet, which offers so many possibilities for connection and communication but also enables people to be increasingly solipsistic. We can browse, swipe, move on: if something doesn't hold our interest, we don't need to persist. We can seek out those who we like and who are like us. I see the effects of this in class in a reluctance to tackle difficulty, a creeping resistance to engage. The books we read in school are vital in introducing young people to ideas and experiences that lie beyond their own immediate concerns and that they would not necessarily choose to explore. Imagining what it's like to be in someone else's position, to walk around, as Atticus Finch says, in their skin: books nudge us out of our familiar worlds and forge an encounter with what lies beyond.

This book has been, in part, a love letter to English teaching, the profession that has sustained me for the whole of my working life. Love alone, though, is not going to be enough to sustain English teaching, because it is a profession that is under increasing threat. The teaching profession as a whole is crumbling, due to a number of factors: the pressures of a target-driven system, of Ofsted, of years of underfunding, of the effects of the Covid-19 pandemic, of a lack of aware-ness of the importance and difficulty of what teachers do. But English faces additional problems. The relent-less emphasis on science, technology, engineering and mathematics – the STEM subjects – means that the number of students opting to take English at A level has dropped. The STEM subjects, at this level, feel safer than English to many students, as they involve clear bodies of factual knowledge and straightforward tech-niques that can be memorized and mastered, rather than the complications of nuance and interpretation. They also, so teenagers and their parents are told, offer a path-way to a lucrative career. As a result, fewer students are embarking on English degrees. And, with a sick inevit-ability, fewer graduates are applying to train to teach

English. Many of those who do train leave the profession within five years, worn down by the workload and the constant need to spin plates and juggle competing demands, and lured by the promise of higher salaries and better conditions elsewhere.

English deserves more than this. It deserves more than this because it matters. For one thing, the ability to read sensitively and write precisely is vital, not only in many workplaces but also to participating in the life of a democracy. We need to be able to spot when others are using words to manipulate us; we need to be able to critique and challenge and hold to account. As consumers, and as voters, we need to be able to detect false promises and see through weasel words. And as human beings, we need to use language for a host of reasons: to build relationships and reach out to others, to express our thoughts and frustrations, to persuade and entertain and imagine and create, to share joy, deliver bad news and offer comfort. We would not be who we are without the words through which we connect with both others and ourselves. English is the subject that helps us to shape our relationship with words and the many ways in which humans have used them. It teaches us to experiment and question, to read between the lines. We need these skills more than ever.

We are often told that studying English is an indulgence in a world that needs more scientists and engineers. Degrees in English and other arts and humanities subjects have been derided in recent years by politicians who have criticized them as a fruitless waste of time. They do not increase earning potential; they do not contribute enough to the economy. Yet a briefing published by the House of Lords in December 2022 stated that the creative industries contributed £109 billion to the UK economy in 2021, and that the UK was the world's fifth-largest exporter of creative services. And the skills fostered by studying English are widely valued by employers. In her book *The New Education: How to Revolutionize the University to Prepare Students for a World in Flux*, Cathy N. Davidson cites the findings of Project Oxygen, a 2013 study carried out by Google to identify 'the qualities that lead to promotion and a successful career'. Project Oxygen discovered that the top six skills for success included empathy, critical thinking, communicating and listening well, and possessing insights into others, including their different values and points of view. In a subsequent project, Google found that its most effective teams were not those containing the most skilled technologists, but those whose members displayed 'generosity, curiosity towards the ideas of . . . teammates, empathy, and emotional intelligence'. A report published by the British Academy in 2020 pointed out that eight of the ten fastest-growing sectors of the UK economy employ more graduates from arts, humanities and social science subjects than STEM disciplines, and highlights the role of the arts and humanities in developing 'active citizens who can think for themselves and hold authority to account'.

Reading matters in our wider lives too. It brings comfort and improves our mental health. The charity Shared

Reading brings together thousands of people each week to listen to stories read aloud by volunteers. It supports people living with mental and physical health problems, families under stress, children in care and individuals struggling with addiction, and has had a particular impact in the criminal justice system, where it offers a space for offenders to discuss texts, reflect on stories and share their vulnerabilities. Initiatives such as the Reading for Wellbeing project, launched in 2021 by the crime writer Ann Cleeves, have been shown to reduce social isolation and offer a means of escape from the grind of everyday life. Cleeves comments: 'Stories can be healing. If we're drowning in chaotic thoughts of our own, to step inside someone else's head, just for a while, is a kind of freedom.'

It's vital, then, that we continue to fight for the importance of books, and that we give our children the chance to read and explore all the many ways in which people have interpreted the world through texts. Novels and plays and poems, memoirs and nature writing, films and songs and spoken-word poetry, animations and video games and television drama: all part of an ongoing conversation about the world, and a conversation that our young people need to join.

The books we read at school contribute to our lives in many ways. They ask us questions that are not asked in other lessons, with answers that are not necessarily right or wrong. They reach out beyond the classroom and alert us to aspects of the world that seem bewildering and unfair. They are by no means perfect: they might reflect parts of our culture, our shared past, that demand interrogation, and we need to be able to challenge them and unpick the complexities they contain. Perhaps most importantly, they prompt us to examine ourselves, thinking about our own reactions and values, how we might behave in the situations they explore. Going back to these books, after a gap of perhaps many decades, reminds us that the conversations they spark, the arguments and ideas and interpretations, are potentially endless. The best reading lessons never really finish. There is always something else to say.

# Acknowledgements

Writing – like teaching – is never a solitary pursuit, and in writing this book, I've benefited from the support, encouragement and guidance of many people. My agent, Charlotte Atyeo, at Greyhound Literary helped me to shape the idea I had in the early spring of 2020 into the outline of a book, and my wonderful editor, Helen Garnons-Williams, at Fig Tree – plus assistant editor, Ella Harold – steered me through the process of bringing *Reading Lessons* into being. Charlotte, Helen and Ella have been an absolute joy to work with and I cannot thank them enough for their judicious advice, their close and careful reading, and for the cheerleading that kept me going at the times when combining writing with being a full-time Head of English seemed like utter madness. It's been quite a journey, but one that I feel very privileged to have been able to make.

My career as an English teacher has been a journey all of its own, and in this book there are traces of many of the friends and colleagues I've taught alongside over the years. A special mention must go to Richard Cave, with whom I've worked for over two decades now: I've drawn on his wise counsel more times than I can remember, in many areas of my life. Ela Donnelly, my Duke of Edinburgh Award buddy, was by my side during a particularly memorable journey to the Lake District, and, just like my imaginary Mrs Lintott, knows exactly when biscuits are necessary. My friends in the wider English-teaching community have helped me to develop, question and refine my thinking about the subject, and I'd like to thank Gary Snapper, Barbara Bleiman, Bob Eaglestone, Sean McEvoy, Andrew Green, Marcello Giovanelli, Julie Blake, John Hodgson, Jenny Stevens, Pamela Bickley, Steve Willshaw, Yvonne Williams and the late Sue Dymoke for all they have done to keep the subject alive – not to mention defiant, beautiful and intellectually rigorous – in the time they've been involved in the profession.

Many thanks and much love to Janet Nevin, the A-level English teacher who did more than anyone to shape the course of my life. I have no idea where I'd have ended up – or what I'd have ended up doing – if she hadn't encouraged me to study English and apply to Oxford, and I owe her an enormous amount for opening up the world of books and literary study to me. Lucy Newlyn and Kate Ward-Perkins took a gamble on me as a very raw comprehensive school applicant to St Edmund Hall back in the winter of 1990: I think it paid off. Josephine Guy supervised my PhD at the University of Nottingham, and she – along with Philip Smallwood and the late Ron Carter, my very thoughtful and encouraging examiners – did much to help me to think about the discipline of English Literature and the complicated beast it has become.

Dermot Fitzsimons and Steve Fogarty, two of my old schoolfriends, were extremely generous in sharing with me their experiences of growing up under Section 28.

My former student Penny Copping kindly allowed me to quote from her message about the impact that *Oranges Are Not the Only Fruit* had on her as a teenager. Emma Davis shared her thoughts about teaching the stage adaptation of *Noughts & Crosses* at her school in Peterborough. Claire Stoneman drew my attention to Michael J. Sandel's book *The Tyranny of Merit: What's Become of the Common Good?* in a post on her blog www.birmingham teacher.wordpress.com, and I'd like to thank her for sparking off the thoughts that shaped my chapter on *Death of a Salesman*. Twayna Mayne and Al Coates interviewed me for their podcasts about the ways in which adoption is portrayed in school set texts, and I'd like to thank them for helping me to refine my ideas and present them to a wider audience. My lovely friends Elly Spilberg, Linda Hill, Jan Flanagan, Simon Mozley and Eleanor Martindale have all encouraged me, bounced ideas around, read drafts of chapters and fed me cake.

As I hope I've demonstrated in this book, the young people I've taught have played a hugely important role in pushing me to think clearly about the place of literature in education, and to make their lessons challenging and thought-provoking. I'd like to extend particular thanks to Ryan, Sayang, Anderson, Brian and Andrew, the members of my sixth-form reading group, for their careful exploration of *Noughts & Crosses* and *I Know Why the Caged Bird Sings*; to Ruby, for recommending Rutger Bregman's *Humankind: A Hopeful History*; to Hannah, for her long and thoughtful email about Maya Angelou;

and to my A-level English groups of 2021–23 and 2022–24, whose lessons on *Death of a Salesman* helped to shape my thinking as I wrote my chapter on Arthur Miller. My Year Eight class of 2022–23 made their own inimitable contributions to my chapter on *Great Expectations* and reminded me of the importance of doing all the different voices. Isaac, Beon and Jacob allowed me to quote from their wonderful work.

My parents, Frank and Eileen, did not live to see this book published, or indeed the many years of my career that preceded it. I've spent more than half my life without them, but they are part of me in ways that I am still learning about, and I hope they'd be proud of who I've become and the digging I have done. My brother and sisters, Peter, Julie and Susan, have supported me all the way and I am more grateful than I can possibly say for everything they've done for me, including turning a blind eye to those early raids on their bookshelves.

The greatest of thanks, and lots of love, to my husband, Matthew, and my son, Levi, who have given me their unstinting support – and brought me many cups of coffee, and done my share of the housework – during the many weekends I've spent hunched over a laptop. I couldn't have done any of this without them.

And finally, to all the shadow colleagues who've shared my classroom over the years, both those I've written about in this book and the many others: thank you for the lessons in reading that you have helped me to give to so many young people.

# References and Further Reading

One of my aims in *Reading Lessons* has been to send readers back to the books I've explored, to rediscover old favourites or reassess books they might have hated years ago. All of the set texts I've discussed are widely available, some in a range of editions. All of the poems I've referred to can be found easily online, and if *Reading Lessons* has helped to rekindle a love of poetry, I'd recommend spending some time on the Poetry Archive website (www.poetryarchive.org), which contains thousands of poems, accompanied by recordings of poets reading their own work.

## Introduction

The quotations about reading that I refer to are from Emily Dickinson's poem 'There is no Frigate like a Book' (1890), Roald Dahl's classic *Matilda* (Jonathan Cape, 1988), Nora Ephron's memoir *I Feel Bad About My Neck: And Other Thoughts on Being a Woman* (Alfred A. Knopf, 2006) and Alan Bennett's *The History Boys* (Faber, 2004).

## 'My Last Duchess'

Browning's poem can be found on the Poetry Archive website (www.poetryarchive.org/poem/my-last-duchess), where there is also a recording of the poem being read aloud by Anthony Thwaite. It's also available at www. poetryfoundation.org, along with a commentary by Camille Guthrie.

The websites I refer to in my discussion of gender-based violence, misogyny and coercive control are www.every daysexism.com, www.everyonesinvited.uk and www. isthisokgm.co.uk. The Duluth Power and Control Wheel can be found at www.theduluthmodel.org.

A huge amount has been written about Andrew Tate since his rise to prominence in the summer of 2022. Shanti Das's *Guardian* article 'Inside the violent, mis- ogynistic world of TikTok's new star, Andrew Tate' (6 August 2022; www.theguardian.com/technology/2022/ aug/06/andrew-tate-violent-misogynistic-world-of- tiktok-new-star) is a good starting point.

Margaret Atwood's short story 'My Last Duchess' is in her collection *Moral Disorder* (Virago, 2006). Maggie O'Farrell's novel *The Marriage Portrait*, based on the story of Lucrezia de' Medici, was published by Tinder Press in 2022. Naomi Wolf's *The Beauty Myth* – a book that made a huge impression on me as a nineteen-year-old – was published by Vintage in 1990; a shortened edition, with a new Introduction, was published by Vintage in 2015.

## An Inspector Calls

If you're revisiting *An Inspector Calls* – or exploring it for the first time – then there are a number of dramatizations available online, including the 1954 black-and-white version with Alistair Sim as Inspector Goole (www.archive. org/details/AnInspectorCalls1954_201508), and the BBC's 1982 version with Bernard Hepton (www.youtube.com/ watch?v=giW3d8hvyq4). The most recent version, and the one I refer to in the chapter, is the BBC's 2015 production, with David Thewlis on excellent form as the Inspector. Purists might quibble with this version, as it uses flashbacks to show us scenes from the life of Eva Smith, but dramatically it is very powerful, and has a stellar cast that includes Ken Stott and Miranda Richardson as Mr and Mrs Birling. If you're able to see Stephen Daldry's stage production, it is highly recommended – its staging adds another dimension to Priestley's attack on the ignorance of the moneyed classes, and makes a neat connection between the play's setting and the wars that Mr Birling so pompously dismisses.

J. B. Priestley's *English Journey* was published in 1934 and is worth a read for its portrayal of England in the interwar years, though be prepared for Priestley's idiosyncrasies. The most recent edition was published by HarperNorth in 2023.

There's a lot of J. B. Priestley-related material on the internet. BBC Radio 4's *Great Lives* series featured Priestley in an episode first broadcast 11 January 2011, with Barry Cryer and Martin Wainwright: it can be found on the BBC Sounds website (www.bbc.co.uk/sounds/play/b00x95hm?scrlybrkr=82822dc4). Also on Sounds (www.bbc.co.uk/sounds/play/b00sfotg) is an episode of *Archive on 4* focusing on Priestley's *Postscripts*, first broadcast 22 May 2010, which gives a sense of the writer's wartime broadcasts and the controversy they caused. On the British Pathé website (www.britishpathe.com/asset/81058/) you can find the episode of *Personalities* that I refer to, first issued 20 November 1944.

Georg Weerth's scathing quotation about Bradford is taken from Martin Greenwood's article 'Bradford's rich history has shaped its UK City of Culture bid', *Bradford Telegraph and Argus*, 8 April 2022 (www.thetelegraphandargus.co.uk/news/20051561.bradfords-rich-history-shaped-uk-city-culture-bid).

There are many articles online about the appalling death of Awaab Ishak: Mark Brown and Robert Booth give an account of his inquest in their *Guardian* article of 15 November 2022, 'Death of two-year-old from mould in flat a "defining moment", says coroner' (www.theguardian.

com/uk-news/2022/nov/15/death-of-two-year-old-awaab-ishak-chronic-mould-in-flat-a-defining-moment-says-coroner).


## To Kill a Mockingbird

There are several different editions of *To Kill a Mocking-bird*, including various schools editions: there's also a wonderful graphic novel version, adapted and illustrated by Fred Fordham (Heinemann, 2018). The 1962 film, directed by Robert Mulligan and starring Gregory Peck and Mary Badham, is definitely worth a watch. Charles J. Shields's biography of Harper Lee, *Mockingbird: A Portrait of Harper Lee* (Henry Holt, 2016), is a fantastic source of information about the writer herself.

*To Kill a Mockingbird* features in lots of lists and surveys. I refer to the BBC Big Read (www.bbc.co.uk/arts/bigread/top100.shtml), the Museums, Libraries and Archives Council's list of thirty books every adult should read before they die (www.listchallenges.com/museums-libraries-and-archives-societys-30) and Amnesty International's 2016 survey of parents on books that develop empathy (www.forreadingaddicts.co.uk/polls-and-discussion/parents-choose-10-books-they-believe-build-empathy).

The American Library Association's Banned and Challenged Books website is a fascinating – and troubling – source of information about censorship and book-banning, including the objections raised to books across the US. It runs an annual Banned Books Week that celebrates the freedom to read, and offers support and resources for schools, libraries and individuals. It can be found at www.ala.org/advocacy/bbooks.

In writing about the arguments surrounding *To Kill a Mockingbird*, I've drawn on a range of articles, including Osamudia R. James, 'Now We Can Finally Say Goodbye to the White Savior Myth of Atticus' (*New York Times*, 15 July 2015; www.nytimes.com/roomfordebate/2015/07/15/how-should-schools-deal-with-the-new-atticus-finch/now-we-can-finally-say-goodbye-to-the-white-savior-myth-of-atticus), Tanya Landman, 'Is *To Kill a Mockingbird* a racist book?' (*Guardian*, 20 October 2015; www.theguardian.com/childrens-books-site/2015/oct/20/is-to-kill-a-mockingbird-a-racist-book-tanya-landman), Kristine Phillips, 'A school district drops *To Kill a Mockingbird* and *Huckleberry Finn* over use of the n-word' (*Washington Post*, 7 February 2018; www.washingtonpost.com/news/education/wp/2018/02/07/a-school-district-drops-to-kill-a-mockingbird-and-huckleberry-finn-over-use-of-the-n-word), Khaleda Rahman, 'Schools Drop *To Kill A Mockingbird* From Reading List After Race Complaint' (*Newsweek*, 25 January 2022; www.newsweek.com/schools-drop-kill-mockingbird-required-reading-list-

1672563) and Lamiat Sabin, 'Edinburgh school cancels *To Kill a Mockingbird* as book "promotes white saviour narrative"' (*Independent*, 6 July 2021; www.independ ent.co.uk/news/education/education-news/ edinburgh-school-to-kill-a-mockingbird-b1878806. html).

My exploration of Aaron Sorkin's stage adaptation was informed by Bob Ashby, '*To Kill a Mockingbird* at Kennedy Center opens us to our political onus today' (DC Theater Arts website, www.dctheaterarts.org), David Sims, 'A New Way of Looking at *To Kill a Mockingbird*' (*Atlantic*, 17 December 2019; www.theatlantic.com/entertainment/ archive/2019/12/aaron-sorkin-finds-new-edge-to-kill-mockingbird/603652) and Katherine Cowles, 'Aaron Sorkin's *To Kill a Mockingbird* is a fierce, funny and near-flawless stage adaptation' (*New Statesman*, 1 April 2022; www.newstatesman.com/culture/theatre/2022/04/ aaron-sorkins-to-kill-a-mockingbird-is-a-fierce-funny-and-near-flawless-stage-adaptation).

Information about agriculture in the Fens was drawn from the National Farmers' Union report *Delivering for Britain: Food and farming in the Fens* (April 2019; www. nfuonline.com/archive?treeid=117727). Information about the UK daffodil harvest is from the Warwick Crop Centre at the University of Warwick (www.warwick. ac.uk/fac/sci/lifesci/wcc/research/crop_research/ narcissus).

## *Jane Eyre* and *Wide Sargasso Sea*

There is an endless amount to read on Charlotte Brontë, and indeed on the rest of her family. You could start – as I did – with Winifred Gérin's *Charlotte Brontë: The Evolution of Genius* (Oxford University Press, 1967), or you could go back to Elizabeth Gaskell's 1857 *The Life of Charlotte Brontë*, but you absolutely must also read Juliet Barker's *The Brontës*, first published in 1994 and reissued in a revised edition by Abacus in 2010. Once you've finished, move on to Barker's *The Brontës: A Life in Letters* (Overlook Press, 2002). I'd also recommend Lyndall Gordon's *Charlotte Brontë: A Passionate Life* (1996, reissued 2008 by Virago) for its exploration of the writer as a 'rising character' full of spark and anger, and Claire Harman's *Charlotte Brontë: A Life* (Penguin, 2015). Lucasta Miller's *The Brontë Myth* (Vintage, 2002) offers a fascinating look at our image of the Brontë family. Virginia Woolf's *A Room of One's Own* (1929) examines the barriers faced by women writers, including the impact of Brontë's 'hunger, rebellion and rage' on her creative expression.

The Silver Petticoat Review's ranking of its top fifteen *Jane Eyre* adaptations can be found at www.silverpetticoatreview. com/jane-eyre-movies-adaptations-ranked. My own favourite is the BBC's 2006 adaptation, with Ruth Wilson as Jane, but Cary Fukunaga's 2011 film version, with Mia Wasikowska as Jane, comes a very close second.

If all of this has piqued your interest, and if you're able

to do so, you could visit some of the places I describe at the end of the chapter. Haworth needs no introduction, but North Lees Hall, near Hathersage, is especially worth a visit.

*Wide Sargasso Sea* is available in the Penguin Modern Classics series. It was adapted for television by the BBC in 2006, with Rebecca Hall as Antoinette and Rafe Spall as Rochester, and is available on DVD. Miranda Seymour's biography *I Used to Live Here Once: The Haunted Life of Jean Rhys*, published by William Collins in 2022, was an invaluable source of information about Rhys's life.

Finally, David Lodge's novel *Nice Work* (Penguin, 1988), which prompted me to read *Jane Eyre* and *Wuthering Heights*, is well worth a read for its satirical take on 1980s politics and culture, as well as its exploration of the contrasting worlds of industry and academia.

## Oranges Are Not the Only Fruit

*Oranges Are Not the Only Fruit* was first published by Pandora in 1984; the most recent edition is the Vintage paperback. The wonderful 1990 BBC adaptation, starring Charlotte Coleman and Geraldine McEwan, is available on DVD and on various streaming services. *Oranges* was explored over four consecutive Saturdays in John Mullan's Book Club series for the *Guardian* in 2007: the first of

Mullan's articles, which offer fascinating insights into Winterson's narrative methods, can be found at www.the guardian.com/books/2007/oct/20/jeanettewinterson. Winterson's memoir *Why Be Happy When You Could Be Normal?* was published by Vintage in 2011.

There's an extremely moving episode of BBC Radio 4's *Soul Music* devoted to Bronski Beat's song 'Smalltown Boy' and what it has meant to various listeners over the years. It was first broadcast on 14 July 2021 and is available on BBC Sounds at www.bbc.co.uk/sounds/play/m000xr7r?scrlybrkr=82822dc4.

Matthew Todd's article 'How Section 28's painful legacy is still being secretly felt three decades on', published in *Attitude* in May 2018 (www.attitude.co.uk/culture/sexu ality/how-section-28s-painful-legacy-is-still-being-felt-three-decades-on-295974), gives a sense of the fear that surrounded this appalling piece of legislation. The American Library Association's Bibliography for Gay Teens is at www.ala.org/rt/rrt/popularresources/teens.

The TV adaptation of *Oranges* features in Tim Lusher's list 'The Guardian's top 50 television dramas of all time', published on 12 January 2010 (www.theguardian.com/tv-and-radio/tvandradioblog/2010/jan/12/guardian-50-television-dramas); information about the response of members of the Elim Pentecostal Church is taken from Julia Stone and Alan Rimmer, 'Church in TV lesbians row', published in the *Sunday Mirror* on 14 January 1990 (www.britishnews paperarchive.co.uk/viewer/bl/0002137/19900114/015/ 0011). John Mullan's *Guardian* article 'You write from a wound' (10 November 2007; www.theguardian.com/ books/2007/nov/10/jeanettewinterson) and Chitra Ramaswamy's interview with Jeanette Winterson in the *Scotsman* (1 November 2011; www.scotsman.com/arts-and-culture/interview-jeanette-winterson-writer-1655474) both refer to the death of Mrs Winterson during the broadcast of *Oranges Are Not the Only Fruit*.

In the chapter, I also refer to Susan Hill's 1983 novel, *The Woman in Black*, now available in an edition by Vintage, and to Philip Larkin's collection *The Whitsun Weddings* (Faber, 1964), a book that taught me so much about the study of poetry. Joan G. Robinson is perhaps most famous now for her 1967 novel, *When Marnie Was There*, which was adapted by Studio Ghibli in 2016, but if you can track down a copy of *Charley* (Armada Lions, 1971), it's an absolute delight.

## Great Expectations

There are many different editions of *Great Expectations*, including some excellent graphic novel and manga versions: the Classical Comics graphic novel adaptation (2009), which uses Dickens's own words, is particularly good. There are also many TV and film adaptations. The one we use in school is the BBC's 2011 version, with Douglas Booth as Pip, Ray Winstone as Magwitch and Gillian Anderson as Miss Havisham, but there is also the 2023 BBC adaptation, with Olivia Colman as Miss Havisham, and of course David Lean's classic 1946 film, starring John Mills as Pip.

Peter Bazalgette's thought-provoking *The Empathy Instinct: How to Create a More Civil Society* was published by John Murray in 2017. Lynsey Hanley's *Estates: An Intimate History* (Granta Books, 2007) helped me to understand the wall in my own head, as well as being a hugely important book in its own right; Hanley's *Respectable: Crossing the Class Divide* (Penguin, 2017) is also recommended.

Tony Harrison's poem 'Book Ends' can be found in his *Collected Poems* (Penguin, 2016), and also on the Poetry Archive website (poetryarchive.org/poem/book-ends). Seamus Heaney's 'Digging' was first published in *Death of a Naturalist* (Faber, 1966) and can be found on the Poetry Foundation website (www.poetryfoundation. org/poems/57040/death-of-a-naturalist); a search on YouTube will lead you to a number of recordings of Heaney reading his own work.

## A Kestrel for a Knave

*A Kestrel for a Knave* is available as a Penguin Modern Classics edition, although you'll need to track down a second-hand copy if you want one with the iconic V-sign cover. It should go without saying that Ken Loach's film *Kes* (1969) is a must-watch.

The *Guardian* published a number of articles on Barry Hines to mark the writer's death on 18 March 2016. Mark Hodkinson and Tony Garnett's obituary was published on 20 March 2016 (www.theguardian.com/books/2016/mar/20/barry-hines-obituary-a-kestrel-for-a-knave-author), and was followed on 21 March by John Hall's 1970 interview with Barry Hines (www.the guardian.com/books/2016/mar/21/barry-hines-1970-interview-kes-archive) and Ian McMillan's tribute 'Yorkshire found its voice in *Kes*' (www.theguardian.com/commentisfree/2016/mar/21/yorkshire-barry-hines-kes-barnsley-yorkshire-poetry).

Greg Davies's fascinating documentary *Looking for Kes*, featuring an interview with Dai (David) Bradley, was first broadcast by BBC4 on 19 November 2019, and can now be viewed on YouTube (www.youtube.com/watch?v=sg99OdsvfXI).

Information about Kirk Balk Academy, the school Billy would attend nowadays, is taken from its website: www.kba.northerneducationtrust.org.

The books I remember reading in my early years at secondary school are Eve Garnett's *The Family from One End*

*Street* (Frederick Muller, 1937), John Rowe Townsend's *Gumble's Yard* (Hutchinson, 1961), Keith Waterhouse's *There is a Happy Land* (Michael Joseph, 1957) and Elizabeth Stucley's *Magnolia Buildings* (Bodley Head, 1960). I reread them while researching this chapter and was transported back to the English classrooms of the mid 1980s.

## Noughts & Crosses

*Noughts & Crosses* was first published in 2001; the most recent edition was published by Oxford University Press in 2021. A graphic novel version, adapted by Ian Edginton and illustrated by John Aggs, was published by Doubleday in 2015. Dominic Cooke's stage adaptation was published by Nick Hern Books in 2007. The 2020 BBC adaptation of the novel is available on DVD and on BBC iPlayer. Malorie Blackman's autobiography, *Just Sayin': My Life in Words*, was published by Merky Books in 2022.

John Agard's poem 'Checking Out Me History' can be read on the Poetry by Heart website at www.poetrybyheart.org.uk/poems/checking-out-me-history. I'd also recommend the BBC's short film of Agard reading his poem and talking about its composition: it's at www.bbc.co.uk/teach/class-clips-video/john-agard-checking-out-me-history-analysis/zdbkqp3?scrlybrkr=82822dc4. This poem, along with 'Half-Caste' and 'Flag', is explored in detail by Daljit Nagra on the British Library's Discovering

Literature website at www.bl.uk/20th-century-literature/ articles/close-readings-of-john-agards-checking-out-me-history-flag-and-half-caste.

If you want an insight into the earliest version of the National Curriculum, have a look at *The Cox Report: English for ages 5 to 16*, published by HMSO in 1989 and available at www.education-uk.org/documents/cox1989/cox89. html. The development of this curriculum – one that aimed to be vibrant, creative and respectful of students' own backgrounds and cultures – formed the backdrop of much of my teacher-training course, and Brian Cox's injunction that English should teach students to be 'active makers of meaning' has steered me through my career.

As stated in the chapter, Malorie Blackman is mentioned in two songs: 'Superheroes' by Stormzy, from his 2019 album, *Heavy is the Head*, and 'Written in the Stars' by Tinie Tempah, from the 2020 album *Disc-Overy*.

The polls that feature *Noughts & Crosses* are 'The 100 best books of the 21st century', published in the *Guardian* on 21 September 2019 (www.theguardian.com/books/2019/ sep/21/best-books-of-the-21st-century), and the BBC's Big Read (www.bbc.co.uk/arts/bigread/top100.shtml).

Candice Carty-Williams's praise for Blackman is quoted on the Penguin Books website at www.penguin. co.uk/series/XANDOS/noughts-and-crosses, and Ruth

Borthwick's description of Blackman's work is quoted in Sarah Shaffi's article 'Malorie Blackman's "dynamic imaginary worlds" win her the PEN Pinter prize', the *Guardian*, 21 June 2022 (www.theguardian.com/books/2022/jun/21/malorie-blackman-wins-pen-pinter-prize).

Jeffrey Boakye's *I Heard What You Said: A Black Teacher, A White System* (Picador, 2022) and Chelsea Kwakye and Ọrẹ Ogunbiyi's *Taking Up Space: The Black Girl's Manifesto for Change* (Merky Books, 2019) are both essential reading on issues surrounding education and diversity.

You can read about Lit in Colour, the initiative launched by Penguin Random House and the Runnymede Trust in 2020 to broaden the range of texts taught at GCSE and A level, at www.litincolour.penguin.co.uk.

Chimamanda Ngozi Adichie's 2009 TED Talk, 'The danger of a single story', is on the TED website at www.ted.com/talks/chimamanda_ngozi_adichie_the_danger_of_a_single_story.

### Lord of the Flies

The standard edition of *Lord of the Flies* is published by Faber, although various educational editions are also available.

There's a fascinating discussion of *Lord of the Flies* in Sarah Dillon's 'Literary Pursuits – Golding's *Lord of the Flies*', broadcast on BBC Radio 3 on 2 June 2019 and available on the BBC website at www.bbc.co.uk/programmes/m00o5np2. Peter Brook's *Lord of the Flies* (British Lion Film Corporation, 1963) is a must, as is Richard Dale's documentary *Time Flies*, first broadcast on BBC2 on 23 November 1996 and available on YouTube (www.youtube.com/watch?v=V5YnE1pPqfY&t=3s). You could, if you want to, watch Harry Hook's 1990 film – the one I wouldn't let my Year Tens watch – but be prepared for it to be very different from Golding's novel! It's definitely worth reading Marianne Wiggins's novel *John Dollar* (Secker & Warburg, 1989) for an even more disturbing twist on the trope of abandonment.

Jeffrey Boakye's *I Heard What You Said: A Black Teacher, A White System* was published by Picador in 2022.

Rutger Bregman's *Humankind: A Hopeful History*, which contains some fascinating perspectives on Golding's novel, was published by Bloomsbury in 2020.

Jimmy McGovern's *Hearts & Minds* was broadcast by Channel 4 from 16 February to 9 March 1995; all four episodes are available on YouTube (www.youtube.com/watch?v=TmapBpywobY).

## Coram Boy

*Coram Boy* was first published by Mammoth in 2000. A stage adaptation by Helen Edmundson was published by Nick Hern Books in 2005. Jamila Gavin's website is at www.jamilagavin.com.

There is a wealth of information about the history of the Foundling Hospital and of adoption in the UK in general. Three books I'd recommend are Gillian Pugh's *London's Forgotten Children: Thomas Coram and the Foundling Hospital* (The History Press, 2007), Jenny Keating's *A Child for Keeps: The History of Adoption in England, 1918–45* (Palgrave Macmillan, 2008) and Hunter Davies's *Relative Strangers: A history of adoption and a tale of triplets* (Sphere, 2003). If you're in London, do pay a visit to the Foundling Museum in Coram's Fields: it is now run by CoramBAAF, the UK's largest charity for adopted and care-experienced children, and holds regular exhibitions exploring themes related to childhood, parenting and care.

Lemn Sissay's poem 'Superman was a Foundling' can be read on the Foundling Museum's website at www.found lingmuseum.co.uk, as well as on the walls of its study space. Information about Woodrow Phoenix's view of superheroes was drawn from the exhibition 'Superheroes, Orphans & Origins: 125 years in comics', Foundling Museum, London, 1 April–28 August 2022.

I've written about the way adoption is depicted in school set texts in 'Images of Adoption: Adoption in Literature and in the English Classroom', published in the Spring 2016 issue of *Teaching English*, the magazine of the National Association for the Teaching of English. In this article, I explore Susan Hill's *The Woman in Black* (1983) and Willy Russell's musical *Blood Brothers* (1983). I've also spoken about this topic on two podcasts: Twayna Mayne's Loco Parentis podcast (16 September 2018) and Al Coates and Scott Casson-Rennie's Adoption and Fostering podcast (21 August 2021).

There are many accounts of adoption reunion and the complex emotions it involves. I've quoted Nicky Campbell's *Blue-Eyed Son: The Story of an Adoption* (Pan, 2004), but I'd also recommend Jackie Kay's *Red Dust Road* (Picador, 2010), *Family Wanted: Adoption Stories*, edited by Sara Holloway (Granta, 2006) and, of course, Jeanette Winterson's *Why Be Happy When You Could Be Normal?* (Vintage, 2011). Katy Giebenhain's poem 'What Typesetters Call Them' is in *Tokens for the Foundlings*, edited by Tony Curtis and published by Seren in 2012.

## Of Mice and Men

The most recent edition of Steinbeck's novel is the Penguin Modern Classics version. There are two film adaptations: the 1939 version, starring Burgess Meredith as George and Lon Chaney Jr as Lennie, and the 1992 version, starring Gary Sinise as George and John Malkovich as Lennie. John Steinbeck's 1938 letter to Claire Luce can be found at www.hellesdon.org/documents/missluce.pdf.

Michael Gove's feelings about *Of Mice and Men* were documented in a number of newspaper articles in the early summer of 2014, including Maev Kennedy's '*To Kill a Mockingbird* and *Of Mice and Men* axed as Gove orders more Brit lit' (*Observer*, 25 May 2014; www.theguardian.com/education/2014/may/25/mockingbird-mice-and-men-axed-michael-gove-gcse), Yakub Qureshi's 'Education secretary Michael Gove set to ban children's classic *Of Mice And Men* from British classrooms' (*Mirror*, 26 May 2014; www.mirror.co.uk/news/uk-news/education-secretary-michael-gove-set-3604971) and Antonia Molloy's 'Michael Gove "axes" American classics including *To Kill a Mockingbird* from English literature GCSE syllabus' (*Independent*, 27 May 2014; www.independent.co.uk/news/education/education-news/michael-gove-axes-to-kill-a-mocking bird-and-other-american-classics-from-english-literature-gcse-syllabus-9432818.html). For another take on this argument, see Arifa Akbar's 'Never mind Michael Gove, I'd ban *Of Mice and Men* and other over-used set texts' (*Independent*, 28 May 2014; www.independent.co.uk/arts-entertainment/books/features/arifa-akbar-never-mind-michael-gove-i-d-ban-of-mice-and-men-and-other-overused-set-texts-9453657.html).

Judy Blume's classic *Forever* was first published in 1975, and has never been out of print since. A Netflix adaptation was announced in November 2022.

The girls' magazines I refer to, including *Jackie*, are now sadly defunct, although you can get a sense of their contents from D. C. Thomson and Nina Myskow's compilation *The Best of* Jackie *Magazine – The Seventies* (Prion, 2005).

Baz Luhrmann's *Romeo + Juliet* was released in 1996. Arthur Miller's *A View from the Bridge*, first published in 1955, is available in numerous editions.

## I Know Why the Caged Bird Sings

*I Know Why the Caged Bird Sings*, and the subsequent volumes of Maya Angelou's memoirs, are published by Virago, as is her essay collection *Letter to my Daughter* (2012). Angelou's poems 'Still I Rise' and 'Caged Bird' can be found on the Poetry Foundation website (www.poetryfoundation.org/poems/46446/still-i-rise and www.poetryfoundation.org/poems/48989/caged-bird).

There is a huge amount of information about Angelou online, with a website – www.mayaangelou.com – dedicated to her legacy, and a wealth of interviews and speeches available on YouTube, including Angelou's reading of her poem 'On the Pulse of Morning' at Bill Clinton's presidential inauguration in 1993 (www.youtube.com/watch?v=OQQThtav410). Barack Obama's statement on the death of Maya Angelou is in David Hudson's press release 'Remembering and Celebrating the Life of Dr. Maya Angelou', available at www.obamawhitehouse.archives.gov/blog/2014/05/28/remembering-and-celebrating-life-dr-maya-angelou, and Michelle Obama's tribute, delivered at Angelou's memorial service on 7 June 2014, is available at www.obamawhitehouse.archives.gov/the-press-office/2014/06/07/remarks-first-lady-memorial-service-dr-maya-angelou. Afua Hirsch's wonderful, warm 'Maya Angelou appreciation – "The ache for home lives in all of us"' was published in the *Guardian* on 1 June 2014 (www.theguardian.com/books/2014/jun/01/maya-angelou-appreciation-afua-hirsch).

Frances Perraudin's report on the repainting of the Rudyard Kipling mural at the University of Manchester, which includes photographs of the original mural and the new version, was published in the *Guardian* on 19 July 2018 (www.theguardian.com/education/2018/jul/19/manchester-university-students-paint-over-rudyard-kipling-mural).

Brian Keenan's *An Evil Cradling*, which helped me through the spring of 1994, was published by Vintage in 1993.

Sathnam Sanghera's brilliant *Empireland: How Imperialism Has Shaped Modern Britain* was published by Penguin in 2021.

If you want to know more about the lovely concept of 'glimmers', a good starting point is Sara M. Moniuszko's article '"Glimmers" are the opposite of triggers. Here's how to embrace them' (*USA Today*, 23 March 2022; https://eu.usatoday.com/story/life/health-wellness/2022/03/23/glimmers-opposite-triggers-mental-health-benefits/7121353001). There's also an article by J. K. Murphy on the Greatist website at www.greatist.com/discover/embracing-your-glimmers#glimmers-defined.

## Macbeth

As you'd expect, *Macbeth* is available in many versions. In school we use the Cambridge Schools Shakespeare edition, which has colour photographs and handy explanatory notes: as a university student, I used the Arden Shakespeare edition. There are abridged versions, several graphic novels, a manga adaptation (published in the Manga Shakespeare series by SelfMadeHero in 2008) and countless retellings for children. There are also many film and television adaptations available online, on DVD and on various streaming services. The Digital Theatre website, www.digitaltheatre.com, contains recordings of a number of stage versions, including the Royal Shakespeare Company's 2018 production, starring Christopher Ecclestone and Niamh Cusack, and the 2011 Liverpool Everyman production (reviewed by Alfred Hickling in the *Guardian* on 13 May 2011; www.theguardian.com/stage/2011/may/13/

macbeth-everyman-liverpool-review) that I refer to in my chapter. It's also possible to buy a recording of the 2013 Globe Theatre production from the Shakespeare's Globe website, www.shakespearesglobe.com (which is also a fabulous source of *Macbeth*-themed merchandise, including fridge magnets, mugs, cufflinks and the 'Eye of Newt' apron that I refer to in the chapter).

Moniek Bloks's article 'Gruoch – the real lady Macbeth', on the History of Royal Women blog at www.history ofroyalwomen.com/gruoch/gruoch-real-lady-macbeth/, was a fantastic source of information about the historical Lady Macbeth. I also consulted Raphael Holinshed's revised *Chronicles of England, Scotland, and Ireland* (1587), which is available on the University of Oxford's Holinshed Project website at www.english.nsms.ox.ac.uk/Holinshed/.

There is much critical discussion of Lady Macbeth, both in print and online. L. C. Knights's essay 'How many children had Lady Macbeth?' has been reprinted in a number of collections of critical essays on Shakespeare, including Knights's *Hamlet and Other Shakespearean Essays* (Cambridge University Press, 2010). Sandra M. Gilbert's article '"Unsex Me Here": Lady Macbeth's Hell Broth' is a fascinating read that explores the character of Lady Macbeth alongside a number of historical images: it's available on the British Library website at www.bl.uk/shakespeare/articles/unsex-me-here-lady-macbeths-hell-broth. I explore the teaching of *Macbeth* through the lens of social media in my essay 'Teaching

Shakespeare and Social Media: How Many Facebook Friends had Lady Macbeth?' in Pamela Bickley and Jenny Stevens (eds), *Shakespeare, Education and Pedagogy: Representations, Interactions and Adaptations* (Routledge, 2023). The BBC *English File* clips I refer to, 'Shakespeare Shorts – *Macbeth* in the future: Lady Macbeth in her historical context' and 'Lady Macbeth's character', are available at www.bbc.co.uk/programmes/poow1c9c?scrlybrkr=82822dc4.

Emma Smith's lovely description of the 'sheer permissive gappiness' of Shakespeare's work comes from her excellent book *This is Shakespeare: How to Read the World's Greatest Playwright* (Pelican, 2019). In my chapter on *Macbeth* I give three examples of novels that exploit this gappiness – J. R. Thorp's *Learwife* (Canongate, 2021), Jane Smiley's *A Thousand Acres* (Alfred A. Knopf, 1991) and Isabelle Schuler's *Lady MacBethad* (Bloomsbury, 2023) – but there are, of course, many more.

For further information about the concept of the 'wandering womb' – plus other alarming historical ideas about women's bodies – Elinor Cleghorn's *Unwell Women: A Journey through Medicine and Myth in a Man-Made World* (Weidenfeld & Nicolson, 2021) is essential reading.

## Death of a Salesman

*Death of a Salesman* was first published in 1949. It's available in a number of editions; the one used in my school is the Penguin Modern Classics edition. It has been filmed several times, most notably in 1966, with Lee J. Cobb as Willy Loman, and in 1985, with Dustin Hoffman. Arthur Miller's essay 'Tragedy and the Common Man' was first published in the *New York Times* on 27 February 1949, and can be read at www.archive.nytimes.com/www.nytimes. com/books/00/11/12/specials/miller-common.html.

The poems I refer to in this chapter are Gerard Manley Hopkins's 'I wake and feel the fell of dark, not day' (1885), Philip Larkin's 'Aubade' (1977), Wilfred Owen's 'Exposure' (1918), Walt Whitman's 'Patrolling Barnegat' (1881), Thomas Hardy's 'The Voice' (1912) and Mary Oliver's 'The Wild Geese' (1986). The first five can be found on the Poetry Foundation website, www.poetryfoundation.org; 'The Wild Geese' can be found on poetry.com at www.poetry.com/ poem/123017/wild-geese. I also refer to William Shakespeare's *King Lear* (1606), Frank Sinatra's 'New York, New York' (1980) and 'Empire State of Mind', by Jay-Z featuring Alicia Keys, from the 2009 album *The Blueprint 3*.

Michael J. Sandel's *The Tyranny of Merit: What's Become of the Common Good?* was published by Penguin in 2020, and is a deeply thought-provoking read.

## The History Boys

Alan Bennett's original playscript of *The History Boys* was published by Faber in 2004, with an Introduction in which Bennett recounts his own experiences of applying to Cambridge. The 2006 film is available on DVD and via various streaming services.

I explore the arguments surrounding the origins of English Literature as an academic discipline in my book *Defining Literary Criticism: Scholarship, Authority and the Possession of Literary Knowledge, 1880–2002* (Palgrave Macmillan, 2005).

## Afterword

The books I mention are Celeste Ng's *Our Missing Hearts* (Abacus, 2022), Dean Atta's *The Black Flamingo* (Hodder, 2019), Elizabeth Acevedo's *The Poet X* (HarperCollins, 2018), Zana Fraillon's *The Bone Sparrow* (Hodder, 2016), Robert Macfarlane and Jackie Morris's *The Lost Words* (Hamish Hamilton, 2017) and Shaun Tan's *The Arrival* (Hodder, 2006) – a brilliant, passionate, thought-provoking, generous and occasionally angry line-up of books that deserve to be read by anyone, not just teenagers.

The case for reading – and for the arts and humanities more widely – is made in Hugh Hewitt's article 'Why we must read fiction even as terrible times loom' (*Washington Post*, 25 April 2023; www.washingtonpost.com/opinions/2023/04/24/why-read-novels), Cathy N. Davidson's *The New Education: How to Revolutionize the University to Prepare Students for a World in Flux* (Basic Books, 2017), the House of Lords report 'Arts and creative industries: The case for a strategy' (1 December 2022, available via www.lordslibrary.par liament.uk) and the British Academy's 'Qualified for the Future: Quantifying demand for arts, humanities and social science skills' (May 2020, available via www.thebritish academy.ac.uk). A discussion of the role played by reading in fostering our mental health and well-being can be found in Maisie Jeynes's article 'New research provides evidence that shared reading delivers positive change for individuals in prisons and probation services' (*The Reader*, 16 November 2022; www.thereader.org.uk/new-research-provides-evi dence-that-shared-reading-delivers-positive-change-for-individuals-in-prisons-and-probation-services) and in the NIHR Applied Research Collaboration's report 'Can stories help with our health? Author Ann Cleeves takes part in one of the first "Reading for Wellbeing" events in Gateshead' (27 August 2021), which is available at www.arc-nenc.nihr.ac.uk/news/reading-for-wellbeing-chopwell-woods-ann-cleeves.

## And finally . . .

Many of the ideas explored in this book are examined in my blog, 'Passing it On', at www.passing-it-on.com. My discussions of Mr Sugden, in *A Kestrel for a Knave*, and Mrs Lintott, in *The History Boys*, have appeared in the journal *Teaching English* as part of a series on fictional schoolteachers. The British Library's Discovering Literature website, www.bl.uk/discovering-literature, is a brilliant resource for readers, containing critical articles, short films and digitized items from the British Library's collections, such as Brontë juvenilia, Charles Dickens's sketch for a writing desk and items from J. B. Priestley's scrapbook. Go for a browse and it'll be several hours before you emerge. For books on the importance of English, I'd recommend Robert Eaglestone's *Literature: Why It Matters* (Polity, 2019) and Barbara Bleiman's *What Matters in English Teaching* (English and Media Centre, 2020), both of which emphasize the richness and diversity of the subject and its role in our wider lives. Daniel Pennac's manifesto *The Rights of the Reader* (Walker Books, 2006) explores the complex relationships we have with what we read, and Sharon Creech's *Love That Dog* (Bloomsbury, 2006) – part diary, part poetry collection – will appeal to anyone who found themselves baffled by poetry at school. Last but very definitely not least, Emma Smith's wonderful *Portable Magic: A History of Books and Their Readers* (Penguin, 2022) is a fascinating exploration of the physical bookhood of books, and of their lasting appeal.

# Permissions

Extracts on pp. 30 and 31 from 'In Memory of W. B. Yeats' by W. H. Auden

Extracts on pp. 39 and 48 from *An Inspector Calls and Other Plays* by J. B. Priestley, published by Penguin Classics. Copyright © J. B. Priestley, 1947. Reprinted by permission of Penguin Books Limited

Extracts on pp. 40 and 41 from *English Journey* by J. B. Priestley

Extract on p. 42 from *Postscripts* by J. B. Priestley

Extract on p. 43 from 'Personalities', Pathé News, 1944

Extracts on p. 175 from 'Checking Out Me History' by John Agard

Extracts on p. 224 from *Coram Boy* by Jamila Gavin

Extracts on p. 234 from *Blue-Eyed Son: The Story of an Adoption* by Nicky Campbell

Extracts on pp. 236–7 from 'What Typesetters Call Them' by Katy Giebenhain, in ed. Tony Curtis, *Tokens for the Foundlings*

Extracts on pp. 244, 245, 246, 252 and 253 from *Of Mice and Men* by John Steinbeck

Extract on p. 261 from 'Still I Rise' by Maya Angelou, reproduced with permission of the Licensor through PLS Clear

Extract on p. 277 from *Letter to My Daughter* by Maya Angelou

Lyrics on p. 310 from 'New York, New York' by John Kander and Fred Ebb

Extract on p. 311 from 'Tragedy and the Common Man' by Arthur Miller, published in the *New York Times* in 1949

Extracts on pp. 326, 327, 328, 331, 332, 334, 335 and 336 from *The History Boys* by Alan Bennett